W0035941

SAGE was founded in 1965 by Sara Miller McCune to support the dissemination of usable knowledge by publishing innovative and high-quality research and teaching content. Today, we publish over 900 journals, including those of more than 400 learned societies, more than 800 new books per year, and a growing range of library products including archives, data, case studies, reports, and video. SAGE remains majority-owned by our founder, and after Sara's lifetime will become owned by a charitable trust that secures our continued independence.

Los Angeles | London | New Delhi | Singapore | Washington DC | Melbourne

Advance Praise

The international education community observes early childhood in India with respect and awe; educating the world's largest population of preschool-aged children takes imagination and grit. This scholarly yet practical book focuses on 'quality' in eight innovative, multi-age programmes in diverse marginalized communities. The authors distil common elements, underpinning successful education under intense economic and social pressures. The 'grounded theory' analyses and reveals actions and structures which lift children's learning. Lessons include the crucial role of the teacher, differentiated teaching and developing a vision for children. Scaling up the powerful lessons from this book will require financial commitment—but will transform millions of young lives.

—**Kathy Sylva**
Emeritus Professor of Educational Psychology,
University of Oxford, UK

This book, drawn from a landmark multi-site study of early childhood education in India, provides a wealth of culturally and contextually specific approaches to conceptualizing and improving quality in early learning programmes. The lessons of the book—for grounding programmes in culture and local contexts, for meaningful community involvement and for a systems approach to partnerships and scale—will deepen praxis and inform early childhood policy for years to come.

—**Hirokazu Yoshikawa**
Courtney Sale Ross University Professor of Globalization
and Education, Department of Applied Psychology,
NYU Steinhardt, USA

This book is among the first of its kind—bringing together nuanced analysis and engaging case studies—which cuts across different areas such as neurosciences, child development, linguistics, cultural studies, preschool education and sociology. It provides valuable insights into how we could restructure early childhood education, especially for children who are marginalized. The intermeshing of rigorous theoretical knowledge with qualitative insights from case studies has given this volume an edge over purely empirical, data-based studies or theoretical studies. As a resource, it would be of immense value to the larger research community, practitioners and policymakers who engage with social development.

—**Vimala Ramachandran**
Director, Educational Resource Unit (ERU Consultants
Private Limited), Jaipur and Delhi, India

EARLY CHILDHOOD EDUCATION FOR MARGINALIZED CHILDREN in India

EARLY CHILDHOOD EDUCATION FOR MARGINALIZED CHILDREN in India

Deconstructing Quality

Edited by

Monimalika Day
Venita Kaul
Swati Bawa Sawhney

Los Angeles | London | New Delhi
Singapore | Washington DC | Melbourne

Copyright © Monimalika Day, Venita Kaul and Swati Bawa Sawhney, 2022

All rights reserved. No part of this book may be reproduced or utilised in any form or by any means, electronic or mechanical, including photocopying, recording, or by any information storage or retrieval system, without permission in writing from the publisher.

First published in 2022 by

SAGE Publications India Pvt Ltd
B1/I-1 Mohan Cooperative Industrial Area
Mathura Road, New Delhi 110 044, India
www.sagepub.in

SAGE Publications Inc
2455 Teller Road
Thousand Oaks, California 91320, USA

SAGE Publications Ltd
1 Oliver's Yard, 55 City Road
London EC1Y 1SP, United Kingdom

SAGE Publications Asia-Pacific Pte Ltd
18 Cross Street #10-10/11/12
China Square Central
Singapore 048423

Published by Vivek Mehra for SAGE Publications India Pvt Ltd and typeset in 10.5/13 pt Adobe Caslon Pro by AG Infographics, Delhi.

Library of Congress Control Number: 2021945599

ISBN: 978-93-5479-146-8 (HB)

SAGE Team: Amrita Dutta, Shipra Pant and Rajinder Kaur
Cover Photo Credit: Swati Bawa Sawhney

*Dedicated to every young child waiting to
cross the margins.*

Thank you for choosing a SAGE product!
If you have any comment, observation or feedback,
I would like to personally hear from you.

Please write to me at **contactceo@sagepub.in**

Vivek Mehra, Managing Director and CEO, SAGE India.

Bulk Sales

SAGE India offers special discounts
for purchase of books in bulk.
We also make available special imprints
and excerpts from our books on demand.

For orders and enquiries, write to us at

Marketing Department
SAGE Publications India Pvt Ltd
B1/I-1, Mohan Cooperative Industrial Area
Mathura Road, Post Bag 7
New Delhi 110044, India

E-mail us at **marketing@sagepub.in**

Subscribe to our mailing list
Write to **marketing@sagepub.in**

This book is also available as an e-book.

Contents

List of Illustrations

Figures

Tables

List of Abbreviations

ABS	Adaptive behaviour scale
ACDPO	Additional Child Development Project Officer
AECED	Association for Early Childhood Education and Development
AIF	American India Foundation
AWC	Anganwadi centre
AWH	Anganwadi helper
AWTC	Anganwadi Workers Training Centre
AWW	Anganwadi worker
BRT	Block-level resource team
BSPKs	Bal Shikshan Prachar Karyakartas
BSS	Bodh Shiksha Samiti
CAs	Contiguous Anganwadis
CBO	Community Based Organizations
CDPO	Child development project officer
CDR	Centre for Development and Research
CECDR	Center for Early Childhood Development and Research
CECED	Centre for Early Childhood Education and Development
CEO	Chief executive officer
CIFF	Children's Investment Fund Foundation
CLR	Centre for Learning Resources
CML	Children's media laboratory
COCs	Community-owned centres
CSR	Corporate social responsibility
CSWB	Central Social Welfare Board
DAP	Developmentally Appropriate Practice
DFID	Department for International Development
DPEP	District Primary Education Programme

DPM	District programme manager
DUWA	Delhi University Women's Association
ECA	Early Childhood Association
ECCE	Early childhood care and education
ECD	Early childhood development
ECE	Early childhood education
ECEQAS	Early Childhood Education Quality Assessment Scale
FCRA	Foreign Contributions Regulation Act
FGDs	Focus group discussions
GBSK	Gram Bal Shiksha Kendra
IAPE	Indian Association for Preschool Education
ICDS	Integrated Child Development Services
IECEI Study	*India Early Childhood Education Impact Study*
ILA	Incremental Learning Approach
MAYA	Movement for Alternatives and Youth Awareness
MHRD	Ministry of Human Resource Development
MLTC	Mid-level training centre
MMSs	Mandal Mahila Samakhyas
MoE	Ministry of Education
MP	Madhya Pradesh
MPRs	Monthly progress reports
MWCD	Ministry of Women and Child Development
NAEYC	National Association for the Education of Young Children
NCERT	National Council of Educational Research and Training
NCTE	National Council for Teacher Education
NEP 2020	National Education Policy 2020
NGOs	Non-governmental organizations
NIPCCD	National Institute of Public Cooperation and Child Development
NPE 1986	National Policy on Education 1986
OAs	Observation Anganwadis
OBCs	Other Backward Castes
PHC	Public health centre
PISA	Programme for International Student Assessment
RAC	Research Advisory Committee

RAs	Remaining Anganwadis
RTE	Right to Education
SCERT	State Councils of Educational Research and Training
SCs	Scheduled Castes
SDGs	Sustainable Developmental Goals
SDMC	School Development and Monitoring Committee
SERP	Society for Elimination of Rural Poverty
SEWA	Self Employed Women's Association
SHGs	Self-help groups
SRI	School-readiness instrument
SSA	Sarva Shiksha Abhiyan
STs	Scheduled Tribes
TISS	Tata Institute of Social Sciences
TLMs	Teaching–learning materials
USNPSS	Uttarakhand Seva Nidhi–Paryavaran Siksha Sansthan
WEF	Welfare Extension Project

Foreword

I am indeed delighted to be called upon to write the foreword to this eagerly awaited book which brings forth very valuable insights and learnings for reaching children from the margins in diverse social settings through developmentally and contextually appropriate early childhood education. These learnings emanate from a qualitative study leading to a grounded theory building on the basis of an analysis of a set of eight case studies of good practices in early childhood education. The book comes as a culmination of a comprehensive, multi-strand research project titled *India Early Childhood Education Impact Study* (IECEI Study), which commenced about a decade ago, a project with which I was fortunate to be closely associated. The singular strength of the research design of this project, which includes the case studies that become the focus of this publication, is that it dovetails the data obtained at the macro, intermediate and micro levels. It has been a long and exciting journey.

The case studies presented in this book reflect data from the micro or proximal level of children's daily lives as influenced by the ecological environment, including opportunities for schooling and literacy acquisition. Questions have often been raised about the extent to which large-scale quantitative data captures the complexity of real lives and tells the whole story. On the other hand, qualitative data presented with thick descriptions has been questioned in terms of subjectivity. Therefore, triangulation of data at multiple levels using multiple methodologies complements each other and brings together various pieces of the puzzle to form the whole. For this reason, The *Early Childhood Education and School Readiness in India: Quality and Diversity* (Kaul & Bhattacharjea, 2019) and this book need to be read together.

A major challenge that we continue to face in India in our goal of reaching out to every child with high-quality early childhood education, as promised by the National Education Policy 2020 (NEP 2020), is that of addressing the paradox of contextual and cultural diversity along with the need for scaling up. The eight case studies, representing early childhood education initiatives in diverse communities of India, offer a wealth of insights and learnings for the larger system in this context, which have been analysed and very well articulated in this book.

The timing of this publication during the regeneration phase following the devastating pandemic which has negatively affected the lives of young children is also of special significance. One sincerely envisions that these lessons learnt will also assist in bridging the gap of the lost year in children's early learning. That is the hope.

The challenges were many, be it identifying good practices, finding sustained funding for prolonged engagement in the field, ensuring availability of competent researchers or finding the time and opportunity for shared dialogues to refine the design and engage in analysis of data. However, it led to the formation of a community of researchers and a collective sensitivity and nuanced understanding of complexities and possibilities of conceptualizing inclusive early childhood education in India.

Yet the feeling of satisfaction of a job well done is tempered by scepticism following experiential observation and learning. Despite having traversed more than four decades since the formal recognition of the need for universal early childhood education through the inception of the world-acclaimed Integrated Child Development Services (ICDS) scheme in 1975, early education is still struggling for the recognition it well deserves. Having been a participant and an observer in the scenario, many questions continue to plague one's mind. Are we as a nation in a position to ensure that every child citizen has the chance of being empowered with early education from her formative years? Can we rest assured that despite the rising poverty and the setback caused by the pandemic, malnutrition in young children can be arrested such that they can gain from other wellness inputs? Are the physical spaces that house early learning centres safe and fairly well equipped? For how long will the Anganwadi worker, the pivot in the wheel of early education with several complementary inputs, carry the burden with minimum support? Above all, is the budgetary allocation for education adequate, considering that actually additional inputs are required to bridge the gap of the lost year of educational opportunities? For how long will we lag behind in allocation for education when compared to even countries which are smaller and poorer than us?

These questions and more arise because one sees a drastic cut in the budget in the already-modest allocation for early education despite the government's commitment to foundational learning in the NEP 2020. But are not young children the foundation of our development plans? Are they not truly the future citizens of India? Do we only pay a lip service in saying so? Are they not the resources in whom we need to invest wisely so that we can build a nation of young people physically strong and mentally agile to carry on the multiple tasks of building a robust society?

The present book on case studies is a timely publication, as it effectively demonstrates that even under constrained circumstances with limited resources, but with appropriate prioritization, well-mentored teachers and a well-designed and developmentally and contextually appropriate curriculum can make a difference in early learning. But that can in no way let us assume that early education needs only the barest minimum resources and minimally trained and paid workers. Unless and until the nation finds the political will to treat young children as precious resources for the present and the future and commits itself to investing adequately in necessary infrastructure for quality early childhood education and trained human resources to support the same, our commitment to children will remain superficial and unfulfilled. Herein lies the challenge, and the chapters in the present publication show us the way forward.

Reference

Kaul, V., & Bhattacharjea, S. (2019). *Early childhood education and school readiness in India: Quality and diversity.* Springer.

T. S. Saraswathi
Former Professor of Human Development and Family Studies,
The Maharaja Sayajirao University of Baroda, Vadodara, Gujarat

Preface

India has committed to the goal of ensuring high-quality early childhood care and education (ECCE) to all children below six years of age (SDG 4.2 [2015] and NEP 2020) and making Early Childhood Education (ECE)[1] an integral part of the early learning continuum or foundational stage of school education, that is, up to Grades 1 and 2. While these commitments are no doubt laudable, these are likely to pose several challenges in implementation, given India's scale and sociocultural diversity. These challenges emanate from some key questions that need to be addressed, namely: How do we define 'quality' in ECE? What are the structures and processes that constitute 'high quality', and can all these be scaled up and universalized? Will quality in one social context have relevance in another? Also, can there be multiple definitions of quality, given multiplicity of contexts, while staying aligned to the goals of social equity and social justice?

Questions such as these have inspired the preparation and design of this book, which has crystallized from intense dialogues on reports from a community of researchers engaged in a collective case study of known early childhood education programmes for marginalized young children across India, with the intent to deconstruct the notion of quality in early childhood education. This qualitative research was part of a larger, longitudinal, three-strand research titled *India Early Childhood Education Impact Study* (Kaul et al., 2017) by the Centre for Early Childhood Education and Development (CECED) at Ambedkar University Delhi and the ASER Centre. The other two strands of the study, designed to be more quantitative in methodology, scanned aspects of access and quality of ECE services and their impact on school

---

[1] In this document ECCE has been used for policy level interventions however, the focus of the current study is on ECE.

readiness and learning outcomes for young children between the ages of four and eight in the states of Rajasthan, Assam and Telangana.

This qualitative strand aims at developing a more in-depth and nuanced understanding of how 'quality' can be defined in ECE, particularly in the context of preschool education for children from the margins. This study was conceptualized to gain insights into the complex processes of constructing quality from perspectives of multiple stakeholders including administrators, teachers, parents and community members. The book thus presents evidence-based approaches to developing and scaling up good-quality preschool programmes for young children from marginalized communities in India. It captures the influence of societal hierarchies in the forms of caste, gender and religion on young children's education.

The book is divided into two parts. The content of the chapters in Part I is anchored in the case studies presented in Part II of the book. The chapters in the first part present the significance of early childhood education in breaking the cycle of poverty, an overview of early childhood education in India, the grounded theory which delineates the crucial factors which affect quality of preschools in diverse contexts and articulates the need and the method of conducting collaborative research to consolidate evidence from multiple sites. The first few chapters thus offer insights on preschool pedagogy, the role of a preschool teacher, the construction of the curriculum and, based on the above, the emerging principles and approaches to contextualize services and strategies for scaling up good practices to meet the goals presented in NEP 2020 and the SDGs.

The eight models of early childhood programmes presented in the second part of the book and listed below, which capture diversity with quality in ECE, are standalone case studies in rural, urban and tribal areas of the country.

Rural areas:
Chapter 6: Place-based Education in Himalayan Villages (Uttarakhand Seva Nidhi Paryavaran Shiksha Sansthan, USNPSS, in Uttarakhand)

Chapter 13: Public–Private Partnership for Government Preschools in Rural Areas
(Gujrat ICDS in Gujrat)

Urban areas:
Chapter 8: Relationship-based Programme for Semi-urban Communities
(Bodh Sikhsa Samiti in Rajasthan)
Chapter 9: Educating Children from Urban Dalit Communities
(Nidan in Bihar)
Chapter 10: Community-based Programme in Urban Slums
(Pratham, Mumbai in Maharashtra)
Chapter 11: Cooperative Preschools in a Cosmopolitan City
(Prajayatna in Karnataka)

Tribal areas:
Chapter 12: Diffusion Model: Scaling Up Quality in Tribal Areas
(Centre for Learning Resources, CLR in Maharashtra)
Chapter 7: Community-managed Balwadi-cum-Creches in Tribal Communities
(Society for Elimination of Poverty, SERP in Telangana)

Each chapter presents the unique strengths of and challenges faced by the respective programmes. They showcase different approaches to offering early childhood education to children and provide insights into the complex processes of building developmentally appropriate programmes while responding to sociocultural linguistic diversity in these regions. Our emerging understanding is to move away from a 'one-size-fits-all' approach and instead present the core elements or principles of quality that we see embedded in the richness and diversity of multiple pathways which could be followed to construct quality in early childhood education for all children, including children at the margins.

We do hope that our readers will find these insights meaningful and relevant in their respective contexts and that these will enable them to identify enough pegs to not just enhance their understanding of quality in ECE but also move beyond that to create/innovate with more and varied sites for widening and deepening our collective understanding from praxis in diverse contexts. We look forward to continuing this dialogue further.

Reference

Kaul, V., Bhattacharjea, S., Chaudhary, A. B., Ramanujan, P., Banerji, M., & Nanda, M. (2017). *The India early childhood education impact study*. UNICEF.

Acknowledgements

During this very valuable journey that we undertook to explore good practices in India with a view to contribute to expanding the current landscape of indigenous knowledge on early childhood education for children at the margins, we had the privilege of meeting some very innovative 'minds' who had spent several years of their lives in trying to 'make a difference'. Their openness to sharing of ideas with us and willingness to allow their field initiatives to be examined and critically evaluated by us speak volumes for their dedication to this cause.

We particularly acknowledge and thank the leadership of all these projects, namely Dr Lalit Pande at Seva Nidhi, Dr Zakiya Kurrien at Centre for Learning Resources, Yogendra Bhushan from Bodh Shiksha Samiti, Arbind Singh from Nidan, P. D. K. Rao and Manohar Prasad who guided the Society for Elimination of Rural Poverty (SERP) project, Ashok and Mahesh Bhansali who led the Bhansali Trust and Dr Farida Lambay from Pratham.

This project was undertaken under the auspices of CECED, Ambedkar University Delhi. We are indebted to the centre and the university leadership and management for providing institutional anchoring to the project and creating a conducive environment for collaborative research. Our colleagues in CECED were a source of consistent support and facilitation. We thank Sandipan Paul, who provided project management support, Aparajita Bhargarh Chaudhry, who provided training on the CECED tools for the case studies, and Mehla ji, Anil Rawat and Manish Sharma for their accounting and logistical support.

We are grateful to the agencies which made this journey possible for us, particularly UNICEF, India Office, Children's Investment Fund Foundation (CIFF, UK), SERP (Andhra Pradesh), Ministry of Human Resource Development (now Ministry of Education) and CARE India, for providing us financial support and consistently contributing to the process of this research by active participation in the discussions.

Professor T. S. Saraswathi provided our team invaluable mentorship and guidance throughout the research for which we are indeed very grateful. Professor Hiro Yoshikawa participated in our review workshop and provided us with very valuable feedback and guidance on interpretation of our findings, which we deeply appreciate. Our generous thanks to Ms Anjali Gokhale for critical insights and suggestions, Dr Ananta Chauhan who painstakingly edited the content for the case studies, and Professor K. Lakshmi and her team from Andhra Mahila Sabha for being consistent participants in our brainstorming and for providing invaluable support for the SERP case study.

Last but not least, our deep gratitude and appreciation for each of the mentors, Balwadi teachers, Anganwadi workers, helpers, community members, parents and, above all the little children in each of the sites we visited who left us with valuable learnings and insights which have made this book possible.

Part I

Early Childhood Education in India: Quest for Quality

Part 1

CHAPTER 1

Challenges and Possibilities in Early Childhood Education

Venita Kaul and Monimalika Day

1.1. Introduction

India is one of the 150 countries that ratified the recent Sustainable Development Goals Agenda of the United Nations (2015) and in the process committed to a global partnership of working towards the achievement of the 17 Sustainable Developmental Goals (SDGs) agreed upon. These goals provide a 'shared blueprint for peace and prosperity for people and the planet, now and into the future' (UN, 2015). These also reflect a clear recognition of the fact that 'ending poverty and other deprivations must go hand-in-hand with strategies that improve health and education, reduce inequality and spur economic growth'. Of these 17 goals, SDG 4, which commits to education of satisfactory quality for all, includes an important SDG Target 4.2, which stipulates that 'by 2030 all girls and boys have access to quality early childhood development, care and pre-primary education'.

If India is to meet this target, to which it is committed, there is an urgency to scale up high-quality early childhood development[1] (ECD) services for all children across the country. India is, as a nation, characterized by three significant challenges: its phenomenal scale, wide diversity and persisting levels of poverty. It is these major social and geographical challenges that provide the backdrop against which we examine, in this introductory chapter, and in a more nuanced and granular way in the subsequent chapters, India's quest, efforts and achievements to meet the goals of access, equity and quality in the field of ECD, with particular reference to pre-primary education or ECCE for children between the ages of three and six years.

1.2. Indian Context

Being the world's largest democracy in terms of scale, India has a federal structure comprised of 28 states and 8 union territories and population of 1.2 billion (Kak & Govindraj, 2018), with an estimated number of 164 million children under the age of 6 years (MWCD, 2011). Of these, an estimated 70 million children are between the ages of 3 and 6 years. With one child out of every five from across the globe residing in this country, India inevitably plays a significant role in influencing the global status of children's development and learning.

India's diversity is its other major challenge, with the coexistence of 2,000 ethnic groups, 29 official languages (and many dialects) and all religions of the world represented within its population, in addition to diversity related to gender, class, caste and ability. Diversity is also clearly evident across its 29 states, with states like Assam, Meghalaya, Rajasthan, Chhattisgarh, Madhya Pradesh, Jharkhand, Uttar Pradesh and Bihar lagging behind in terms of their ranking on the Young Child Outcomes Index, scoring below the national average (Mobile Creches, 2020). Aligned to these two defining features of

---

[1] ECD and early childhood care and education (ECCE) are interchangeably used to refer to a holistic and integrated set of provisions for children below the age of six years in India. At the policy level, the acronym ECCE is accepted. Early childhood education (ECE) is used with specific reference to the early learning provision.

India are also its intersecting concerns with its high levels of poverty, particularly in the rural sector. The percentage of India's population below the poverty line, which in 2011 was estimated to be 21.9 per cent as per the Census of India, had according to a report risen to about 23 per cent in 2017–2018, accounting for almost 30 million people below the poverty line (Bhattacharya & Devulapalli, 2019). Over 385 million children live in extreme poverty across the world. Of these, India is home to 30 per cent, the highest in South Asia (Save the Children, 2017).

This situation has further exacerbated with the onset of the COVID-19 pandemic in 2020, leading to severe physical, social and economic distress for a large number of families in India, the repercussions of which will be evident soon on the health and educational status of children in the country. UNICEF (2020b) refers to it as the 'pandemics of violence and poverty in India' with its recent survey, indicating 74 per cent of main wage earners reporting reduction in their monthly income, only 64 per cent families reporting having enough food to eat in the following week as compared to 79 per cent earlier and 75 per cent reporting a debt burden due to the pandemic. In urban areas, almost 25 per cent of mothers shared their uncertainty about whether their child would be able to even go back to school (UNICEF, 2020b)!

We begin by situating this discussion in the social and economic challenges in the context of the science of ECD which has clearly demonstrated the critical importance of the early years of life and of ECCE for children's lifelong learning and development. We then examine how the above-mentioned social challenges juxtapose with the country's commitment to the SDGs and their vision and efforts for universal and equitable ECE services of satisfactory quality, which should unequivocally be a fundamental right of every child. We then delve into a historical analysis of ECCE in India as it moved from a socialistic ethos into a more neoliberal and market-driven social and economic system and dissect the ways in which these changes have impacted the quality and equity dimensions of ECCE in contemporary India. We conclude the chapter with identification of some emerging challenges.

1.3. Why Is ECCE Significant for Learning and Development?

Research in the multidisciplinary domains of neuroscience, economics and child development has over the last few decades provided credible evidence which assures that investing in the early childhood years is of crucial importance. The underlying rationale for this assurance is that as per neuroscience research, the pace of development of the brain is most rapid in the earliest years of life (Philips & Shankoff, 2010).

> The basic architecture of the brain is constructed through an ongoing process that begins before birth and continues into adulthood. Brain architecture is thus comprised of billions of connections between individual neurons across different areas of the brain which enable communication among neurons that specialize in different kinds of brain functions. One can get a sense of the rapidity of the brain growth from the fact that more than 1 million new neural connections are made per second in the child's brain and these are essentially related to child's direct experiences within his/her environment. Simpler neural connections and skills form first, followed by more complex circuits and skills. (Center on the Developing Child, 2019)

As a result, this early phase of life contains some 'critical and sensitive periods' when the child's receptivity towards development of some foundational linguistic, socio-emotional and cognitive competencies, which are important for later learning and development, is at its peak and the child requires a supportive and interactive environment for their development. These factors also make a strong case for ensuring an experientially rich environment for children's learning and development in these foundational years.

The fact that neural connections that get formed in the earliest phase of life cumulatively provide the foundation for the connections that get formed later explains why learning and development are both cumulative and continuous processes, with upward and not downward continuity, as is often mistakenly believed. This principle becomes important from the perspective of designing curriculum for early childhood, since whatever learning the child experiences in the preceding stage sets the foundation for the curriculum for the succeeding stage. The pedagogy and curricular content for the early years should therefore be age/stage specific and planned in a vertical, spiral and 'bottom-up' mode, to ensure the child's seamless movement upwards into the next stage of education. This again reinforces the need to ensure age and contextually appropriate quality and content of any ECE programme for it to have the desired impact.

It is commendable that the recently approved National Education Policy 2020 (NEP 2020; Ministry of Education, 2020) in India has not only acknowledged this important principle but also recommended the carving out of a separate foundational learning stage through a process of curricular restructuring, which would constitute three years of ECE and two years of early primary, that is, for children from three to eight years of age. This sub-stage is being carved out to especially address the demands of foundational, child-initiated learning along the early learning continuum through play-based and contextually relevant pedagogy.

1.4. Childhoods in India and the Interplay of Social and Economic Challenges

As we explore the dimension of quality in ECE, an important attribute we mention above is that of 'contextual' relevance. A vital question is: How do the social, geographical and economic contexts influence children's development and what are the implications for their learning? Data indicates that of the 159 million children below the age of 6 years in India, 21 per cent are undernourished, 36 per cent are underweight and 38 per cent do not receive full immunization (Mobile Creches, 2020). We move on to examine each of these three specific challenges, that is, scale, diversity and poverty, and the overall effects of marginalization of any kind on children's well-being and development.

1.4.1. Challenge of Scale

India's scale can be estimated from the fact that it covers a total area of 3.28 million km², which is about 2.4 per cent of the total geographic areas of the world! This extensive geographical spread has very obvious implications for ensuring universal provision of acceptable quality of any community-based service, especially for young children, since these services would inevitably require to be completely decentralized and habitation based and therefore in large numbers.

India's Integrated Child Development Services (ICDS) for young children below the age of six years, which is celebrated as the largest public sponsored programme for young children in the world, is a case in point. The ICDS, which aims to reach out to each and every village if not habitation in the country, has within its fold 1.4 million centres[2] across the country for delivery of its six services related to health, nutrition, education and community development. These are delivered by as many as 1.28 million community-based Anganwadi workers. One of these six services focuses on ECE. A recent three states' longitudinal survey team reported seeing an ICDS centre in every village which was visited across the three project states (Kaul et al., 2017).

While this is in itself a significant achievement for a country of India's size and scale, there can be no doubt that ensuring adequate financial and human resources for staffing, provisions, monitoring and support to these centres, which are all essentials for quality of services, would clearly be a phenomenal challenge. This challenge inevitably influences the content, quality and outreach of the ICDS (Rao & Kaul, 2017). We will discuss this aspect in greater detail later in the chapter.

1.4.2. Challenge of Diversity

India's cultural and social diversity, which by itself may well be considered a potential learning resource and a cause for celebration, poses another kind of challenge for designing and delivering services for young children. While planning and designing of quality inputs for ECE assume a 'normative childhood' governed by some universal child development principles, the social reality and related sociological theory defy this assumption of 'normative childhood'; instead, it poses the challenge of finding ways to address the complexity of customizing policies and provisions to align with the specifics of what has been referred to as 'multiple childhoods' resulting from this wide social diversity that defines India (Balagopalan, 2018).

---

[2] Know India, national portal of India, January 2020.

This thesis postulates that childhood is a social construct and can therefore never be segregated from other social variables such as class, caste and gender, which introduce the diversity (Kagitcibasi, 2012; Menon & Saraswathi, 2018). From a psychological perspective too, Super and Harkness (1986) propose the concept of 'developmental niche' based on their cross-cultural research on parenting in different countries to explain how the context may influence children's development. From a systemic perspective, Bronfenbrenner's (1977) ecological systems theory provides further insight into how policies, programmes and experiences at the distal and proximal levels may influence children's growth and development.

In the Indian context, the society is largely defined by the hierarchies inherent in the caste system of the Hindu religion, which become further marked through intersecting social class divisions. These divisions tend to have become more pronounced in recent years with the neoliberal and market-driven political landscape in the country and the growing dependence on the private sector, especially in education. Raman (2018) in her analysis of this relationship states, 'The experiences of Indian children vary both horizontally and vertically. While diversity refers to regional, sociocultural and linguistic dimensions, caste organizes this diversity along a defined hierarchy'. This social and cultural diversity, as well as the uneven economic development that characterizes the Indian society, influences access to education and children's participation in school, as reflected in the sharp disparities in school enrolment and completion rates between different social and economic groups (NCERT, 2005). Despite India being governed by a secular constitution, periodic spurts in rise of communalism and religious discrimination also add to these disturbing dimensions, creating experiences of superiority/subordination among children and influencing social interactions and self-esteem in children.

1.4.3. Challenge of Poverty

Poverty is another dimension that intersects these diverse social categories. Research indicates that the specific aspects of child deprivation

> cannot be divorced from the overall deprivation and poverty of the household. Chronic undernutrition and malnutrition have been

the plight of large numbers of children and a majority of them are children of the SCs and STs and the overwhelming majority of whom are separately poor. (Saxena, 2016)

'While the number of young children living in the poorest and richest households varies tremendously across states, about 25 percent of children under the age of five in India live in households belonging to the poorest quintile' (Mobile Creches, 2020). Thus, millions of young children do not reach their full potential because of poor health, inadequate nutrition, exposure to stress, a lack of love and early stimulation, and limited opportunities for early learning (WHO, 2018).

1.5. Social Marginalization and Children's Learning

We further explore how the social contexts which contribute to children being marginalized also tend to influence their learning opportunities. Jerome Bruner (1975) indicates three interconnected influences associated with poverty: (a) The first is encouragement and management of goal-seeking and problem-solving. This involves aspects such as what is it that the child strives for, how does she go about the task of means end analysis, her expectations of success and failure, the approach adopted towards the delay of gratification, and her pacing of goal setting. All these are not only crucial for overall learning but also influence how the child uses language, deploys attention, processes information and so on, and these are impacted by poverty. (b) The second influence is in the domain of linguistic competence since by exposure to many situations and through the application of many demands, children come to use language in different ways, particularly as an instrument of thought, of social control and interaction, of planning and so on. Bernstein (1964) postulates that children in underprivileged situations tend to have limited exposure to language and as a result demonstrate use of more restrictive rather than elaborative codes of speech, which negatively impacts their school achievement. (c) The third influence comes from the pattern of reciprocity into which the child is placed in terms of what parents expect, what teachers demand and what peers anticipate, and all of these operate to shape the outlook and approach in the young one.

More recent research along the similar lines in the cognitive sciences indicates a significant relationship between socio-economic status and development of 'executive functions' in children, with children from higher socio-economic status families displaying better executive functions. Executive functions and self-regulation skills are those mental processes which 'enable us to plan, focus attention, remember instructions and juggle multiple tasks successfully'. These skills which involve brain functions such as working memory, cognitive flexibility and self-regulation therefore become very critical for all learning and development (Center on the Developing Child, 2019). In addition to other learning outcomes, these cognitive processes are fundamentally involved in learning to read and write (Haft & Hoeft, 2017).

An important insight provided by research is that children are not born with these skills; instead, they are born with the potential to develop these skills. Children's potential can therefore be developed by 'scaffolding' the development of these skills through good-quality early learning or ECE programmes. Children learn these skills in early childhood years through appropriate role models, establishing regular routines, supportive relationships and hands-on activities which foster creative play, vigorous exercise and social connections (Haft & Hoeft, 2017), all of which characterize a good-quality ECE programme which has the potential to address challenges of social inequity.

Shonkoff (2011) introduces a more scientific perspective as he states,

> Curricular enhancements in early childhood education that are guided by the science of learning must be augmented by protective interventions informed by the biology of adversity. The same neuroplasticity that leaves emotional regulation, behavioural adaptation, and executive functioning skills vulnerable to early disruption by stressful environments also enables their successful development through focused interventions during sensitive periods in their maturation. The early childhood field should therefore combine cognitive-linguistic enrichment with greater attention to preventing, reducing, or mitigating the consequences of significant adversity on the developing brain. Guided by this enhanced theory of change, scientists, practitioners, and policy-makers must work together to design, implement, and evaluate innovative strategies to produce substantially greater impacts than those achieved by existing programs.

1.6. Schooling without Learning: The Role of ECE

This discussion assumes particular significance in the context of the current trend across countries in the Global South, including India, of what is being referred to as 'schooling without learning' or 'learning poverty' (World Bank, 2018). The concern stems from the fact that 250 million children worldwide cannot read, write or do basic mathematics and 130 millions of these are actually in school (UNESCO, 2013–2014)!

A recent longitudinal research in India[3] which tracked a cohort of 14,000 rural 4-year-olds across 3 states for a period of 5 years found the cognitive learning levels of children in schools to be dismally low (Kaul et al., 2017). The study also demonstrated a significant linear relationship between children's school-readiness levels in the cognitive domain at the age of five years and their learning levels in mathematics and language in primary school in the subsequent years, thus validating the role of cognitive-readiness levels as a critical factor in school learning.

A third important finding of the study was that while almost 80 per cent of the 4-year-olds were attending an ECE programme, either public or private, their school-readiness levels in terms of cognitive competencies assessed at the age of 5 were very low. This disturbing finding was found to be significantly associated with the quality of preschool education which children were exposed to across the three project states. The classroom observations indicated the pedagogy to be dominated primarily by formal instruction of alphabet and numbers through rote and repetitive learning methods, referred to as 'schoolification' of ECE, or a minimalist curriculum in terms of content with predominance of a few repetitive rhymes and songs. Other than in a few innovative programmes included in the sample, there was almost no opportunity given to children for any creative play, stories or what are termed as developmentally appropriate and interactive activities.

---

[3] This is a multi-strand longitudinal study with Strand 1 adopting a survey mode, Strand 2 a quasi-experimental method and Strand C a qualitative study of good practices. The present book is based on the findings of Strand C and includes case studies in Part II of the book which were developed under this qualitative strand.

An interesting comparative analysis of school-readiness levels between a sub-sample of the cohort attending an innovative ECE programme and another attending a mainstream fee-charging private ECE provision demonstrated that

> A good quality preschool programme can bridge the gap between more and less privileged children. Even though the children from less privileged families had much lower scores at the baseline, those who attended innovative centers caught up with their more privileged peers by the end line one year later. (Kaul et al., 2017)

This again points to the need to prioritize good-quality ECE provisions for children from marginalized groups to mitigate any cognitive deficits they may have acquired in their early years due to a less-enabling environment.

1.7. ECCE in India: A Historical Perspective

ECCE has been conceptualized in India as 'integrated services for holistic development of all children along the continuum from the prenatal period to six years of age ... towards ensuring a sound foundation for survival, growth and development of the child' (Ministry of Women and Child Development, 2013). This conceptualization is consistent with the global definition of ECD, although the age band is often now being considered as extended up to eight years to address the early learning continuum and need for upward continuity and smooth transition to primary education (Ministry of Education, 2020). The age band up to six years is further subdivided into two segments, that is, from prenatal or birth to three years and the other from three to six years. The former sub-stage, which includes the 'first thousand days' is acknowledged as the most significant period for brain development with good health, nutrition security, responsive care and opportunities for early cognitive stimulation or learning considered areas of priority. The three–six sub-stage, while it continues to require a holistic treatment and nurturance of all domains, gradually shifts priority in relative terms from the health domain towards early learning or preschool education.

ECE has been a part of the policy discourse in India for several decades now, and there has been some understanding of its importance as a formative stage, with the major ICDS scheme on the ground since 1975. However, the experience/expertise in this area has been largely in the non-governmental sector or in the academic institutions. It has not been given its due priority at the government level in terms of developing institutional capacity or promoting quality, as also in terms of ensuring it becomes a fundamental and justiciable right of every Indian child for a sound foundation for life.

We demonstrate this lacuna as we briefly trace the historical journey of ECCE in India with specific reference to ECE/preschool education for children from three to six years of age and review related research, policy and programmatic initiatives undertaken in this field over the past years. We will also review the current status of provisions in ECCE and raise some issues and challenges in the Indian context with regard to defining and implementing quality programmes for children, particularly from the margins.

1.7.1. Cultural Legacy

This understanding of the need for nurturing holistic development of children below six years of age is not a new phenomenon borrowed from the West in India. India's ancient scriptures, the Vedas and in particular the Ayurveda, viewed both mother and child as a symbiotic unit and emphasized *samskaras,* or age-wise rites of passage and childcare practices, reflecting a developmental perspective. Based on the age of the child, these *samskaras* sequenced the optimal physical and psychological progress in each phase of the life cycle of the child, marked by distinct developmental milestones (Khalakdina, 2011). This ancient understanding is also reflected in the emphasis, among other recommended practices, on exclusive breastfeeding till six months of age and alongside in the rich repertoire of traditional culture-specific infant games, lullabies, stories, rhymes and riddles and folk toys, prevalent among India's diverse social communities, which evidently had developmental significance for the child and could well be considered in today's parlance as 'early stimulation activities' for infants. These were an integral part of childhood and childcare practices across India till a few generations back. Unfortunately, in the more recent times, with social structures moving towards nuclear families and demand for surrogate childcare becoming the norm rather than exception, as well as due to the onslaught and influence of technology, this legacy of holistic, contextually relevant, pro-child development practices and traditional toys is gradually getting extinct.

1.7.2. Organized Preschools—The Western Influence

While developmentally appropriate activities such as those mentioned above were part of the Indian legacy across states in terms of child rearing, these were expected to be the primary responsibility of the home and the family. The scriptures refer to a child's rearing at this stage as *lalayat* or indulgent child rearing, with free play, exploration and choice-based activities dominating a child's life. There was no organized system of early or preschool education for the young child in India till the late 18th century. This institutionalization of ECCE or preschool education needs to be examined in the context of the 'aftermath of colonization of India by the British empire and its impact on the socio-cultural life of Indian society, particularly in the context of education' (Kaul & Sharma, 2018).

It was during this period of British occupation that the first set of infant schools were established in eastern India by early missionaries, which were again seen largely as 'attempts at moral and spiritual redemption of the natives, particularly native Christian' (Kaur, 2006). This concept of organized kindergarten or preschool education came into India in the 19th century with a focus on teaching of English and literacy by European missionaries, who came and gradually influenced other parts of the country. These programmes were, however, still accessible only to a privileged few. Largely, the practice of addressing children's learning needs at this stage was home based and closely related to the immediate context of the child.

A major impetus to organized preschool education came in the early 20th century when Maria Montessori visited India at the invitation of Mahatma Gandhi and conducted training in what is now known as the Montessori Method of early education at several locations in the country. The setting up of an institutionalized system and the emphasis on English and literacy led to the distancing of the curriculum—including in many cases through the language of instruction—from real life contexts' (Kaul & Sharma, 2018). This remains an issue even today, although the research has clearly indicated the importance of educating children in their home language in the early years and the Indian policies have committed to promote this practice.

1.7.3. The Indian Balwadi

The first attempt to reach out with organized preschool education to the more marginalized sections in India came when Tarabai Modak from the Nutan Bal Shikshan Sangh (trained by Maria Montessori) established what she called Balwadis or 'children's gardens' using a locally improvised Montessori Method for tribal children in Kosbad in Thane district of Maharashtra (Tschurenev, 2021). Her belief was that if children cannot come to preschools, preschools can go to them into their courtyards or gardens! The nomenclature Balwadi has since been adopted to describe low-cost preschool centres, supported by the government or from other funding sources and run by non-governmental organizations (NGOs) as a welfare measure for education of children from impoverished families. These have all along been supported through direct funding or government funds under various schemes routed through the Central Social Welfare Board and later the Indian Council for Child Welfare. These Balwadis in most cases offered only preschool education and not integrated services for children, and these too, possibly due to lack of resources, were often of minimal quality.

1.8. Current Provisions in ECE: Increase in Quantity but Poor in Quality

Currently, in terms of provisions for ECE, India has made remarkable progress, with a recent survey indicating that 80 per cent of four-year-olds across rural India are enrolled in a preschool programme, whether public or private (ASER Centre, 2020). India's most significant accomplishment perhaps is the ICDS, which we had briefly mentioned earlier, and which has preschool education as one of its six services within an integrated child development framework. We will now examine the ICDS preschool education component in greater detail, along with the other major ECE provider in the country, that is, the private sector.

1.8.1. Integrated Child Development Services

The concept of integrated child development, in acknowledgement of the interdependence of health, nutrition and preschool education, was introduced formally in the 1960–1970s through the conceptualization of the ICDS. This is a government-sponsored programme, modelled to an extent on the Head Start programme of the USA, to meet the foundational needs of children below six years of age, particularly from the marginalized and poorer sections of the society. This programme, which follows a life cycle approach, started as a pilot in 1975 in 35 administrative blocks of the country and is today universalized across the country with 1.4 million Anganwadis or early childhood centres, making it the world's largest integrated programme for children below six years of age and for services for pregnant and lactating women in accordance with a life cycle approach. This programme offers six services to children, namely immunization, supplementary nutritional supplementation, health check-up, referral services, preschool non-formal education, and nutrition and health education.

While the fact that in India an integrated approach was adopted as early as in 1975 for children's development is really commendable and also consistent with contemporary thought, the issue is its quality of implementation. It has faced relative neglect of ECCE since its inception and has been constrained by resource and capacity deficits (Mobile Creches, 2020). The six services are expected to be provided single-handedly by a local community-based multipurpose Anganwadi worker with limited academic qualification and a helper. A single worker handling six diverse services requiring different skill sets and that too with minimal training and facilities has proven to be an extremely challenging expectation which has inevitably impacted the quality of services. The other issue is the 'one-size-fits-all' standardized model of the ICDS and within it that of the preschool education component which does not always respond to the country's wide social and cultural diversity (Rao & Kaul, 2017). As a result, while this service is free and available across the country, undoubtedly to the credit of the government, the quality of preschool education offered to children is in most cases of very uneven quality with wide state differences (Kaul et al., 2017). In terms of priority too, the focus of the programme is largely on the nutrition supplementation component, which is more closely monitored and attended to. In comparison, the preschool education or ECE component is very weakly monitored with the help of only two indicators: (a) number of children enrolled in preschool and (b) number of days in the month in which preschool education was offered. As a result, in most cases, the ECE service is limited to getting children to recite a few rhymes by way of preschool education (Kaul & Sankar, 2016). The longitudinal research referred to earlier empirically confirms this observation.

1.8.2. Private Preschools

With poverty levels on the rise in India over the years, a positive development has been that whereas earlier parents had to be persuaded to send children to schools, parental aspirations are also now rising and the demand for alternative better quality services has risen. Since the 1990s, with the liberalization of the Indian economy and emergence of the neoliberal governance paradigm with strong emergence of market forces, private provisions in preschool education have seen a rapid expansion across the country, even in rural and urban slum areas. These are in most cases structurally part of larger composite schools and range from expensive, high-end preschools to the more 'affordable' preschools of minimal quality.

These private provisions tend to offer significant competition to the Anganwadis or ICDS centres and government schools in terms of diverting their enrolments. As indicated in the *India Early Childhood Education Impact Study* (IECEI Study), these affordable private preschools/schools tend to be more responsive to parental demand in designing their curriculum in terms of the quality offered, which in most cases focuses on 'English-medium' education and formal teaching of the three Rs. In practice, however, this amounts to some smattering of English phrases and nursery rhymes in English and a focus on rote and repetitive learning of numbers and the alphabet with scarce attention to developmentally appropriate practices (Kaul et al., 2017).

It was in response to these developmentally inappropriate practices that the National Policy on Education 1986 (NPE 1986) had categorically stated, 'There shall be no formal teaching of the 3R's at this stage of education.' But in the absence of any system of regulation, these practices have persisted with scant regard for children's maturational or experiential readiness, thus leaving them with a weak foundation for lifelong learning and poor levels of school readiness (Kaul et al., 2017).

1.8.3. Other Initiatives

In addition to Anganwadis and private preschools which are the two facilities which majority of children attend, there are a few very sporadically located low-cost preschool programmes of better quality, small in scale and either running independently as Balwadis or as projects supporting the ICDS in a partnership mode. These are either sponsored by funding agencies as projects or run by some well-known NGOs catering to the marginalized communities. These have been referred to as 'known practices' in the context of this research, and these tend to be seen in a few cases as pace setters or exemplar practices, particularly in the context of offering demonstrations of contextualization of curricula to meet the challenges of diversity of 'multiple childhoods'.

1.9. Policy Framework for ECCE in India

Education, and within it ECCE, is a concurrent subject in the business arrangement of the Government of India. This implies that in India's federal structure, both the federal government and the state or provincial governments have the responsibility for this subject, with the delivery of service and service providers essentially allocated to the state.

India's policy framework for ECCE is fairly robust and well intentioned. Interestingly, the Constitution of India, which was formulated in 1950 when India became a republic, articulated as Article 45 the state's commitment to free and compulsory education for all children 'up to the age of fourteen years within ten years of promulgation of the Constitution'. This has been interpreted to include the stage of ECCE as well. The NPE 1986 also devoted a complete chapter to ECCE as a feeder programme for primary education and dwelt extensively on the need for a play-based approach for this stage of education.

The formal school system of public education has, however, consistently across states been structured to include Grades 1–8 only as also defined in the Ministry of Human Resource Development (MHRD) document titled 'Ten Years of School Education', and preschool education has traditionally been kept out from this structure altogether. The more recent Right to Education Act (MHRD, 2009), which made education up to Grade 8 the fundamental right of every Indian child, again omitted the first six years from its ambit, which in a way reversed the constitutional provision. However, after considerable advocacy and reaction from the civil society, a Section 11 was inserted in the Act which now includes a commitment by all states to endeavour to provide preschool education for all children between three and six years of age as a preparation for primary education. It still does not make ECCE a justiciable right. An amended Article 45 in the Constitution also includes ECCE as a commitment and not a right. As mentioned earlier, the recently approved NEP 2020 is a landmark in this context as it not only integrates ECCE in terms of the curriculum into the school structure as the foundational stage but also commits to universalization of ECCE by not later than 2030. The NEP 2020 also places the responsibility for ECCE for three- to six-year-olds with the Ministry of Education. This is being seen as a significant reform which will give a boost to ECCE in terms of relative priority in the education sector.

Historically, in 2006, the subject of preschool education or ECCE was shifted in terms of responsibility from the erstwhile MHRD to the Ministry of Women and Child Development (MWCD), which is also the nodal ministry overseeing the ICDS programme. As mentioned earlier, the challenge with this alignment was that with the mandate to ensure delivery of six ICDS services by a single worker, the focus in most cases remained on nutrition supplementation, with preschool education receiving little attention. However, in 2013, the MWCD brought preschool education centre stage to an extent, by formulating a National ECCE Policy (2013), which focused on care and early learning of children below six years of age. This policy was accompanied by a National Curriculum Framework, which prescribed the contours of a developmentally appropriate curriculum and discouraged formal teaching of the three Rs. To further supplement this framework, the MWCD also developed quality standards for ECCE at the national level. These generated some sense of priority to ECCE in the integrated structure of the ICDS, and all states prepared an ECCE curriculum to be used in their respective ICDS Anganwadis in accordance with the National Curriculum Framework. However, there is no available documentation to date of the process followed in developing these and the quality of their implementation by the respective states.

As proposed in the NEP 2020, the National Council of Educational Research and Training (NCERT), an advisory body to the Ministry of Education, has now been tasked with the responsibility of preparing the curriculum for ECCE and a framework for the foundational stage which will incorporate both the early childhood and early primary stages.

1.10. National Initiatives for Strengthening ECCE Quality

Although there is no reliable official database on ECCE access and participation, a recent large-scale rural survey by Pratham (ASER Centre, 2020) indicates presence of 80 per cent of the four-year-olds in preschools/ICDS centres. This finding reflects that the challenge of access to ECCE/preschool education is gradually getting addressed across the country, barring in some pockets, especially with the expansion in private provisioning. However, the challenge of quality of preschool education continues to be a major issue, raising the inevitable and persisting debate about quantity vs quality and equity, especially in the context of the ICDS.

As early as in the early 1970s, when the significance of preschool education was globally gaining prominence, some initiatives were taken in India as well, to contextualize preschool education methods and materials to the Indian context while ensuring quality. These efforts were initiated with support from the UNICEF, in which the first author (Venita Kaul) had the privilege of directly working as a junior researcher.

There is no available documentation of these initiatives, and what is presented below is on the basis of her own lived experiences and close engagement with these activities as a young professional.

Children's media laboratory: A children's media laboratory (CML) was established in NCERT around this time in response to a survey which indicated that there was a dearth of any reading or audio-visual material for children below six years of age. The objective of the CML was to develop prototypes of developmentally appropriate play and learning materials in multiple media including print for the very young child. Picture storybooks for infants, toddlers and preschoolers with locally generated stories were developed and printed as prototypes in graded format as 'breakthrough readers' for publishers to adapt/replicate. Since most children came directly into school at the age of six years without any preschool education, a six-week-long school-readiness programme kit was developed to be used as an initial preparation with children in Grade 1. This was field tested in many states with favourable results. Surveys were conducted across states of traditional infant and childhood games and toys, and their significance for children's early stimulation and development was examined and documented.

ECE project: The CML project subsequently evolved into a multi-state ECE project with the objective of making available decentralized resource support and expertise in ECE to state governments and thus create institutional capacity for planning and implementation of ECE in the country. This project involved setting up of resource centres for ECE in eight states of the country, with six located in the State Councils of Educational Research and Training (SCERT) and two in central universities in Andhra Pradesh and Gujarat. In addition, preschool sections were established as adjuncts to over 500 primary schools across the 8 states on a pilot basis. The project was coordinated by NCERT at the national level. A major longitudinal research conducted retrospectively after five years of this experience on about 38,000 children across the 8 states established a significant positive impact of preschool participation on children's continuation in primary schools, with the dropout rate reduced by 15–20 per cent across the states over the 5 primary grades (Kaul et al., 1994).

Another major research subsequently undertaken on readiness levels of children in Grade 1 across several states confirmed that a majority of children in government schools were coming into school directly with no preschool experience (Upadhyaya, 1996). Each state resource centre developed state-specific play and learning materials for this age group, developed contextualized storybooks and developed their own preschool curriculum and training packages, thus creating a decentralized momentum for good-quality ECCE. However, with the project coming to a close in the mid-1990s, the momentum also waned.

While these initiatives were undertaken under the ECE project and supported by the UNICEF, a few resource centres such as M. S. Swaminathan Research Foundation, Chennai; Centre for Learning Resources (CLR), Pune; and Mobile Creches in Mumbai and Delhi also came up in the non-government sector with expertise in preschool education or ECE. Andhra Mahila Sabha in Hyderabad, which had been established as one of the resource centres under the ECE project, has continued over the years to serve as a technical resource institution for the local government and developed some excellent kits for ECE. In addition to some pilots of innovative practices, these institutions also developed and disseminated useful training and curricular materials and provided technical support. M. S. Swaminathan Research Foundation brought out an excellent series of case studies titled 'Suraksha Series' which covered different kinds of ECE programmes on the ground. Similarly, CLR brought out very stimulating curricular guides along with a full kit of activity materials for promoting developmentally appropriate classroom practices and conducted training in the states on these materials.

ECCE in District Primary Education Programme (DPEP) and Sarva Shiksha Abhiyan (SSA): Attention to issues of access, equity and quality in preschool education at the government level was again revived in the late 1990s and 2000 onwards when the externally funded DPEP was implemented across states. ECE was included in these projects as an important component, from the dual perspective of (a) providing a sound foundation in children for primary education and more importantly (b) for facilitating participation of older girls in primary education/schooling by providing surrogate care facility for their younger siblings through the ECE centres. In this context, many ICDS Anganwadis were relocated to primary schools in some states and, in others, new centres were set up and their timings synchronized with the primary schools. Evaluation studies conducted under the DPEP indicated very promising results of this initiative, in terms of both increasing girls' enrolment and creating a child-friendly, play-based learning environment in the schools, since initiatives were also taken to extend the preschool pedagogy to the early primary classes in the mode of what was termed as 'joyful learning' (Kaul & Sankar, 2016). Subsequently, some of these initiatives in ECE were incorporated into a newly established national scheme in education titled Sarva Shiksha Abhiyan or Education for All, by MHRD. The ECE activities were undertaken with funds under the SSA's Innovation Fund for strengthening ECE in ICDS. These initiatives continued till around 2012–2013, and gradually this support faded away, possibly due to a persisting lack of convergence and coordination with the nodal ministry for ICDS and ECE, that is, MWCD. With the SSA funds drying up, many innovative or quality improvement initiatives in ECE at the state level also came to a close.

Initiatives to strengthen the evidence base: In 2009–2010, a new initiative was undertaken by two universities—Ambedkar University Delhi (a state university) and Jamia Millia Islamia, New Delhi (a central university)—to establish centres for promotion of research and advocacy in the area of ECE/ECD. Both these centres—Center for Early Childhood Education and Development (CECED) and Center for Early Childhood Development and Research (CECDR)—were set up in a parallel mode but with common objectives to (a) expand the base of professional human resource in ECD and (b) enhance the landscape of indigenous research in this field to contribute to policy development. Both universities are currently supporting/offering postgraduate academic programmes in ECE/ECD, which have created some valuable human resource capacity in the system in this domain. In addition, CECED has also led a major longitudinal research titled *India Early Childhood Education Impact Study* (Kaul et al., 2017) in collaboration with ASER Centre in three states mentioned earlier. One of the three strands of the IECEI Study was qualitative in nature involving preparation of analytical case studies of good practices in ECCE, and these case studies (included in Part II of this book) have informed the structure and content of this publication.

The centres have also engaged in quality promotion activities in ECCE, and these along with CLR and Mobile Creches and a few other resource organizations are emerging as specialized institutions in this area. Given India's international commitment previously to Education for All (2000) and more recently to the SDGs (2015), both of which include ECCE as a goal/target as well as its own policy on ECCE, some states have currently initiated action with the support of the UNICEF on fine-tuning initiatives in ECCE, specifically from the perspective of capacity building and quality promotion. But these initiatives are all still at a nascent stage and need to be supported further, strengthened and scaled up. The most recent NEP 2020 has given a further spurt to ECCE by including it as the first stage in the structure of school education and making a strong case for carving out of a foundational stage along the early learning continuum from 3 to 8 years of age for special attention to the foundational learning and curricular continuity with primary education. These recommendations are still in the process of getting implemented.

1.11. Question of Quality: Challenges and Dilemmas

As discussed above, India can and should celebrate the fact that it has been offering a public-sponsored ECCE provision of an integrated design for children below 6 years of age since 1975, which despite the challenge of scale has been almost universalized with 1.4 million centres across the country. This is certainly no mean achievement. Evaluation studies, though not always very robust, have hinted at gains in terms of better nutritional outcomes, improved health indicators and higher enrolment in schools (NIPCCD, 2009). However, as discussed earlier, the challenges of quality, equity and institutional capacity remain. We conclude with a discussion of some of these challenges with a view to foreground the context for the chapters that follow.

1.11.1. Universalizing and Scaling Up with Equitable Quality

A major challenge to quality and effectiveness of ECCE provisions in India is the process of scaling up of these provisions to reach the 70 million preschool children across the country. The ICDS model with its 1.4 million centres clearly demonstrates the pros and cons of this exercise with uneven quality and limited, though positive, outcomes. A significant collateral of attempting this scale has evidently been the need to resort to a welfare-based 'minimalist' approach to quality, given the availability of limited resources to reach out to each child 'equitably' across the country. This is clearly evident in terms of limitations observed in ICDS centres with regard to both structural and process indicators of classroom quality such as physical facilities, adult–child ratio, training of staff, regularity of daily duration of preschool education and weak monitoring and on-site support, all of which have got compromised over the years with large-scale expansion. As a result, with the quality of ECCE offered being uneven, despite significant number of children attending the ECE programme of the ICDS for at least a year, if not two, the school-readiness levels in terms of cognitive and language competencies at the age of five years are across states still very low (ASER Centre, 2019; Kaul et al., 2017).

Another related challenge is the integrated nature of the ICDS model which would undoubtedly be privileged technically over an unidimensional 'educational' model, since it resonates with the globally accepted concept of holistic ECD. However, the challenge lies in its implementation design, the quality of which rests solely on a single ICDS worker with limited educational qualifications, a short, highly inadequate multi-domain training of a month's duration and poor compensation, who is required to serve as a multi-skilled, multi-tasking service provider, and that too with each of the six services requiring a different skill set! This design clearly deserves revisiting. A recurring recommendation over the years to provide for a second worker for the ECE component for 3- to 6-year-olds has not been responded to, possibly due to the enormous implications for the budget, by doubling the numbers from 1.4 million workers to 2.8 million!

1.11.2. Addressing Diversity with Equity and Quality

Given India's social and cultural diversity, a larger issue that emerges is: should there be a standardized 'one-size-fits-all' model, especially for young children for whom the learning principle of 'familiar to unfamiliar' is most significant? As discussed earlier too, the Indian context is characterized by wide diversity in terms of language, religion, castes, class, gender and ability in addition to geographical, cultural and topological aspects, particularly among the indigenous communities. Each of these factors, single-handedly or in combination, have implications for the teacher quality, interpersonal relationships, content, scope and processes of the ECCE curriculum and practice with children.

A developmentally appropriate curriculum by definition implies one that is 'appropriate to children's age and developmental status, attuned to them as unique individuals, and responsive to the social and cultural contexts in which they live' (NAEYC, 2009, p. 11). This points towards the need to prioritize decentralization of decision-making related to contextualization of curriculum to the level of preschools and teachers, since every set of children may be unique and may require the curriculum to be customized to their needs, although within the contours of a broad curricular framework recommended at the state level, to ensure a developmentally appropriate experience for children. Issues of home language vs regional/school language, secular vs religious symbolism, cultural priorities especially in tribal pockets, gender discrimination and neglect of children with special needs are also other issues which need to be engaged with, but all these tend to remain as a part of mere academic discourse.

The emerging issue is that to what extent can decentralization of decision-making with regard to the curriculum be feasible in a federal set-up like India's. Education is essentially a state subject, but the federal government also has a concurrent responsibility of laying down a policy. The Government of India has brought out a National Curriculum Framework (2014) and more recently the NEP 2020, both of which adhere to a developmentally and contextually appropriate and theoretically sound professional perspective. India's IECEI Study further demonstrates the superiority of the developmentally appropriate curriculum as advocated in the policy documents over the prevailing practice of formal teaching of the three Rs in terms of school-readiness outcomes (Kaul & Bhattacharjea, 2019).

The policy intent is to lay out the broad framework of objectives and essentials of curricular domains and pedagogy but allow for more decentralized accommodation and adaptations. A major challenge in this context is the dearth of capacity at decentralized levels in the country to take this recommended process forward. With dearth of institutional capacity and understanding of the concept of developmental appropriateness in ECCE, the response by default or design is to revert to formal teaching of the three Rs, which is more teacher controlled and syllabus driven and also the preference of most parents and which is therefore a visibly prevalent practice across the 'more coveted' affordable private school sector.

1.11.3. Strengthening Institutional and Professional Capacity

Although the vision is for the teachers to be able to have adequate understanding and skills to be able to adapt the National Curriculum Framework into a need-based curriculum for their respective centres as per local contextual needs, realization of this vision has various impediments including lack of good-quality teacher preparation. Despite ICDS being an integral part of the government system since 1975 and ECCE having been given importance at the policy level since 1986 (Ministry of Education, 1986), there are hardly any government-sponsored teacher education institutions dedicated to preparing ECCE teachers in India. The few that are in existence are in the private sector and are inequitably distributed across states (CECED, 2011). This lacuna is primarily an issue of both supply and demand. There had been no provision in the past to provide preschool education in the school system by the provincial governments, except for a few municipal corporations in a few metro cities such as Delhi, Chennai and Mumbai. As a result, there is hardly any pre-service training provision in the public sector across states. Although there are a few inequitably distributed private initiatives in some states, they are often not able to sustain themselves due to lack of demand. With ECCE being an unregulated sector coupled with the absence of a notified cadre of teachers at preschool level (unlike other stages of education), there is no incentive for potential teachers to invest time and resources in getting trained when they can get jobs without it. Private preschools, especially in the affordable category, tend to appoint teachers who are untrained or are trained for higher levels of schooling.

The ICDS also, in its efforts to universalize, has been compromising on its training component. The design of the initial job training of ICDS workers of three months' duration has been reduced to a short-term induction-cum-refresher approach, which is not only inadequate in terms of time allocation but also being cross-disciplinary in content, allows at best for a surface understanding of the ECCE domain. Historically, there has also been the issue of the ECCE workers being minimally qualified academically, but this limitation is gradually receding with better qualified individuals seeking these positions. The challenge is not only at the level of teachers but also at higher levels in terms of dearth of institutional capacity to train, mentor/monitor or supervise programmes. In the absence of adequate trained human resources in the country, the challenge of decentralizing curricula and practice and making it developmentally and contextually appropriate for children, while retaining priorities of quality and equity, appears a distant dream.

1.11.4. Reaching Consensus in Defining Quality

A major issue in addressing quality in ECCE is a lack of common understanding among various stakeholders of what constitutes good-quality ECE which will not only prepare children for school but also provide a foundation to them for lifelong learning. While policies and professionals prescribe what is referred to as developmentally appropriate curriculum with a focus on all-round development, through play-based methods, most programmes, in both ICDS and the private sector, follow in practice a curriculum which is actually a downward extension of the primary curriculum with a clear focus on teaching of the three Rs at this stage (Kaul et al., 2017).

Parental understanding of what is good-quality ECCE appears to be also in most cases along similar lines limited to their understanding of schooling and teaching of the three Rs. In addition to these misplaced priorities, there is also an attraction to English-medium education across the country, which is seen as a ladder for upward social mobility, and which dictates to a considerable extent the expanding demand for private schools.

Another perspective which is important to consider in this context is that in ECCE there is often a 'reflection of a cultural dissonance between western thought and Indian belief systems as is evident between the current policy prescriptions for pedagogy informed by Piaget and Vygotsky and actual classroom practice' (Kaul & Sharma, 2018). Gupta (2006) relates this phenomenon to the cultural dissonance with the pan-Indian understanding of process of learning as 'handed down' or as a process of transmission from teacher to taught, rather than that of 'co-construction' with the active agency of the learner. Teachers, therefore, despite having received training, often get influenced by their own past beliefs and experiences of the schooling system and tend to easily revert to a didactic pedagogy which is more in sync with their understanding of how children learn.

Given the above challenges, some questions that confront us are: How should and can these varying perspectives be reconciled? While there is a National Curriculum Framework (2013) in position and an NEP 2020 which envisages four diverse models of preschool education for three- to six-year-olds to flourish in the country, can a single definition of quality in ECCE be applicable to all? And if not, how do we ensure equity across models? Again, is what is possible and considered good quality in a limited-sized pilot project amenable to sustainability and scaling up? Can we identify some non-negotiable ingredients of a good-quality programme which could be universally applicable while also catering to the contextual diversity? What could be effective modalities to create a consensus on the vision for quality in ECCE as a prerequisite to developing community ownership of a programme? And finally, can we learn from some known good practices in ECCE in our efforts to address some of these emerging but vital questions for envisioning 'equitable quality' in ECCE?

1.12. Deconstructing Quality in ECE: A Collaborative Research Endeavour

Questions, such as those raised above, motivated us to initiate a collective and collaborative research endeavour by bringing together a community of researchers from diverse backgrounds with expertise in ECE, to explore and deconstruct the concept of 'quality' in ECE, especially for children living in marginalized communities. The research agenda for a collaborative study is primarily shaped by the concern for equity and attempts to strengthen democratic processes by strengthening the evidence base (Bruce & Pine, 2010).

This collaborative research was primarily conceptualized to study the phenomenon of quality in preschool education, especially in the context of India's scale and wide diversity. The theme of deconstructing quality in ECE was considered to be extremely topical, given the attention ECE is receiving internationally and nationally in the context of India's policy framework and the SDGs coupled with the acknowledged need for high-quality ECCE to address the persistent problems of 'schooling without learning'. The main objective of this study was to deconstruct the notion of 'quality' of preschool education in India from a qualitative paradigm, with a view to complement the findings of the two quantitative strands of the IECEI Study and thus facilitate a more granular and nuanced understanding of this dynamic social construct (see footnote).[4] The study was intentionally

---

[4] This collaborative research was undertaken by the CECED at Ambedkar University Delhi. This was a part of the multi-strand longitudinal research titled IECEI Study which was implemented between 2011 and 2017 by CECED and ASER Centre with support from several international and national organizations including UNICEF. The IECEI Study was conceptualized to comprehensively explore the domain of ECCE and examine some of the dilemmas related to quality in ECE in the Indian context. Quantitative methods were applied in the design of the first two strands of the study which examined trends in participation and quality of preschool programmes and the effects of participation of children on their school-readiness levels and subsequently on learning levels in primary grades. The first strand was a survey of 13,868 children in 1,616 centres in 362 villages. The second strand was a quasi-experimental study to capture the effects of quality variation in ECCE on school-readiness levels and subsequently on learning levels in primary schools. The data for the first two strands were collected in the states

conducted from an interpretive rather than a positivist paradigm and both the ontology and the epistemology were taken into consideration. Our collaborative initiative led to the development of a collection of qualitative case studies of 'known practices' in the country.

The ECE programmes identified for study were recommended by a group of ECE experts as innovative practices. The case studies thus focused on capturing the unique features and struggles of each programme within specific sociocultural contexts with a view to present thick descriptions of these known practices, rather than focus on evaluating them. These rich narratives give a glimpse of how the idea of quality is approached by different stakeholders in various parts of the country, and this study allows for delineation of an emergent theory by examining specific issues across case studies. This book thus provides an analytical documentation and interpretation of the qualitative data obtained from the case studies, leading to the grounded theory, and deriving from that identifies some domain-specific lessons for the larger system.

As we draw this chapter to a close, we attempt to provide a brief glimpse into the structure and content of this book. The book furthers the discourse on quality from an evidence-based perspective by integrating the data from the study with current literature. It is, therefore, an important resource for practitioners, policymakers and scholars in this field.

The book is divided into 'two' parts.

Part I presents a nuanced and analytic discussion of crucial issues related to promoting quality in ECE in India based on the data and existing literature. While Chapter 2 explains the research process and the emerging grounded theory, Chapters 3 and 4 critically examine the implications for the two major constituent domains of preschool

---

of Assam, Rajasthan and Telangana. The third strand, which has culminated in this publication, was an in-depth, qualitative and collaborative endeavour designed to document through nine qualitative case studies the complex ways in which quality is conceptualized, constructed and contextualized, and to meet the needs of children in different contexts, in preschool programmes which are well known for the quality of their services in varied locations of the country.

quality, that is, curriculum and teacher development and professionalization. Chapter 5 distils the learnings from all the chapters and theorizes on the emerging constructs related to quality in ECE.

Part II presents a compilation of eight case studies of preschool programmes for marginalized children in different states of India, which provide the evidence from which issues were drawn for higher-level analysis in Part I. We were unable to get permission to publish one of the nine case studies which were conducted. Each case study portrays the complex ways in which multiple stakeholders interact to build early learning programmes which are responsive to the needs of young children and to the demands of their families in diverse contexts. The case studies also explore various dilemmas related to addressing quality and innovative approaches to address them.

References

ASER Centre. (2019). *Annual status of education report (rural)*. https://img.aser-centre.org/docs/ASER%202018/Release%20Material/aserreport2018.pdf

ASER Centre. (2020). Annual status of education report (rural): 'Early years'. http://img.asercentre.org/docs/ASER%202019/ASER2019%20report%20/aserreport2019earlyyearsfinal.pdf

Balagopalan, S. (2018). Colonial modernity and the child figure: Refiguring the multiplicity in 'multiple childhoods'. In T. S. Saraswathi, S. Menon, & A. Madan (Eds.), *Childhood in India: Traditions, trends and transformation* (pp. 23–43). Routledge.

Bernstein, B. (1964). Elaborated and restricted codes: Their social origins and social consequences. *Anthro Source, 66*(6), 55–69.

Bhattacharya, P., & Devulapalli, S. (2019). India's rural poverty has shot up. *Mint.* https://www.livemint.com/news/india/rural-poverty-has-shot-up-nso-data-shows-11575352445478.html

Bronfenbrenner, U. (1977). Toward an experimental ecology of human development. *American Psychologist, 32*(7), 513–531. https://doi.org/10.1037/0003-066X.32.7.513

Bruce, S. M., & Pine, G. J. (2010). *Action research in special education: An inquiry approach for effective teaching and learning.* Teachers College Press.

Bruner, J. S. (1975). Poverty and childhood. *Oxford Review of Education, 1*(1), 31–50. http://www.jstor.org/stable/1049995

CECED. (2011). *Preparing teachers for early childhood care and education.* https://www.earlychildhoodworkforce.org/sites/default/files/resources/Preparing_Teacherins_for_Early_Childhood_care_and_Education.pdf

Center on the Developing Child. (2019). Executive function & self-regulation: Key concepts. https://developingchild.harvard.edu/science/key-concepts/executive-function/

GoI. (2011). Annual report 2011 -2012. Ministry of Women and Child Development. https://wcd.nic.in/sites/default/files/AR2011-12.pdf

Gupta, A. (2006). Early childhood education, postcolonial theory, and teaching practices in India: Balancing Vygotsky and the Vedas. Palgrave Macmillan.

Haft, S., & Hoeft, F. (2017). Poverty's impact on children's executive functions: Global considerations. New directions in child and adolescent development, 158, 69–79.

Kagitcibasi, C. (2012). Sociocultural change and integrative syntheses in human development: Autonomous-related self and social–cognitive competence. Child Development Perspectives, 6(1), 5–11. https://doi.org/10.1111/j.1750-8606.2011.00173.x

Kak, M., & Govindaraj, R. (2018). Evaluating integration in the icds: Impact evaluation of an awc-cum-creche pilot in madhya pradesh (Report No: AUS0000253). World Bank. https://documents1.worldbank.org/curated/en/493951537776051558/pdf/Impact-Evaluation-of-an-AWC-cum-creche-pilot-in-Madhya-Pradesh.pdf

Kaul, V., & Bhattacharjea, S. (Eds.). (2019). Early childhood education and school readiness in India: Quality and diversity. Springer.

Kaul, V., Bhattacharjea, S., Chaudhary, A. B., Ramanujan, P., Banerji, M., & Nanda, M. (2017). The India early childhood education impact study (p. 76). UNICEF.

Kaul, V., Ramachandran, C., & Upadhaya, G. C. (1994). A study of impact of preschool education on retention in primary grades. NCERT.

Kaul, V., & Sankar, D. (2016). Early childhood care and education in India. In R. Govinda & M. Sedwal (Eds.), Elementary education in India. Oxford University Press.

Kaul, V., & Sharma, S. (2018). Early childhood policies in India: A historical analysis. In L. Miller, C. Cameron, C. Dalli, & N. Barbour (Eds.), The SAGE handbook of early childhood policy. SAGE Publications.

Kaur, B. (2006, 30 November–4 December). Gathering the destitute child: A case study in India [Paper presentation]. 14th Reconceptualizing Early Childhood Conference, Rotorua, New Zealand.

Khalakdina, M. (2011). Human development in the Indian context: A socio-cultural focus (Vol. II). SAGE Publications.

Menon, S., & Saraswathi, T. S. (2018). Introduction. In T. S. Saraswathi, S. Menon, and A. Dewan (Eds.), Childhoods in India: Traditions, trends and transformations (p.7). Routledge.

Ministry of Education. (1986). National policy on education. Government of India.

Ministry of Human Resource Development. (2009). The Right of Children to Free and Compulsory Education Act (RTE). Government of India.

Ministry of Women and Child Development. (2013). *National policy on early childhood care and education.* Government of India.

Mobile Creches. (2020). *Status of the young child in India* (South Asia ed.). Routledge.

NAEYC (National Association for the Education of Young Children). (2009) Developmentally appropriate practice in early childhood programs serving children from birth through age 8. A position statement of the National Association for the Education of Young Children. https://www.naeyc.org/sites/default/files/globally-shared/downloads/PDFs/resources/position-statements/PSDAP.pdf pp 11

NCERT. (2005). National curriculum framework. https://ncert.nic.in/pdf/nc-framework/nf2005-english.pdf

NIPCCD (National Institute of Public Cooperation and Child Development). (2009). *Research in ICDS: An overview (1996–2008).*

Office of the Registrar General & Census Commissioner. (2011). Census of India. Ministry of Home Affairs, Government of India.

Raman, V. (2018). India's children and the brave new world. In T. S. Saraswathi, S. Menon, & A. Madan (Eds.), *Childhoods in India: Traditions, trends and transformations* (p. 74). Routledge India.

Rao, N., & Kaul, V. (2017). *India's Integrated Child Development Services scheme: Challenges for scaling up in child—Care, health and development* [Case Report]. John Wiley & Sons.

Save the Children. (2017). What is the impact of poverty on children in India. Available at: https://www.savethechildren.in/poverty-and-inclusion/what-is-the-impact-of-poverty-on-children-inindia/#:~:text=Children%20who%20live%20below%20the,stimulating%20environment%20for%20their%20children

Saxena, N. C. (2016). Malnourished and marginalised. *Budget Track,* 11, 15–17.

Shonkoff, J. (2011). Protecting brains not simply stimulating minds. *Science,* *333,* 982.

Shonkoff, J. P., & Phillips, D. A. (Eds.). (2010). *From neurons to Neighborhoods: The science of early childhood development.* National Academy Press.

Super, C., & Harkness, S. (1994). The developmental niche: A theoretical framework for analyzing the household production of health. *Social Science & Medicine, 38*(2), 217–226.

Super, C. M., & Harkness S. (1986). The developmental niche: A conceptualisation at the interface of child and culture. *International Journal of Behavioural Development, 9*(4), 545–569.

Tschurenev, J. (2021). Montessori for all? Indian experiments in 'child education', 1920s–1970s. *Comparative Education.* https://doi.org/10.1080/03050068.2021.1888408

Upadhyaya, G. C. (1996). *Identifying numeracy and reading readiness levels of entrants to Class I: A synthesis report.* NCERT.

UNESCO. (2013–2014). 250 million primary school age children can't read, write or do basic math: UN report. https://globalnews.ca/news/1117609/250-million-primary-school-age-children-cant-read-write-or-do-basic-math-un-report/#:~:text=link%20Copy%20link-,At%20least%20250%20million%20of%20the%20world's%20650%20million%20primary,by%20the%20U.N.%20education%20agency.&text=UNESCO's%20U.N. (Accessed on 28 March 2021).

UNICEF. (2020a). Impact of COVID-19 crisis on the lives of children in India. Panel discussion with media for World Children's Day 2020. https://www.unicef.org/india/media/4811/file/Impact%20of%20COVID-19%20crisis%20on%20the%20lives%20of%20children%20in%20India%20-%20Panel%20discussion%20with%20media%20for%20World%20Children's%20Day.pdf

UNICEF. (2020b). Protecting the most vulnerable children from the impact of coronavirus: An agenda for action. https://www.unicef.org/coronavirus/agenda-for-action

United Nations. (2015). *Transforming our world: The 2030 agenda for sustainable development*. https://sustainabledevelopment.un.org/content/documents/21252030%20Agenda%20for%20Sustainable%20Development%20web.pdf

World Bank. (2018). *World development report*. https://www.worldbank.org/en/publication/wdr2018

World Health Organization. (2018). *Nurturing care for early childhood development: A global framework for action and results*. https://www.who.int/maternal_child_adolescent/child/nurturing-care-framework-first-draft.pdf

World Health Organization, United Nations Children's Fund, & World Bank Group. (2018). *Nurturing care for early childhood development: A framework for helping children survive and thrive to transform health and human potential*. World Health Organization.

CHAPTER 2

Deconstructing Quality
Grounded Theory from Multiple Case Studies
Monimalika Day

We embarked on an ambitious journey to conduct a collective case study of early childhood education programmes, known to experts for the quality of services provided to young children and families living in poverty. This was a collaborative endeavour involving a diverse group of researchers. The purpose was to capture the complexities of designing, sustaining and scaling up such programmes, with a specific focus on gaining a nuanced understanding of preschool quality. The study was conceived to bring evidence which can be easily considered by policymakers and programme developers committed to promote excellence in early childhood education. A total of nine case studies were conducted simultaneously in eight states of India by researchers from different disciplines, through a collaborative research project led by (Centre for Early Childhood Education and Development) CECED. The background and the purpose of the research have been explained in Chapter 1. In this chapter, we elaborate on the collaborative research process, research design for the multiple case studies and the emergent theory grounded in the empirical data.

2.1. Collaborative Research: Diversity, Dilemmas and Dialogues

Collaborative research from a postmodern paradigm is often conducted with an agenda to study a phenomenon which is of great significance at a specific period of time in relation to the social and cultural contexts (Bruce & Pine, 2010; Meyer et al., 1998). Such research is grounded in the concern for equity and is an attempt to strengthen the democratic processes. Often, this is a topic which has received little attention from mainstream researchers. The coming together of experts from various backgrounds to a common platform reflects the urgency to study the topic. Collier (1945) initiated a collaborative action research in the USA to reverse the discriminatory practices against Native American people and preserve their culture and language. A consortium for collaborative research was formed by Meyer et al. (1998) to document the ways in which children with disabilities socialize and form relationships with their peers. Similarly, a research consortium with five universities was formed by Odom et al. (2002) to document the strategies for inclusion of children with disabilities in preschools in different regions of the USA. Moreover, Charmaz (2011) argues that grounded theory method can be applied to social justice enquiry in the 21st century by examining issues of equitable resources, fairness and oppression. The need for collaborative research also stems from the need to bridge the gap between research and practice.

According to Cheruvelil et al. (2014), the success of collaborative research rests on three caveats: first, a team consisting of diverse researchers committed to a specific goal; second, the interpersonal relationships between researchers, which gives cohesion to the group and fosters social sensitivity and emotional engagement; and third, capacity-building processes to engage in the fieldwork. Further, the authors identify three main features of strong collaborations as positive interdependence of team members, effective communication, and both individual and group accountability. These elements are reflected in the nine stages of this collaborative enquiry from conceptualization to completing this manuscript, presented in the Table 2.1. The process of collaboration was inductive and developed based on the needs of the project as well as the researchers. Needless to say, it was far from a linear predictable process. A discussion on the various dilemmas which emerged at each stage is beyond the scope of this chapter, but the major issues are presented in the table. A discussion on the various dilemmas which emerged at each stage is beyond the scope of this chapter, but the major issues are presented in Table 2.1. These dilemmas were critical to pursuing an inductive research design.

Several scholars have emphasized the need to have a diverse group of researchers in order to conduct a collaborative enquiry from an interpretive paradigm as the various lenses they bring to the project ensure diversity of perspectives and help to address the issue of subjectivity right from the process of deciding what should be the focus of the study be to the theory-building process (Cheruvelil et al., 2014; Meyer et al., 1998). There was much thought that went into the process of bringing together the community of researchers, each of whom were charged with conducting a case study. The principal investigator for each study brought together a small team of one or two research assistants to conduct the enquiry. While a few of the researchers had conducted qualitative research prior to joining this project, majority did not have that experience. There was a need to create a platform for dialogues to create opportunities to share perspectives and allow development of intersubjectivity among the researchers. A summary of the stages of the research process, major tasks and related dilemmas are presented in Table 2.1.

As a lead organization, CECED at Ambedkar University Delhi needed to (a) create the space for collaboration, (b) organize information and (c) engage in ongoing communication to remind the researchers of the activities to be completed. Thus, it was essential to have a dedicated team for this project, with different roles and responsibilities. Professor Venita Kaul ensured synergy between the different strands of the IECEI Study. I was given the charge to conceptualize the methodology, plan the workshops and lead the study. Swati Bawa Sawhney took the responsibility to monitor the implementation of the project and provide administrative support to each research team.

The journey began with a workshop with the Research Advisory Committee (RAC) to identify the objectives of the study and develop a conceptual framework, to ensure a common platform for the researchers. According to Miles and Huberman (1994), developing

Table 2.1. Stages in the Collaborative Research

S. No.	Purpose	Process	Dilemmas and Questions	Outcome
1.	Design a qualitative study which complements other strands of the IECEI Study	Workshop with RAC	–	Initial conceptual framework
2.	Review a concept note on the research methodology	Workshop with researchers identified for the case studies, RAC members and funders	How to connect findings from different research strands which were designed based on different research paradigms?	• Agreement on the need for qualitative case studies • Research questions • Criteria for selection of programmes • Initial list of researchers • Identifying the lead researcher for the collaborative research
3.	Finalize a research proposal on a collective case study	• Workshop with researchers for the case study and RAC members • Workshop to finalize research proposal • Detailed discussion on data collection strategies and decide tools • Introduction to qualitative enquiry and data collection processes	• Negotiating the tension of rigour and feasibility • Prolonged engagement vs short visits • Variation in researchers familiarity with qualitative paradigm	• Forming a community of researchers • Final research proposal • Guiding questions • Steps for data collection • Tools for data collection

4.	Creating a community of researchers	• Finalizing contracts for each case study	• Expertise in early childhood education • Expertise in qualitative enquiry • Availability of experts	• Identifying the principal investigators for each study
5.	Workshop on data analysis	• Presenting data from the first visit to the sites • Peer debriefing on data collected in the first visit • Introducing data analysis using constant comparative method • Workshop on software for qualitative methods	• Tensions between inductive and deductive approaches • Tensions between etic and emic codes • Resources for the qualitative analysis software	• Emerging research questions for each case study • List of etic codes • Request for interactions with lead researcher from some teams • Resources were not available to provide access to software for each team
6.	Facilitating data analysis in various teams	Lead researcher conducted data analysis workshops with various teams	• Tensions between inductive and deductive approaches • Tensions between etic and emic codes • Negotiating the tension between generalization and specificity • Lack of linearity in the process	• Emerging codes and themes from each case study • Developing claims

(Table 2.1 Continued)

(Table 2.1 Continued)

S. No.	Purpose	Process	Dilemmas and Questions	Outcome
7.	Developing research reports including member checking and peer debriefing	• Workshop to share the case study reports • Review of each case study report by peer researcher and an expert • Member checking and review of case study report by the programme studied	• Negotiating tension between insider and outsider perspectives • Negotiating critical feedback from peers • Negotiating the tension between generalization and specificity	• Critique and feedback on each case study report • Incorporating feedback to develop final reports for each case study which were submitted to the respective funders
8.	Presenting the emergent theory from the multiple case studies	• Workshop with representatives of programmes studied, national and international experts • Presenting each case study • Presenting the grounded theory	• Complementing information from other strands of the study vs a stand-alone piece • Asymmetries in the case studies	• Feedback on grounded theory • Feedback on each case study
9.	Research reports to manuscripts	• Review of case studies by a content editor • Exploring publishers • Editing of case studies by lead researcher • Writing thematic chapters	• Critical feedback from content editor • Summarizing vs retaining thick descriptions • Asymmetries in the case studies • Retaining uniqueness vs developing uniformity across case studies	Manuscript for the book

a conceptual framework in advance is necessary even in a study with emergent design, as it helps to focus data collection and enables comparison across different cases when conducting multiple case studies. Following which, a community of researchers was brought together to refine the research questions, debate on the method of study and decide on the selection criteria for identifying the sample of the study. The primary research questions for the study were as follows:

1. What are the key elements of quality in terms of curricular, organizational, financial, management and professional development in early childhood education interventions which are conducive to creating a learning environment which promotes the intended learning and developmental outcomes in children in different contexts?
2. How do the known programmes engage with special categories of children (girls, special needs, minority language groups, schedule caste, tribal population, etc.)?
3. What are the scaling-up implications in terms of finance, training and management in running quality programmes on a large scale?

A set of guiding questions was later developed at the request of researchers to focus the data collection process and allow comparisons across case studies. To follow an iterative process, data collection for each case study was conducted in two visits. Since we pursued an interpretive approach, the research design for each case study was further refined based on the data collected during the first visit to each programme. Individual researchers presented the primary findings from the data analysis of the first visit in a workshop and received feedback from the entire community of researchers. Through discussions, the researchers identified salient questions which required deeper exploration based on the initial analysis of evidence and modified the data collection plan for the second visit to address these issues.

The initial level of analysis was conducted through a constant comparative method for each case study, which is presented in Part II of this book. The third section in this chapter presents the grounded theory from a second level of analysis of the themes and claims which emerged from the nine case studies by identifying key concepts related to quality, the ways in which they were related and the various issues which facilitated or hindered development of good programmes, with an intent to deconstruct quality by studying variations within and across the case studies.

Dilemmas are eminent in a collaborative project of this magnitude. They make us uncomfortable yet create windows of opportunities for deeper explorations of the topic. Since this was a national-level study, and researchers came together from various parts of the country, the workshops provided a critical platform for learning, dialogue, planning and problem-solving. These interactions helped to sustain the momentum of the study and to engage in perspective taking to develop shared understanding of issues and concepts. More importantly, these dialogues were critical in developing the grounded theory on quality of preschools for young children in the margins.

2.2. Method for Multiple Case Studies

This section presents the research design for the individual case studies and rationale for the decisions taken. According to Bell (2005, p. 10), while conducting case studies of organizations researchers need to '...identify various interactive processes at work, to show how they affect the implementation of systems, and influence the way an organization functions'. Researchers can obtain valuable information about a programme by observing the routine activities and engaging in authentic dialogues with the stakeholders to understand and document their experiences. According to Stake (2008), a well-known expert on this methodology, case studies may be divided into three different categories based on the purpose for which they are undertaken and related methodological decisions: intrinsic, instrumental and collective. He further defines collective case study or multiple case study in the following words:

> A number of cases may be studied jointly in order to investigate a phenomenon, population, or general condition. I call this multiple case study or collective case study. It is instrumental study extended to several cases.... They may be similar or dissimilar, with redundancy and variety, each important. They are chosen because it is believed that understanding them will lead to better understanding

and perhaps theorizing, about a still larger collection of cases. (Stake, 2008, p.123)

There is a crucial need to strengthen the evidence base of early childhood education in India to improve the quality of programmes for children from marginalized groups. The community of researchers decided to use the 'multiple case design' recommended by Yin (2009) to study the 'nine early childhood programmes' and identify the various components and factors related to the quality of preschool education. The following sections present the process of sampling, tools and techniques for data collection, procedures for data analysis and strategies used to ensure the credibility of the study. Although these four processes are discussed separately, they are closely interconnected and often occur simultaneously as reflected in Table 2.1.

2.2.1. Purposive Sampling

The aim of this study was to deconstruct the notion of quality in early childhood education programmes; it was, therefore, essential to begin by identifying programmes known to experts for their 'good practices'. A 'purposive sampling' technique was applied to select the nine programmes. This strategy was especially useful, as programmes and participants were chosen based on their relevance to the subject of enquiry (Glaser & Strauss, 1967). The three steps in the sampling process were selection of programmes, selection of two centres within each programme and selection of participants connected to the programmes and the centres.

An initial list of programmes was identified using two criteria. First, known practices were selected from Strand B of the IECEI project for the case study research on the basis of scores on classroom quality (Early Childhood Education Quality Assessment Scale [ECEQAS]), preparation for school (school-readiness instrument [SRI]) and children's annual attendance. Bodh Shiksha Samiti in Rajasthan and Society for Elimination of Rural Poverty (SERP) in Telangana were selected using this criterion. In addition, 'seven new programmes' were identified by the group of experts. The following criteria were applied for selection of the additional programmes:

1. Programmes should represent different sectors (government and non-governmental organizations [NGOs]) in urban, rural and tribal sites from different states.
2. They should offer services primarily to children from the low socio-economic groups and marginalized communities. Therefore, private preschools were not included.

A list of programmes and the principal investigators for each case study was identified based on their expertise, knowledge of programmes in that region and their availability following intense deliberations. The list of programmes, principal investigators and type of programmes is presented in Table 2.2.

Table 2.2. List of Programmes

S. No.	Researcher	Programme	Category	State
1.	Dr Nandita Chaudhary	Bodh Shiksha Samiti (Chapter 8)	Semi-urban	Rajasthan
2.	Dr Usha Nayar and Dr Reeta Sonawat	Pratham (Mumbai) (Chapter 11)	Urban	Maharashtra
3.	Dr Deepa Jain	Gali Gali Sim Sim Collaboration with Integrated Child Development Services (ICDS) (Mumbai)	Urban	Maharashtra
4.	Dr Usha Abrol	Prajayatna	Urban	Karnataka
5.	Dr Suman Sachdeva	Nidan (Chapter 9)	Urban	Bihar
6.	Dr Harini Rawal	ICDS Gujarat, Collaboration with Bhansali Trust (Chapter 13)	Rural	Gujrat
7.	Dr Monimalika Day	Uttarakhand Seva Nidhi Paryavaran Shiksha Sansthan (USNPSS) (Chapter 6)	Rural	Uttarakhand
8.	Dr Usha Abrol	SERP (Chapter 7)	Tribal	Telangana
9.	Professor Venita Kaul	Centre for Learning Resources (Chapter 12)	Tribal	Maharashtra

Second, though each organization operated multiple centres, the principal investigator for each case study in discussion with programme administrators 'selected two centres': One that demonstrated good practices and another that was facing challenges. Yin (2009) argues that comparative case study method is a specific form of multiple case studies which provides insights into variations of the phenomenon being documented. This allowed us to explore variations in quality within programmes and to study the construct of quality in considerable depth in these two centres. ECEQAS, a tool used in the longitudinal IECEI Study, was used to measure classroom quality in these centres.

The judgements of the experts regarding the quality of the early childhood education programmes selected for the case studies were confirmed by the ECEQAS scores collected during the first visit. A comparison of the ECEQAS scores of programmes selected for the case studies (Strand C of the IECEI study) (as shown in Table 2.3) and programmes which participated in the longitudinal study (Strand B of the IECEI Study) indicates that the mean score was higher for former. It is necessary to note that the averages for the major domains in ECEQAS for preschools in the case studies were calculated by considering the scores of the two centres: one that functioned well and another which faced challenges which affected the quality of the centre. The data from four of the programmes was incomplete and therefore not included. The data for the longitudinal study was taken from the CECED (2015) report and presents information on quality of early childhood programmes studied in the three states of Assam, Rajasthan and Telangana.

Third, participants and key informants were identified for observations, interviews and focus group discussions. This included programme administrators, supervisors and front-line workers (e.g., Balwadi teachers and Anganwadi workers). In addition, 'three target children' were selected to administer the SRI and adaptive behaviour scale (ABS) in the age range of four–six years in each centre.

Fourth, specific events such as Balmela (children's fair) or meetings with parents were selected to understand the process of curriculum transaction and community interactions.

Table 2.3. Comparison of ECEQAS between the Case Studies and the Longitudinal Study

Programmes Items of ECEQAS	Strand C (Scale of 10)						Strand B (Scale of 10)				
	Centre for Learning Resources	ICDS Gujarat	Bodh Shiksha Samiti	Pratham	USNPSS	Mean	Known Practice Programmes (n = 22)	AWC (n = 171)	Private Preschool (n = 97)	Government Preschool (n = 14)	Mean
Language and reasoning experience	8.50	4.75	8.75	8.25	8.25	31.90	7.20	6.10	5.70	5.80	20.45
Fine and gross motor activities	8.33	5.83	6.25	7.08	9.17	29.33	3.70	1.90	0.90	1.30	6.83
Creative activities	9.29	4.64	8.57	9.64	8.57	33.86	6.20	4.30	3.50	0.90	14.23
Social development	5.71	7.50	5.00	7.86	7.50	27.57	6.30	5.20	5.50	5.50	18.38
Teacher's disposition	8.33	1.67	3.33	6.67	3.33	20.67	7.40	6.40	5.20	4.80	20.20

Table 2.4. *Summary of Qualitative Strategies*

Qualitative Tools	Participants
Interviews	Administrators, supervisors, front-line workers, including Anganwadi workers and Balwadi teachers, and families
Participant observations	Classroom observations, community meetings and unique activities of the programme
Focus group discussions (optional)	Balwadi teachers, families of children attending the programme and community members
Documents and artefacts	Annual report, newspaper clippings, teacher's diary, logbook of teachers, lesson plans, etc. Curriculum, brochure, assessment documents, minutes and agenda Artefacts: Photographs, films and sample work of children
Videos	Focus on activities which demonstrate exemplary practices: lessons, meetings with families, etc. Videos were taken only after classroom observation and administration of ECEQAS

2.2.2. Process for Data Collection

This was a qualitative enquiry, and various strategies used for data collection including participant observations, ethnographic interviews, document analysis and focus group meetings, as indicated in Table 2.4. The primary purpose of the study was to understand and document the experiences and perspectives of the participants who were closely associated with the selected programmes along with the history of the programmes, their efforts to address quality multiple perspectives on quality and challenges encountered. Researchers were encouraged to establish the rigour of the study by supporting their arguments by triangulating data from multiple participants and methods of data collection. In addition, a few quantitative tools used in Strand B of the IECEI Study were used to describe the sample characteristics and link the findings to the other strands of the research and are listed in Table 2.5.

Participant observation was a valuable strategy to document the transaction of the curriculum and classroom interactions. It allowed

Table 2.5. *Quantitative Tools Used for Data Collection*

Name of the Instrument	Source of Data Collection
Observation ECEQAS	Examines quality of preschool classroom, including physical environment, children's participation and teacher disposition conducted in the two selected centres
ABS	Provides information on social–emotional development of children A total of six parents of the selected children from each programme
Assessment: SRI	A total of six children between the ages of four and six years from each programme, three from each centre

us to capture variations in the quality of preschool activities, pedagogical processes, participation of children, participation of families and teacher disposition. This process was also used to document parent meetings or community events. The process of observation allowed us to gain insights into existing hierarchies of caste, gender and other social issues. Participant observations differ from ordinary observations primarily because of reflexivity of the researchers (Glesne & Peshkin, 1992). Researchers address the issue of objectivity not by maintaining an objective stance but by describing how they were influenced or may have influenced the events. Anandalakshmy et al. (2008, p. 36) suggest that

> The essence of good research lies in consciously knowing when to distance and when to close in. Perhaps, some of the indicators lie in the actual distance between the researcher and the researched. When there is distance we need to work inwards, and when one is part of a social reality, then step a little outside.

For this purpose, researchers were encouraged to write reflective memos with observation notes. Some events were later photographed or videotaped to document specific aspects of the phenomenon. We later learned that the quality of most videos was not good enough to create documentaries.

Ethnographic interviews were conducted in each programme with administrators, supervisors, Balwadi teachers or Anganwadi workers and parents to explore the notion of quality from multiple perspectives. In some sites, additional interviews were conducted with community members or founder members to understand the history and evolution of the programme. Spradley (1979, p. 9) describes ethnographic interviews simply 'as a strategy for getting people to talk about what they know' by establishing a rapport with them. While a protocol was developed for interviews with administrators, educators, mentors and families, subsequent questions often emerged based on the responses from the participants and provided more in-depth information (Lincoln & Guba, 1985). Researchers audiotaped most interviews with permission and wrote analytical notes. Our experience supports Anandalakshmy et al.'s (2008, p. 40) observation that researchers need to remain flexible and include 'a constellation of people' in the dialogue with parents or other caregivers, as in India it is natural for neighbours and relatives to join a conversation regarding children.

A variety of documents were collected such as annual reports, government orders, monthly progress reports (MPRs), teachers' diaries, lesson plans, logbooks of teachers, brochures, minutes and agendas, which may be used to substantiate or verify data obtained from other sources. Yin (2009, p. 103) proposes that 'For case studies, the most important use of documents is to corroborate and augment evidence from other sources.' Documents were primarily used to triangulate data obtained from other sources. Artefacts such as programme brochures, publications, photographs, films, work samples of children's work and assessment records were collected by the researchers.

Researchers were given the option of conducting focus group discussions with participants, if needed. Many researchers used a semi-structured or unstructured approach to collect information from a group of teachers, families or community members. The concept of focus group meetings has been borrowed from market research (Denzin & Lincoln, 2008) and involves a group discussion which is usually conducted to capture a diversity of perspectives on a specific topic.

2.2.3. Data Analysis

The constant comparison method of data analysis was originally developed by Glaser and Strauss (1967). It is considered to be 'a foundational pillar of classic GT [grounded theory] in which data are analyzed as they are collected and are constantly compared to with previously collected data for interchangeable indicators of emerging concepts' (Holton & Walsh, 2017, p. 210). Therefore, analysis was initiated after the first round of data collection. The data analysis for individual case studies had seven steps: coding the data (categorizing), identifying themes (integrating categories), analysis of data from tools, developing claims (primary findings from each case study), writing the case study report, member check and review by experts. The analysis was an iterative process, and the various steps are often overlapped to refine the data collection, especially for the second visit. Codes are small units of meaning. We developed codes by comparing incidents and labelling them to form categories. Developing coding categories is an inductive and recursive process which begins with data collection and ends when we reach a point of saturation only, and there is no further need for categorization (Glaser & Strauss, 1967). Both etic and emic codes (Lincoln & Guba, 1985) were developed to capture insider and outsider perspectives. A list of predetermined codes (etic) based on existing literature was identified prior to data collection. Emic codes emerged by capturing the perspectives of the participants. The codes were grouped together to develop themes. This was a higher-level analysis which helped the researcher to examine the relationships between the different codes and explore various constructs.

The data from the quantitative tools were presented in a descriptive analysis as these were collected from a small purposive sample. While some researchers stopped after the thematic analysis, others developed claims and supported them with evidence. Each team was required to develop and present the case reports to the community of researchers, representatives of the programmes studied and outside experts.

2.2.4. Ensuring Credibility

We primarily used three major strategies to ensure credibility of the study, which were: data triangulation, peer debriefing and member checking (Lincoln & Guba, 1985). Data triangulation was applied in multiple ways, including using different methods to explore the phenomenon, documenting perspectives of several participants and sampling events over time. Peer debriefing refers to a process through which the investigators become aware of their biases and receive support from their peers in interpreting the data, refining the methodology and developing the reports (Lincoln & Guba, 1985). The community of researchers met in several workshops to present findings and received critical feedback. In addition, every report was reviewed by a member of the research collective, a member of the RAC and the lead researcher. Finally, member checks involve verifying the data interpretations and conclusions with the respondents. This was an ongoing process, where each research team confirmed various findings with participants. The final report of the case study was shared with each organization for comments. Moreover, programme representatives attended a workshop, where each case study and the grounded theory was shared at the culmination of the study. A limitation of the study was the inability to engage in the field for a prolonged period of time due to shortage of resources and unavailability of researchers.

There were various ethical issues encountered by the research team, a few of them have been highlighted in the Table 2.1 on collaborative research. Obtaining informed consent tends to be more complicated in such a qualitative enquiry as participants and events selected for the study may change over time. We followed the recommendations of Miles and Huberman (1994) to use the ongoing negotiations with participants for informed consent. While the programme managers agreed to participate in the study, researchers explained the study verbally to the adult participants and sought their verbal approval, as some of them were not literate or had limited literacy. We have retained the names of the programmes and founder members to maintain authenticity, but pseudonyms have been used for all other participants.

2.2.5. Case Study Reports

Teaching and learning are sociocultural processes which need to be understood in specific contexts. The goal was to capture the experiences of the participants and explore the meaning of their experiences.

For example, how do children, parents, teachers and community members engage with education and what does it mean to them? The goal was also to identify the important concepts embedded in the data. To develop case reports, researchers were encouraged to present detailed narratives of events, activities, relationships and classroom processes; 'explore the factors' which influence the lives of children; and 'compare information' from different contexts (the two centres) to learn from the similarities and differences (Descombe, 2007). In reporting findings from an interpretive enquiry, Geertz (1973) has argued that 'thick description' of the data is essential to examine and interpret the meaning assigned to various practices and the use of symbols and document the complexities in the phenomenon being studied.

2.3. The Emergent Theory on Quality of Preschool Education

The final process of developing a grounded theory was completed by carefully analysing the findings from each case study presented in Part II of this book and synthesizing the information to develop explanations of how quality was constructed by various stakeholders in different context, the variations in quality or the circumstances when it was lacking. Glaser and Strauss (1967) originally developed this approach and argued that theories developed from this framework are ecologically valid, fit the context of enquiry and are understandable to participants and the ordinary people. Glaser (1978, p. 2) defined it as 'GT is the systematic generation of theory from data that has itself been systematically obtained.' Later, Holton and Walsh suggested that the grounded theory reflects both the process of conducting the research and the emergent theory which is anchored in empirical data. According to Lincoln and Guba (1985, p. 205), 'No a priori theory can anticipate the many realities that the inquirer will inevitably encounter in the field, nor encompass the many factors that make a difference at the micro (local) level.' The emergent grounded theory was presented to the community of researchers, the RAC and both national and international experts. While discussing analysis in a grounded theory, Holton and Walsh (2017, p. 78) assert that 'Concepts remain buried amid detailed empirical accounts, and it is difficult if not impossible to see the simple elegance in the relationships between concepts that together integrate a grounded theory and provide its explanatory power.'

According to Gregor (2006), essentially, there are five different types of theories, which are: analytical, explanatory, predictive, explanatory and predictive design and action. The grounded theory presented in this book is primarily explanatory in nature, as it attempts to answer questions such as: What is quality? What are the main components of quality? How do the different components relate to each other and influence quality? Which components are essential and must be given priority? Where is the programme situated, and how do they respond to specific needs of the local children and families? Why? The three foundational components of the grounded theory are: emergence, constant comparison and theoretical sampling (Holton & Walsh, 2017). The emergent theory from the multiple case studies suggests that the following issues must be taken into consideration in conceptualizing and scaling up quality of early childhood education programmes in India.

2.3.1. Multiple Childhoods and Marginalization

While this topic was not the primary focus of the study, the collective evidence from different case studies indicate that the nature of early childhood varies considerably across different geographical, social and cultural contexts in India, and it is essential to document these variations to develop contextually relevant early childhood programmes. A few examples would help to illustrate the three kinds of variations.

While conducting the case study of Seva Nidhi in Shama district of Uttarakhand, located in the high altitudes of the northwestern Himalayas, we came across the practice of the use of *doka*, a basket designed to keep children safe and comfortable while mothers worked in the fields. Conversations with local villagers indicated that such baskets were primarily used for infants and toddlers but may have been used for children till the age of six years in the past. This practice indicates the critical need for childcare services, a need voiced by various communities across the nation. Moreover, the prolonged hours spent by the babies in these baskets questions existing science of early stimulation and suggests the need to explore alternative developmental pathways. The concept of parental ethnography (Harkness et al. 2009) and developmental niche proposed by Super and Harkness (1986) is particularly useful in studying such practices. While conducting research to study the concept of early stimulation for babies in nine countries, they concluded that the meaning of the phrase varies considerably across countries.

Considering the social milieu, we notice the specific concerns in urban and rural sites. For example, Nidan's work with marginalized children in Patna reveals that children who belong to lower castes begin to encounter several barriers to access education early in life. Even in government schools, some of the Dalit students experienced various kinds of marginalization, and therefore parents preferred to enrol children in the preschool started by the NGO. Furthermore, young children in urban migrant communities sometimes had to miss preschool to support their parents in menial jobs, which could be hazardous. On the other hand, the Gujarat ICDS study reports that regularity was a major concern for children of agricultural labourers. Even when parents were interested in educating their young children, they had to move from one place to another in search of work and found it difficult to ensure regular participation in the Anganwadis.

From a cultural perspective, while visiting Bodh, researchers observed that in a Muslim community, children above the age of four years went to the local madrasa to read 'Sipara' from the Quran and learn Urdu in the afternoon. The Balwadi programme took into consideration this cultural activity as they developed the preschool routine. Chapter 3 on presents examples of use of cultural artefacts and activities in the curriculum of various preschool programmes.

2.3.2. Curriculum: A Dialectic between Policy and the Context

There were interesting variations in the curriculum developed by the different programmes. The variations emerged primarily from attempting to adapt policy recommendations to the local needs of the community. Four pedagogical approaches were observed in the classrooms: the thematic approach, activity-based approach, place-based education and relationship-based approach. The first two have been recommended in different policies on early childhood education including the ECCE Policy (GoI, 2013a), the ECCE Curriculum Framework (GoI, 2013b) and the recent NEP 2020 (GoI, 2020). The latter two approaches had evolved from the values and perspectives of various stakeholders. Nuanced analyses of these practices are presented in Chapter 3. The structure of the curriculums and the activities were anchored in different philosophical perspectives including Gijubhai Badheka, Tarabai Modak, Maria Montessori, Jean Piaget and Lev Vygotsky. The curriculum of CLR and Bodh were exemplary and were informed by recent research on young children's learning and development. Multiple languages were used in classrooms in rural, urban and tribal areas. Preschools, especially in urban areas, were challenged to create multicultural classrooms. A range of good practices were documented on literacy, but activities focusing on numeracy required further strengthening in most of the programmes. The influence of Gijubhai Badheka's work was evident in many programmes in the way that local low-cost materials were used to facilitate learning (Kaul, 2009; Tschurenev, 2021). Consistent with findings in other studies (Kaul, 2019), it was found that good infrastructure was necessary but did not always lead to high-quality learning environment.

2.3.3. Crucial Role of the Teacher

The most important finding of this collaborative enquiry is that the quality of a preschool is determined primarily by the quality of the teacher. It is worth noting that every case study presents a claim on the crucial role of the teacher; this is a powerful testimony, especially considering the diversity of location, philosophy and structure of the programmes. Furthermore, this is supported by the findings from the other strands of the IECEI Study (Kaul & Bhattacharjea, 2019). First, we present the emerging categories of variations in the quality of the teachers. Second, we explore some of the reasons behind the positive relationship between the quality of the teacher and the preschool classroom. Third, we discuss the importance given by programmes to teacher recruitment and capacity building.

Teaching young children is a difficult task, especially in multi-age classrooms. The variations in the quality of teachers which emerged from classroom observations may be grouped into three categories as indicated in Table 2.6. First, some teachers struggled to conduct the preschool activities in a meaningful way and were not fully cognizant of the purpose of the activities. Many of these educators were new to the programme (Bodh, Gujarat, Seva Nidhi) and were not yet familiar with the curriculum and had not acquired the necessary skills to understand the needs of the children and respond to them in developmentally appropriate ways in a consistent manner. Others had been in the programme for many years, and while they could succeed in keeping children engaged through song, dance and other activities, there was a lack of understanding of learning objectives and the larger curriculum (Seva Nidhi). In this situation, the classroom often became chaotic, as the teachers had difficulty engaging the children consistently. Second, there were teachers who followed the script of the curriculum closely and conducted lessons based on the training and mentorship they had received. They were generally successful in maintaining order in the classroom and engaging children for most of the time. Third, there were teachers who went beyond what they had learned from the trainings and created innovative lessons, demonstrated a nuanced understanding of children's developmental abilities, were able to modify activities to suit their needs and followed children's interest (CLR, SERP, Seva Nidhi). Such teachers were able to relate to young children and engage in perspective taking and were not easily perturbed even when children misbehaved. Moreover, the observation data indicates that they had succeeded in developing supportive relationships with the children in their class. As children were meaningfully engaged and excited about the activities, there were fewer conflicts in the classroom. Day and Hernandez (2015) present a detailed account of a thematic lesson conducted by such a teacher in a Himalayan village. According to a trainer and mentor of Seva Nidhi, the level of education influenced teachers' performance; those with higher levels of education had a more nuanced understanding of children's developmental abilities.

It is essential to note that these categories are not static and should not be used simply to label teachers. Rather, such categories may be used to determine the nature of training and mentoring that they need. The evidence from the case studies clearly indicates that the quality of teaching changes significantly when individuals receive

Table 2.6. Variations in Quality of Early Childhood Teachers

Above Average	Average	Emergent
Enjoys working with young children	May or may not enjoy working with young children	May or may not enjoy working with young children
Understands nuances of child development	—	—
Appreciates children's curiosity	—	—
Follows the prescribed routine and demonstrates fluency	Follows the prescribed routine and demonstrates fluency	Has difficulty following the routine and conducting activities
Is able to keep children engaged most of the time	Is able to keep children engaged most of the time	Attempts to keep children engaged but experiences difficulties
Demonstrates a warm relationship with children in their interactions	May or may not demonstrate a relationship with children	May or may not demonstrate a relationship with children
Uses positive approach to discipline and appears to relate to them	Uses positive approach to discipline children more consistently	Has difficulty in maintaining a positive approach / May use threats or rewards
Smooth transition between activities	Some down time / Flow of activities may or may not be logical	Down time filled with songs, slogans and dances to fill up time
Is able to plan thematic activities on their own	May plan specific activities	Does not demonstrate planning activities
Is able to modify activities to meet children's developmental needs	Conducts activities based on the groups suggested in the curriculum but may not modify activities on their own	Conducts activities based on the groups suggested in the curriculum but may not modify activities on their own
Demonstrates initiative in planning lessons	Does not demonstrate initiative in planning lessons	Does not demonstrate initiative in planning lessons

appropriate mentorship and coaching. In Gujarat ICDS study, a supervisor reported that they supported an Anganwadi worker who was initially extremely nervous to reach the highest level of performance (Grade A) in their system. There were similar transformative narratives presented in other studies including CLR, MAYA and Seva Nidhi. Observations indicate that good infrastructure and adequate materials for the children were not sufficient to create a good learning environment. The quality of the teacher was critical in determining the quality of the classroom interactions.

2.3.4. Scaffolding the Capacity of Teachers: Integrating Training, Monitoring and Mentoring

Teachers need to have opportunities to develop: the necessary knowledge, skills and disposition to work with young children and create a vibrant learning environment. Many of the early childhood programmes discussed in Part II of this book created a seamless capacity-building system by integrating in-service training, with mentoring and monitoring (e.g., Bodh, CLR, Gujarat ICDS, Prajayatna, Seva Nidhi). This helped to establish a natural feedback mechanism. When trainers visited preschools, they conducted observations and were able to ascertain the extent to which issues discussed in the training were implemented in the field. Moreover, following the observation, the trainers engaged in a reflective dialogue with the teachers to help them identify what went well, areas of improvement, goals to improve the activities and strategies to address the goals. It is important to keep in mind that teachers in most programmes were local women from the community who had completed middle school or high school. Moreover, gender issues and literacy were two areas which were addressed in both the training and mentoring processes. Only SERP had some male teachers; however, retention was a problem, as they moved out of the village when they came across better opportunities. This integrated system of capacity building helped to foster learning and transformation. Teachers need to have opportunities to develop: the necessary knowledge, skills and disposition to work with young children and create a vibrant learning environment.

Training was considered to be an ongoing capacity-building process by all organizations. Many of the programmes began the academic year with an intense two weeks or a month of training followed by workshops, the frequency of which varied across programmes (monthly to half-yearly). Much emphasis was given to the process of observation. In some organizations, new recruits were required to work in a preschool for a month before they received the induction training. Moreover, classroom demonstrations were used during the actual training sessions. Prajayatna used a stratified approach—teachers had to attend monthly cluster-level (10 centres) trainings by coordinators, which were followed by weekly circle-level (3 centres) trainings by lead teachers. Given the level of education of the teachers and limited opportunities for engaging in literacy activities, most programmes felt that it was necessary to engage the teachers deliberately in reading and writing. For example, in Bodh, teachers were required to read books such as *Totto-Chan*, *Bal Hridaya ki Gahraiyan* and *Pehla Adhyapak*. They were encouraged to reflect and write about classroom experiences and various aspects of their lives. During the in-house training in Seva Nidhi, teachers were encouraged to maintain a diary and share their reflections; the trainers reviewed and responded to these writings privately. Each day ended with a cultural programme in the evening, where teachers were encouraged to dance, sing and engage in other local activities to help them overcome their hesitation to express themselves and participate in activities.

In all programmes, the trainers went for monitoring visits. Monitoring and evaluation were emphasized by many of the programmes, including Dharni, Bodh, Prajayatna and ICDS Gujarat. Some programmes like Dharni had designed a checklist for monitoring. This gave the trainers an opportunity to observe and record the functioning of the preschool in a systematic way, which informed the critical dialogues that followed and informed the programmatic decisions. In Gujarat ICDS, a two-tier feedback and monitoring system was implemented. First, the supervisors assessed the quality of all centres based on the checklist, and then the Additional Child Development Project Officer (ACDPO) reassessed the quality of a smaller sample. Anganwadis were categorized into 3 groups (A, B and C) based on the monitoring tool which had 21 indicators. Moreover, cross-visits were planned for the purpose of learning through observations, after strengths and needs were identified. Sometimes, trainers who were also the mentors conducted demonstration lessons during follow-up visits to support teachers in areas they needed to improve.

Mentoring was an essential aspect of capacity building and facilitated transformative changes in several teachers. A systematic approach to mentorship was reported in majority of the case studies. In Dharni, mentors not only provided critical feedback on classroom activities but also created a safe nurturing relationship with the mentee and were there to listen to the various challenges women experienced in other aspects of their lives, thus humanizing the workspace. They were described by many teachers as a philosopher and guide. The dialogues they had with the teachers were perceived as emancipatory, as they could confide with the mentor and discuss various dilemmas they encountered. Many teachers reported that the nature of these relationships was often very different from some of the oppressive interactions they encountered in their families and communities in a society which is fragmented by gender discrimination. It is necessary to note that reflexivity was an essential component in these dialogues. Some of the organizations required the teachers to maintain a diary of classroom activities and a personal diary. In addition to facilitating writing, these diaries provided opportunities to reflect together and plan ahead. In discussing reflective practice, Schon (1991) emphasizes the need to reflect before the action, reflect in action and reflect following completion of an action. The synergy between the above practices created a fertile ground for teachers' growth and transformation. Many of the case studies reported short narratives from the teachers which captured radical changes in their perspective and their self-esteem after they joined these organizations.

2.3.5. Preschool: A Platform for Building Cohesive Communities

Majority of the programmes emphasized the need to involve parents and develop a partnership with the communities. The NGOs created a common platform to begin discussion on issues related to young children, such as the need for childcare, education and nutrition. Further, once the major needs were identified, the external organizations provided the necessary technical support to help the community, considering various programmatic options and select what would be appropriate for their context. The organizations engaged the communities in various steps including needs assessment, programme planning, implementation and evaluation/reflection. The role of the external agency was important in initiating and maintaining this iterative process. In Prajayatna, after working with communities in many areas, the administrators concluded that communities do not usually come together to collectively identify programmatic needs. Further, the programme leaders felt that the role of an external agency is especially critical in bringing together communities which are not homogenous as they are fragmented by social differences in caste and religion.

It is important to note that for many organizations, the early childhood education programme provided a stable platform to bring community members together and address issues of gender, domestic violence, health, sanitation and preservation of the environment (Bodh, Pratham, Prajayatna, Seva Nidhi). For example, when preschool centres of Seva Nidhi had to close down because of lack of resources, village women reported an increase in domestic violence and problems related to alcoholism in men. They also mentioned disruption in their efforts to work on issues of *jal jangal aur zamin'* (water, forest and land) in the Himalayan villages. The disruption in these activities due to the closure of the preschool programmes provides evidence of how they influence social processes in these communities. However, the director of the organization expressed concern that the changes in the community were temporary and lasted only while Seva Nidhi was present, indicating the need to further explore issues of sustainability.

2.3.6. Catalyst Needed: Role of External Agencies

From a system's perspective, the partnership with an NGO or a private trust helped to facilitate change in a systematic manner by promoting flexibility and innovation. The study of CLR's partnership with ICDS in Dharni is a case in point. CLR first developed quality ICDS centres using evidence-based approaches which were then replicated in a stepwise manner. Various NGOs such as Bodh, Pratham and Prajayatna developed their own Balwadi programmes and used them primarily as laboratory schools to contextualize the curriculum and experiment with various ideas. Once they had identified the key components of addressing quality in that area, they partnered with the ICDS to scale up. One of the limitations of large government programmes is the bureaucratic structures which may not allow sufficient space to be responsive to immediate needs of the communities and opportunities or to experiment with new approaches. The three-way partnership between Gujarat ICDS, UNICEF state office and the Bhansali Trust was partially successful in creating a flexible space where the goals for preschool education could be prioritized. Further explanation of this model is presented in the next section. However, there is a need to consider issues of dependency and plan for sustainability from the initial phase and gradual phasing out of the external agency. Some of the models of collaboration which led to scaling up of evidence-based approaches are presented in the following section.

2.3.7. Models for Scaling Up Quality: Collaborations with ICDS

Children belonging to poor families receive early childhood education primarily from Anganwadis and to some extent from the Balwadis operated by NGOs. The ICDS programme of the Government of India is clearly the largest provider for early childhood care and education in India and is an important platform for scaling up preschool education. However, the quality of early childhood education in ICDS centres has often been criticized by various researchers (Chawla-Duggan, 2016; Kaul & Bhattacharya, 2019; Kaul & Shankar, 2009). The findings from the case studies presented in this book indicate that partnership with NGOs or a public trust can create a space which introduces greater flexibility in the system to address the areas of need, augment existing practices and develop innovative models. Three different types of partnerships were captured in the case studies of CLR, Pratham and Gujarat ICDS, where they worked with the government programmes. However, a fourth approach reveals how NGOs which have significant experience can support other NGOs to engage with preschool education through technical assistance and mentorship, as is evident in the relationship between Bodh and Nidan.

The study of CLR's programme in Dharni presents an exemplary approach to create space for innovation and scale up good practices in three phases through the diffusion model. The primary strategies were to develop model demonstration centres, develop the capacities of ICDS functionaries through intense monitoring and mentoring and develop a plan for sustainability. The underlying principle of 'seeing is believing' inspired the vision of the model demonstration centres. In the first phase, 19 model demonstration centres known as Observation Anganwadis (OAs) were established with intense support from CLR. During the second phase, 72 Contiguous Anganwadis (CAs) were selected based on their geographical proximity to the OAs to replicate the preschool programme and develop capacity. In the final phase, along with intense teaching learning support to the remaining 124 centres in the block, the supervisors worked to increase awareness on significance of preschool in the community and among government officials. Using this strategy, CLR was able to substantially improve the quality of early childhood education in the Anganwadi centres. However, unlike some of the other early childhood programmes which began by engaging the community from the planning phase, it was brought in only in the final phase. This probably affected the sustainability of the programme, as when researchers conversed with local villagers they were not able to describe the programme or its benefits. Inspired by this approach, the state of West Bengal launched the Shishu Aloy programme to systematically scale up good practices in early literacy and numeracy in the state ICDS programme (Ghosh, 2021) by developing model Anganwadi centres.

The Pratham preschools, on the other hand, were community-driven programmes, which involved the community members from the preparatory phase. The Balwadi programme in Mumbai was launched with the intent to develop a model which could be replicated in various parts of the country by identifying the non-negotiable. The primary strength of the organization was their ability to mobilize local people from the very beginning and involve them in all aspects of planning, implementation and monitoring. In addition, they tried to bring on board key stakeholders such as government officials and local politicians through strong advocacy. By combining the basic framework of preschool education with local demands, they were able to scale up the Balwadi programme in 10 different states by 2021 (Pratham, 2021). Based on the experience of developing Balwadis in Mumbai, they subsequently partnered with various state governments to provide training and technical assistance. Lastly, the organization valued corporate partnerships and diversified sources of funding to ensure sustainability.

The case study on Gujarat ICDS portrays a third approach to scaling up quality preschool education. The collaboration between the ICDS programme, Bhansali Trust and UNICEF facilitated systemic changes and initiated changes in the quality of education. In this initiative, the Child Development Project Officer (CDPO) was the primary link between the organizations and had a lot of freedom to make decisions. The trust provided the resources needed to hire additional personnel and computerize record keeping so that supervisors could spend more time in the classrooms and communities, which was a priority for the programme. The trust hired additional personnel to address the chronic shortage of supervisors in the ICDS programme ensure quality. UNICEF provided technical assistance to improve the quality of the programme by providing a preschool kit for each centre and strengthening the content for capacity building.

A fourth approach is evident as we examine the relationship between Bodh in Rajasthan and Nidan in Bihar. Here, Bodh acted as a mentor organization and provided technical assistance to Nidan, as they did not have experience of working in the field of early childhood education. This relationship provides an example of replicating by contextualizing an existing conceptual framework. Bodh provided the necessary support for curriculum development and capacity building through training and mentoring. A few people from Nidan also had the opportunity to visit the preschools of Bodh for observation. However, Nidan had a strong history of working with local communities and a clear understanding of the needs and challenges in the area, which was essential for contextualization. Therefore, the Balwadi programme of Nidan was not identical to Bodh, as it was adapted to the needs of the local communities.

2.3.8. Ecology of the Preschool Programme

The evidence from the collective case studies suggests that just as we need to consider the ecology of a setting to understand children's development, similarly it is necessary to consider the ecology of a preschool programme to consider issues of sustainability and scalability. Replication through standardization of classroom practices is problematic. There is a need to acknowledge and live through the tension between the discourse of standardization and contextualization during the scaling-up process. The collective case study indicates that the preschools for children belonging to marginalized groups thrive on a nexus of relationships between the programme and key stakeholders, including parents, community members, local religious organizations, social organizations like clubs and government agencies like the gram panchayat (village council). These collaborations create a supportive system which are similar to the mesosystem described in the ecological systems theory by Bronfenbrenner (1975).

A number of case studies indicate that it is essential to begin dialogues with people in the community during the planning phase to understand local challenges and parents' priorities and conceptualize a programme which is responsive to the needs of the children and families. It also helps in framing evidence-based information based on local priorities, so people are able to connect to the information. This helps to develop ownership of the programme as described in the study of Prajayatna. Although few in number, some of the women's cooperatives succeeded in operating the preschools entirely on their own. The experience in CLR further strengthens this argument as it indicates that it is difficult to sustain the programme if the dialogue is initiated in a later phase. The experience of the various programmes (Bodh, Nidan, Pratham, Prajayatna, SERP, Pratham and Seva Nidhi) further suggests that there is a need to create a robust platform and mechanisms for exchange of ideas. For example, in Pratham, several formal and informal methods were used to involve parents. In addition to seeking information from the community, it is necessary to explicitly articulate the programme philosophy and underlying principles for learning. Some of the basic information on child development, significance of this age and the rationale for the pedagogy of play-based learning need to be explained to parents and community members so that they become critical consumers of preschool education. The role of ecology is also evident in the fact that the platforms created to discuss early childhood education were also used to discuss other local issues related to gender, health, sanitation and environment.

2.4. Lessons Learned and Future Directions

We have learned much from the multiple case studies on what constitutes good preschool education for young children living in poverty in India. The diversity of practices in different programmes provides a glimpse of different pathways to construct quality. The evidence clearly suggests that there is a need to carefully examine classroom processes from a sociocultural perspective and understand the nuances of how contextual issues influence the early childhood programme. The implications of these findings have been presented in great detail in Chapter 5. The quality of the curriculum and the teacher were pivotal in determining the quality of preschool education, and these constructs have been explored in greater detail in Chapters 3 and 4, respectively.

Here, we briefly reflect on the methodology to comment on what we learned and present some of the limitations of the study. First, collaborative research grounded in postmodern paradigm provides insights into complex phenomenon and supports development of indigenous theories. Second, the collective evidence from such studies helps to develop contextually relevant recommendations to improve the quality of services while considering sociocultural issues and diverse perspectives of the stakeholders. Third, it is expensive to conduct such research, considering the resources and time needed for collaboration. Finally, capacity-building processes need to be planned carefully, taking into consideration the needs of the project, goals and capacities of the researchers.

If we consider the total number of hours spent on conducting workshops for the researchers, it is perhaps more than the number of hours spent in a research method course. However, researchers who were new to qualitative research did not get adequate insight into qualitative enquiry to subsequently use this method on their own. It is important for us to question why this is so. One major difference between the academic courses and workshops which was there was relatively limited opportunity to engage with the literature on qualitative enquiry, especially issues of epistemology. The diversity of perspectives and background of researchers led to asymmetries in the case studies. Throughout the study and the process of writing, we struggled to allow the unique perspectives to not only shape the case studies but also find some common platform. The critical perspective especially may be lacking in some of the case studies, including my own. Perhaps, in our enthusiasm to identify good practices, some of us did not focus adequately on the need to maintain a critical stance. The ways to present the views of various stakeholders in sufficient detail while maintaining a critical stance is perhaps best illustrated in the study conducted on CLR, where the authors not only clearly identify exemplary practices but also present a nuanced critique of the programme.

References

Anandalakshmy, S., Chaudhary, N., & Sharma, N. (200)8. *Researching families and children: Culturally appropriate methods.* SAGE Publications.

Bell, J. (2005). *Doing your research project: A guide for first-time researchers in education and social science.* McGraw Hill and Viva.

Bruce, S. M., & Pine, G. J. (2010). *Action research in special education: An inquiry approach for effective teaching and learning.* Teachers College Press.

CECED. (2015). *Quality and diversity in early childhood education: A view from andhra pradesh, assam and rajasthan.* Indian Early Childhood Education Impact Study,1. Centre for Early Childhood Education and Development.

Charmaz. K. (2011). Grounded theory in the 21st century: Applications for advancing social justice studies. In N. K. Denzin & Y. E. Lincoln (Eds.), *Handbook of qualitative research* (3rd ed., pp. 507–535). SAGE Publications.

Chawla-Duggan, R. (2016). Pedagogy and quality in Indian slum school settings: A Bernsteinian analysis of visual representations in the Integrated Child Development Service. *Research in Comparative and International Education, 10*(2), 123–140.

Cheruvelil, K. S., Soranno, P. A., Weathers, K. C., Hanson, P. C., Gosing, S. J., Filstrup, C. T., & Read, E. K. (2014). Creating and maintaining high-performing collaborative research teams: The importance of diversity and interpersonal skills. *Frontiers in Ecology and the Environment, 12*(1), 31–38.

Collier, J. (1945). United States Indian Administration as a laboratory of ethnic relations. *Social Research, 12*(3), 265–303.

Day, M., & Hernandez, D. (2015). *Discovering place-based education in the foothills of the Himalayas* [Occasional Paper Series 33]. Bank Street.

Denscombe, M. (2007). *The good research guide for small scale research projects* (3rd ed.). McGraw Hill and Viva.

Denzin, N. K., & Lincoln, Y. S. (2008). *Strategies of qualitative inquiry.* SAGE Publications.

Geertz, C. (1973). Thick description: Toward an interpretative theory of culture. In *The interpretation of cultures.* Basic Books.

Ghosh, L. (2021). Foundational literacy and numeracy in west bengal. *Economic and Political Weekly, 56*(16), 12–14.

Glaser, B., & Strauss, A. (1967). *The discovery of grounded theory.* Aldine.

Glaser, B. G. (1978). *Theoretical sensitivity: Advances in the methodology of grounded theory.* Sociology Press.

Glesne, C., & Peshkin, A. (1992). *Becoming qualitative researchers.* Longman.

GoI. (2013a). *National policy for early childhood care and education (NPECCE).* Ministry of Women and Child Development.

GoI. (2013b). *National early childhood care and education (ECCE) curriculum framework.* Ministry of Women and Child Development.

GoI. (2020). *National policy on education.* Ministry of Education.

Gregor, S. (2006). The nature of theory in information systems. *Management Information Systems Quarterly, 30*(3). https://aisel.aisnet.org/misq/vol30/iss3/5/

Harkness, S., Super, C., Bermúdez, M. R., Moscardino, U., Rha, J., Mavridis, C., Bonichini, S., Huitrón, B., Welles-Nyström, B., Palacios, J., Hyun, O., Soriano, G., & Żylicz, P. (2009). Parental ethnotheories of children's learning. http://www.celf.ucla.edu/2010_conference_articles/Harkness_et_al_2009.pdf retrieved on 20.5.2021

Holton, J. A., & Walsh, I. (2017). *Classic grounded theory: Applications with qualitative and quantitative data.* SAGE Publications.

Kaul, V. (2009). *Early childhood education programme.* National Council of Educational Research and Training.

Kaul, V., & Shankar, D. (2009). *Education for All-Mid Decade Assessment.* Early Childhood Care and Education in India. NUEPA. https://www.education-forallinindia.com/early-childhood-care-and-education-in-india.pdf

Kaul, V., & Bhattacharjea, S. (2019). *Early childhood education and school readiness in India: Quality and diversity.* Springer.

Lincoln, Y. S., and Guba, E. G. (1985). *Naturalistic inquiry.* SAGE Publications.

Meyer, L. H., Park, H., Grenot-Scheyer, M., Schwartz, I. S., & Harry, B. (1998). *Making friends: The influences of culture and development.* Paul H. Brookes.

Miles, M. B., & Huberman, A. M. (1994). *Qualitative data analysis: An expanded sourcebook* (2nd ed.). SAGE Publications.

Odom, S. L. (Ed.). (2002). *Widening the circle: Including children with disabilities in preschool programs.* Teachers College Press.

Pratham. (2021). *Early childhood education program.* https://www.pratham.org/programs/education/early-childhood-education/

Schon, D. A. (1991). *The reflective practitioner.* Ashgate Publishing.

Spradley, J. P. (1979). *The ethnographic interview.* Harcourt Brace.

Stake, R. E. (2008). Qualitative case studies. In N. K. Denzin & Y. S. Lincoln (Eds.), Strategies of qualitative inquiry (pp. 119–149). SAGE Publications.

Super, C. M., & Harkness, S. (1986). The developmental niche: A conceptualization at the interface of child and culture. *International Journal of Behavioral Development, 9*(4), 545–569.

Tschurenev, J. (2021). Montessori for all? Indian experiments in 'child education', 1920s to 1970s. *Comparative Education,* 1–19. https://doi.org/10.1080/030 50068.2021.1888408

Yin, R. K. (2009). *Case study research: Design and methods.* SAGE Publications.

CHAPTER 3

Curriculum in Multi-age Classrooms

Responding to Developmental and Contextual Challenges

Monimalika Day

'All curricula seek to include and exclude, emphasize and de-emphasize, and embrace and isolate different content knowledge, different identities and different politics' (Au & Apple, 2009). In India, young children living in poverty often receive education in multi-age classrooms, under government (Anganwadis) and non-government (Balwadis) programmes, while their peers from more privileged groups usually attend single-age classrooms in private schools. Although multi-age preschools have been the predominant method for providing education to young children in India, and a number of education policies have promoted this approach, there is a paucity of evidence related to the curricular approaches which have been developed and how it varies across context and its effects on learning. This chapter is written to address this gap in the literature and further the discourse on multi-age preschools for young children. It specifically attempts to critically examine key elements which influence quality in such learning environment while referring to the evidence presented in the case studies in Part II of the book.

In India, multi-age preschool programmes were primarily scaled up to provide access to education to young children living in poverty but with limited investment on infrastructure, personnel and materials. The ASER Centre (2019) survey indicates that majority (90%) of young children between the ages of four and eight years are enrolled in some type of educational programmes. Moreover, 44.2 per cent of four-year-olds and 26.3 per cent of five-year-olds are enrolled in Anganwadis. It indicates that five-year-olds leave the ICDS system to join other programmes. Along with access, it is essential to consider the supportive mechanisms which help children to participate fully in different activities of an educational programme to influence their learning and development. The ECCE Policy (GoI, 2013a) provided an impetus, especially for government programmes, to improve quality, and various states revised the curriculum for preschool education in the ICDS programmes (Ghosh, 2021). Even in the international arena, there is a paucity of the literature on this pedagogical practice (Burns & Mason, 2002); specifically, there are few studies which compare the effectiveness of multi-age classrooms to single-age classrooms. In a longitudinal study, Ansari (2017) reported that five-year-olds in kindergarten made greater gains in numeracy and literacy compared to five-year-olds with combined kindergarten and pre-kindergarten classroom, which included three-, four- and five-year-old children. Therefore, the nature of programmes developed in India needs to be examined, especially as the country attempts to implement the National Education Policy 2020. There is a critical need to integrate the knowledge gained from different research studies with the theoretical perspectives in order to close the learning gap between children belonging to poor families and those from privileged backgrounds. This evidence can also inform other nations striving to ensure both access and quality to achieve the Sustainable Development Goal 4.

Apple (1993) argues that the content of a national curriculum or what is considered 'official knowledge' represents the perspectives of selected groups of people and tends to replicate the existing social inequities in the country. The absence of perspectives of certain groups in what may be considered legitimate knowledge reflects the hegemonic structures of a society which are perpetuated by the curriculum through the process of schooling. His ideas are particularly relevant in the Indian context, as young children from traditionally marginalized groups continue to face systemic oppression due their caste, class and gender and continue to have limited access to quality education (Mobile Creches, 2020). The collective case study presented in this book attempts to document the perspectives of different stakeholders, including parents, teachers and programme administrators on the topic of quality in early childhood education. Since we collected information from programmes providing services to marginalized communities in different parts of the country, the data can inform and influence both policy formulation and practice and partially address Apple's concerns.

The evidence from the multiple case studies presented in Part II of this book together with the theoretical perspectives and current research provides deeper understanding of variations in the quality of multi-age classrooms in India. In this study, the research team conducted detailed qualitative case studies of 18 preschools, including 12 Balwadis and 6 Anganwadis operated by 9 different organizations in various parts of the country, known to the experts for their good practices in early childhood education (refer to Chapter 2). All the programmes offered preschool education to children between the ages of three and six years in multi-age classrooms. This qualitative enquiry using participant observations, interviews and focus group discussions captures the variations in pedagogical processes and children's engagement with learning activities. This chapter synthesizes the learning from the collective case studies to explore various curricular issues, identify elements of good practices and examine the findings in light of existing theories on learning and development and current research. It begins by presenting a description of multi-age preschools in India and current concerns regarding schooling without learning and the need to strengthen the curriculum. We then synthesize and reflect on the data from the case studies in relation to specific aspects of early childhood curriculum, which focuses on emerging curricular approaches and the need for integration, variations in curricular transactions and the need for praxis. We close by highlighting the important lessons learned and their implication for policy and practice.

3.1. Multi-age Preschools in India

In India, experimentation on contextualization of the Montessori approach led to the development of the institutional models for Anganwadi and Balwadi programmes (Kaul, 2009; Tschurenev, 2021). Gijubhai Badheka (1885–1939) '...was one of the pioneers of Early Childhood Education who, inspired by Maria Montessori's pedagogical philosophy and methods, adapted these to suit Indian conditions. He initiated an indigenous education system, imbibing the Gandhian philosophy and integrating it with Montessori's scientific pedagogy' (Kaul, 2009, p. 8). Together with Tarabai Modak (1892–1973), he set up the Nutan Bal Shikshan Sangh in 1926. The models for both Anganwadis and Balwadis were developed later by Tarabai Modak and Anutai Wagh through their dedicated efforts to bring preschool education to marginalized communities in urban and rural Maharashtra (Kaul, 2009; Tschurenev, 2021) through various pedagogical experiments conducted by the Gram Bal Shiksha Kendra (GBSK). It is difficult to scale up the Montessori preschools in their original form in India due to the cost of specific materials, personnel and capacity building. However, drawing on this approach, various experiments were conducted by Indian educationists such as Gijubhai Badheka, Tarabai Modak and Anutai Wagh, which led to the development of low-cost programmes which could be scaled up as Anganwadis and Balwadis. Specifically, the evidence from the experiments in Kosbad in the tribal areas of Maharashtra convinced the Government of India to adopt this model for the ICDS programme when it was launched in 1975 (Tschurenev, 2021). As the programmes were scaled up, it probably became difficult to ensure the quality of education.

Many of the policies on education of young children in India recommend multi-age classrooms as a primary method for providing education. The ECCE Policy (2013) of India, developed by the Ministry of Women and Child Development (MWCD), embraces this approach and articulates some of the theoretical and empirical rationale related to this pedagogy. The ECCE Curriculum Framework also provides guidance on issues which need to be considered when developing curriculum for multi-age classrooms. These policy changes prompted many state governments and ICDS programmes to revise the curriculum for Anganwadis with support from early childhood experts and field test it prior to scaling up, based on the directives from the National Institute of Public Cooperation and Child Development (NIPCCD). Further, the National Education Policy 2020 proposed by the Ministry of Education (MoE) and passed by the Union Cabinet on 29 July 2020 underscores the significance of early childhood education and shifts the responsibility for preschool education from the MWCD to the MoE to ensure continuity with school education. The policy recommends a substantial change in the curriculum structure for school education to 5 years of foundational (ages 3–8 years), 3 years of preparatory (ages 8–11 years), 3 years of middle (ages 11–14 years) and 4 years of secondary education (ages 14–18 years). The first five years of foundation stage include three years of preschool education. This policy emphasizes the urgency to provide quality education to children between the ages of three and six years through four models of preschool education: Anganwadis, co-located Anganwadis in primary schools, pre-primary sections in schools and standalone preschools, most of which are operated by private entities. It gives highest priority to achieving early numeracy and early literacy in primary schools by the year 2025. Further, it endorses the practice of providing education through multi-age classrooms in the ICDS programme as the primary model for scaling up preschool education, and efforts are underway in various states to implement these recommendations. The implementation of this policy is complicated in a context which is ravaged by several economic, political and social uncertainties related to the COVID-19 pandemic which has affected India since 2020 and resulted in closure of schools due to lockdowns imposed at the national and state levels. Government and non-government programmes are struggling to provide access to education. Young children mostly in private schools are required to engage in online learning for prolonged period of time. Recent research indicates that online education has exacerbated the disparities in access to education for children belonging to different socio-economic groups (Shaheed & Chanchal, 2021).

3.2. Schooling without Learning: The Need to Strengthen Curriculum

The ASER Centre (2019) report on early childhood indicates that more than 90 per cent children between the ages of four and eight years are enrolled in some kind of educational programmes. In the later part of the 20th century, Anganwadi and Balwadi programmes expanded significantly with a committed effort in the government and non-government sector to provide access to preschool education to young children from poor families and reduce dropout rates in the primary schools. The *Annual Report* of MWCD 2020–2021 (GoI, 2021) indicates that there are a total of 1,383,955 Anganwadis and mini Anganwadis, and 162,000 children between the ages of 3 and 6 years were enrolled in the preschool programme. However, the quality of education in Anganwadis remains questionable because of the emphasis on nutrition and requirement of the Anganwadi worker to multitask and provide six different kinds of services with little training and support (Chawla-Duggan, 2016; Kaul, 2019; Kaul & Shankar, 2016). The dilemma is articulated succinctly by an administrator in the Gujarat case study:

> As administrators of ICDS, we find it a little difficult. Education is one aspects out of the 6 components of ICDS. Naturally when we focus on one aspect; we cannot concentrate on the other. When the AWW is expected to deliver 6 services then sometimes she cannot focus on one aspect while she is concentrating on the other. (CDPO)

The *Status of the Young Child in India* (Mobile Creches, 2020) report also highlights the neglect of early childhood education in ICDS and recommends the need to increase budgetary allocations in this area. In agreement with Kaul and Bhattacharjea (2019), it recommends the need to establish a regulatory framework at the national and state levels to monitor and promote quality of education in all sectors. While the number of private preschools serving young children has increased exponentially in the past few decades to meet parents' demands, the quality of education remains uneven and does not always align with recommendations of the ECCE Policy. In fact, 'schoolification' of early childhood education in India is a serious pedagogical concern, especially in the private and government sectors (Bhattacharjea, 2019). The findings of the ASER Centre (2019) report indicate that five-year-old children are more competent in completing certain developmental tasks compared to four-year-old children, which underscores the need to create age-appropriate curriculum. However, currently preschoolers, especially from poor communities, are often burdened with a push-down curriculum from the primary level, which is combined with rote learning. Chaudhary and Kaul (2019) compare the effects of a developmentally appropriate activity-based curricula and didactic approach focusing on teaching of the three Rs (reading, writing and arithmetic) on children's cognitive and language development from the longitudinal data of the IECEI Study. The results indicate that developmentally appropriate curricula supported children from disadvantaged backgrounds to make significant gains over a period of one year and score at par with children from privileged communities. The researchers found that formal teaching of the three Rs adds little value and could even be detrimental to children's cognitive and language development. This is consistent with findings from an international study (Crehan, 2018) of top five countries with highest scores on Programme for International Student Assessment (PISA), where they found that preschool education focusing on child-initiated activities helps to facilitate learning when it is conducted by well-trained teachers. After studying six Anganwadis in Mumbai, Chawla-Duggan (2016) concludes that they do not reflect the child-centred pedagogy presented in ICDS documents and portray weak relationships between the worker and the children, as well as between children. The author further explores the notion of intended curriculum and enacted curriculum (Chawla-Duggan, 2019). The researcher concludes that the child-centred pedagogy, grounded in constructivist perspective, was not fully interpreted by the workers who had limited training and viewed children primarily as listeners.

3.3. Who Are the Children Attending the Programmes?

To understand the curriculum and pedagogy, it is essential to develop awareness regarding the background of the students, to understand their needs and participation in the programmes. Majority of the children enrolled in the 18 early childhood centres belonged to poor families and were between the ages of 3 and 4 years. Only a few children were above five years, as most of them had transitioned to the primary schools, even though the Right to Education Act, 2009, recommends enrolment in Grade 1 at the age of six years. Very rarely, children above six years were present in the preschool. However, younger children between the ages of two–three years often attended preschools; most of the time, they came along with their elder siblings but sometimes they were brought by the parents. This phenomenon is perhaps linked to the critical need to develop crèches for families living in poverty, which was voiced by parents and administrators in different case studies.

Young children from traditionally marginalized communities begin to face barriers to access education early on in their lives. Children of migrant workers attended some of the programmes in rural and urban areas, and the teachers explained that the main challenge was to ensure continuity in their learning, as their parents often had to move in order to earn their living. Children from migrant agricultural workers attended the ICDS programme in Gujarat. Organizations such as Nidan and Bodh provided education to urban marginalized groups who had difficulty attending government schools. Nidan catered primarily to children from Dalit groups, many of whose parents worked as sweepers, cleaners or ragpickers. These children also had to support their parents in their employment or in household chores, which affected their participation in the programme. Some of the Balwadi programmes were primarily attended by children who belonged to the lower castes, as they encountered marginalization from teachers and peers in other educational programmes. In SERP, the children from the Savara and Gond tribes attended the Balwadi for their education but visited the Anganwadi for food. This pattern was also observed in some of the other programmes in both rural and urban areas, which indicates the need for an integrated set of services, such as the ICDS programme, and a holistic approach to support young children's development. Although preschool education is one of the six components of the ICDS programme, the environments in these particular centres were not very conducive to learning or they were mini Anganwadis which focused only on nutrition and not on education.

A matter of great concern was that researchers did not find children with disabilities in any of the centres. This is consistent with the findings from the longitudinal IECEI Study and suggests that in

India, children with disabilities experience social exclusion very early in their lives and find it difficult to access educational programmes. The case study on Bodh mentions a special education school providing learning opportunities. However, multi-age classrooms provide excellent opportunities for inclusion of children with diverse abilities as illustrated by Maria Montessori (Crain, 2014).

3.4. Emerging Curricular Approaches and the Need for Integration

An overview of Indian and international thinkers who influenced early childhood education in India has been presented by Kaul (2009). In the current study, the researchers documented four different curricular approaches through classroom observations, review of documents and dialogues with the programme personnel. They are: thematic approach, activity-based approach, relationship-based approach and place-based approach, which were combined in different ways by the programmes. While the first two have been recommended and explained in the ECCE Policy (2013), the importance of the latter two approaches is not explicitly articulated but is of great importance in light of the current social and environmental concerns. Katz (1995) has recommended that all preschool curricula need to address four components: knowledge, skills, dispositions and feelings. Most curricula focus on the first two components, and disposition and feeling are primarily addressed through specific pedagogical approaches. This section not only presents short descriptions of the first two approaches as they are known to educators in India and are articulated in the ECCE Policy (GoI, 2013a) but also provides a more detailed explanation of the two emerging approaches.

3.4.1. Thematic Approach

The ECCE Curriculum Framework (GoI, 2013b) recommends a thematic approach to help young learners to connect and explore topics relevant to their circumstances. All the programmes in the collective case studies used a thematic approach in their curriculum. Themes were selected based on the relevance of topics to their lives, for example, family, animals, plants and transport. However, the activities were sometimes designed to address learning objectives in a single domain and missed opportunities to promote learning in multiple domains, in an integrated manner. In other situations, we observed an integration of different domains, as children were encouraged to engage with a particular topic which addressed various domains of development. The second approach is more naturalistic and provides greater opportunities to promote higher-order thinking skills by individualizing the expectations from children. We observed an example of the latter in a Balwadi in Uttarakhand. A detailed narrative of this exemplary thematic lesson is presented in Day and Hernandez (2014). There were considerable variations in teachers' abilities to transact a thematic curriculum. While some teachers focused on staying within the boundaries of the theme and following the prescribed activities, others demonstrated flexibility and were able to adapt the lesson based on the interest and engagement of children with specific content areas. A thematic lesson can be transacted in a poor way when teachers are unable to fully understand the underlying rationale for such a curriculum. For example, a teacher may keep repeating a song on transport but not engage children on a follow-up dialogue about vehicles. In such circumstances, the teacher often completes the activity in a short period of time and then struggles to fill up the time. Such issues were addressed through mentoring and group discussions in most programmes. Bodh, Nidan, CLR and Prajayatna created opportunities for teachers to plan thematic lessons in small groups with guidance from a lead teacher.

3.4.2. Activity-based Approach

The activity-based approach, together with the thematic approach, holds the potential to develop a contextually relevant curriculum which addresses different domains of development. This approach draws on anthropological perspectives and assumes that there is cultural meaning connected with routine activities conducted by different communities (Dunst et al. 2001; Macy, 2007). For example, simple activities such as eating or toilet training are influenced by various cultural beliefs and values and offer opportunities for embedding learning outcomes. Learning objectives related to various concepts such as colour, texture, taste, smell, shape, patterns and counting may be addressed during these routine activities. O'Donnell et al. (1992) identify the activity setting as a unit of intervention in communities and propose a conceptual framework considering four major components: the physical setting and materials available, purpose of the activity, social environment and the people involved in the activity, when identifying or planning an intervention. This approach is recommended in the ECCE Curriculum Framework (2012) but was not articulated by any of the programmes, which indicates that there is a need to provide more detailed guidance on this approach. However, classroom observations by the researchers indicate that some programmes used routine activities such as snack time or toileting to teach different concepts, while others did not. This could probably be because there was a lack of clear guidelines, and the approach was not fully articulated in most curricula.

3.4.3. Place-based Education: Connecting People to Places

Different programmes in urban, rural and tribal communities paid special attention to use low-cost local materials for early numeracy activities such as matching, sorting and sequencing and early literacy activities such as local songs, stories and poems. Elements of place-based education were observed in many of the curricula but were most evident in Seva Nidhi located in the foothills of the Himalayas and the SERP Balwadis serving the Savara and Gond population of Telangana with an emphasis on valuing the local culture. The case study of Seva Nidhi presents a narrative of a coherent thematic activity designed to help children connect with various concepts related to the environment through an environmental walk discussed in detail in Day and Hernandez (2015). Place-based education is defined as 'The process of using local community and environment as a starting point to teach concepts in language arts, mathematics, social studies, science, and other subjects across the curriculum' (Sobel, 2004, p. 7). Although the phrase was coined in North America in the 1980s, this progressive pedagogy draws on existing theoretical perspectives on experiential learning, critical pedagogy and constructivism. The fundamental principles of this pedagogy are not new to Indian educators and are congruent with the philosophy of Gandhi, Gijubhai Badheka and Tagore. In his work, Tagore viewed the child as someone who connects with the surrounding through an inherent sense of wondering and questioning as is evident in his reflections on childhood and his literary work (Ghosh, 2015). There is a need to revisit these theoretical perspectives and make conscious attempts to address current trends towards globalization, which leads to homogenization of education. Place-based education is of great significance at a time when large sections of the population in India are forced to migrate to earn their living and the world is challenged by climate crisis and serious depletion of natural resources. The nature and magnitude of the problem of not being connected to the place and the people were evident during the lockdown in India in March 2020 due to the COVID-19 pandemic, when millions of migrant workers had to leave the cities and walked hundreds of kilometres to return to their villages, some of them carrying their young children. For common people, this crisis brought to light the magnitude of displacement, especially among the poorer sections of the society. According to Hutchison (2004), with the development of global economy, there are attempts to homogenize education, which presents a single story of prosperity and often fails to help students connect to their local environment and people (Hutchison, 2004).

3.4.4. Relationship-based Approach and Care in Education

Across the board, the early childhood programmes emphasized positive guidance and discouraged teachers from punishing children. Working with young children is challenging for teachers, and they need opportunities to engage in dialogues with supportive adults to reflect, evaluate and plan future actions. The case studies of Bodh, CLR and Prajayatna provide specific examples of structures and institutional processes developed to create nurturing environments. Bodh had developed a strong mentoring system at various levels. The fellow teachers were mentored by mother teachers, both of whom worked directly with children and the latter was mentored by the supervisors. It is not just the mechanisms but also the quality of relationship with the mentor that creates a pathway for transformation for many teachers. In CLR, Prajayatna and Seva Nidhi, various teachers reported that the quality of mentorship they received from their supervisors helped them to go through a process of transformation and engage differently with children. Experiencing a nurturing trustworthy relationship enabled the teachers to establish parallel nurturing relationships with the preschool children. Therefore, the process of mentoring and supportive supervision becomes crucial to provide a platform to reflect, resolve and empathize with young children as articulated in the study of Bodh. These programmes further extended this relationship-building process to parents and the larger community members. Many teachers join the field of early childhood education because they enjoy working with young children. However, the case studies clearly indicate that most programmes required them to engage with families and communities and had to support them in this process of relationship building through coaching and mentorship.

Every programme developed a culture, where students were recognized and praised for positive behaviour but were not punished for disruptive behaviour. Although the expectations were uniform, there was considerable variation between teachers in their ability to create a warm nurturing environment. It is possible that the rationale for this child-centred approach was not clear to all teachers as some of them randomly praised students without giving specific feedback on the nature of actions. For example, a new teacher frequently said 'shabash' (well done) to the children without indicating what action was being appreciated. It is necessary to note that most teachers were women, and some of them experienced oppression in their own family as described in the study of Seva Nidhi; therefore experiencing nurturing relationships with mentors provided a safe space for dialogue and reflection. Such relationships enabled teachers to create a safe environment for the students.

Learning unfolds in the context of relationships which children develop with their teachers and peers. The ability to engage in meaningful interactions with peers and adults to form relationships is a foundational skill which is needed not just for socialization but also for engaging in language and higher cognitive processes. The patterns of interactions which children experience in classrooms influence their self-esteem and ability to relate with peers and participate in classroom activities. It is important to note that this approach is consistent with the most recent recommendation from the National Association for the Education of Young Children (NAEYC) on Developmentally Appropriate Practice (DAP; NAEYC, 2020). Many of the guidelines in this document emphasize on the social–emotional environment of learning. Following are a few examples:

- 'Relationships are nurtured with each child, and educators facilitate the development of positive relationships among children' (p. 15)
- 'Creating a Caring, Equitable Community of Learners' (p. 15)
- 'Engaging in Reciprocal Partnerships with Families and Fostering Community Connections' (p. 18)

To summarize, integration of the thematic approach and the activity-based approach was more successful in keeping children engaged compared to a domain-based approach to planning thematic activities. Both of these pedagogical practices have been recommended in different policies on early childhood education and were used in several programmes. However, teachers, mentors and trainers rarely articulated the underlying principles and the rationale for these approaches. The latter two approaches of place-based education and relationship-based approach seemed to have emerged from the values and experiences of various people in the organizations.

3.5. Variations in Curriculum Transaction and the Need for Praxis

The longitudinal IECEI Study clearly establishes that the quality of preschool environment influences children's learning outcomes in both preschool and primary grades (Kaul & Bhattacharjea, 2019). The ASER Centre (2019) report indicates that there is great variation regarding the expectations from young children in different states of India. The case studies provide deeper insights into existing variations in curricular practices.

It is useful to begin the discussion by considering the definition of curriculum. Au and Apple (2009, p. 103) posit that

> Most of those in the field of education would atleast agree that curriculum includes some set of content knowledge expected to be learned. However, the content of the curriculum also implicates pedagogy, because the selection of content is done with the express purpose of transmitting the said content…. To talk about curriculum means to talk about content, the form the content takes, and the pedagogy that drives the intended transmission.

In this section, we present a snapshot of the emerging variations in curriculum transaction under two major headings of physical and social environment in the preschool classrooms by synthesizing the findings reported in the case studies. Although it is essential to note that the two are intricately connected, we examine existing classroom practices in light of existing policies, theories and research. Physical space includes a description of: infrastructure, availability of outdoor space and teaching-learning materials. Sociocultural environment provides insights: on teacher–child ratio, class routine and activities, importance of play, multilingual and multicultural issues, early literacy and numeracy activities, and differentiated teaching. This chapter ends by focusing on key concerns and recommendations.

3.5.1. Physical Space: Infrastructure and Materials

There were considerable variations in the infrastructure of the preschool centres in rural, urban and tribal areas. These discrepancies were sometimes observed within the same programme. The availability of space and resources for building the classroom was a concern for all programmes. The 'Quality Standards' of MWCD (GoI, 2012) recommend 35 square metres of classroom for a group of 30 children and 30 square metres of outdoor space. Programmes in urban areas such as Mumbai and Patna found it very difficult to meet these standards. Due to lack of resources, organizations struggled to acquire land and construct the buildings for the preschools even in the rural areas. There were very few centres which were able to meet the space recommendations. Differences were observed in the size of the classrooms, availability of outdoor space, light, ventilation and access to toilets. Some centres had concrete permanent structures, while others conducted classes in small mud huts constructed by the local communities. Few of the classrooms met the above standards; they had adequate space for setting up the learning corners and conduct different kinds of group activities. The lower walls of the centres in CLR and SERP were painted in black to encourage children to draw and write to express their thoughts. The floor space of almost all the centres was often used for activities such as drawing, writing, sorting and conducting activities on one-to-one correspondence. There was no child-sized furniture in any of these classrooms. Children typically sat on floor mats. The findings from the longitudinal study of the IECEI research suggests that infrastructure is essential though not sufficient for learning (Kaul & Bhattacharjea, 2019), which was supported by the qualitative data from the case studies. In the absence of proper infrastructure, most preschool centres faced several challenges during monsoon, winter and summer. Occasionally, classes had to be suspended due to heavy rains in areas such as Uttarakhand and Mumbai. During summer, teachers and children struggled to focus on activities, especially when there was poor ventilation and few fans in the room.

3.5.1.1. Materials and Learning Corners

An important feature of most preschool classrooms visited by the researchers was the learning corners, regardless of the size of the class-room. Such classroom arrangements provided children the opportunities to make choices regarding centres and materials, explore various objects based on their interests, engage in sociodramatic play and collaborate with others which led to self-paced learning. The focus of the corners varied from arts, dramatic play, reading and writing, numeracy and cognitive manipulatives (puzzles, lottos). Children had easy access to the material displayed in these corners. However, some materials including various toys were locked up in trunks or put away in shelves as teachers were either unsure of how to use them or concerned about audit in government settings and worried about damage caused by usage.

Gijubhai Badheka's vision of providing education to children from poor families using low-cost and no-cost materials (Kaul, 2009) seems to have inspired many of the programmes. While all programmes used low-cost materials, some programmes paid special attention to selecting local materials. This was evident in both rural and urban settings. In the Balwadis in the villages of Uttarakhand, the dramatic play corner included various types of seeds, brooms made from local grass and dolls made of cloth and clay. In Nidaan, a teacher used objects such as food packets, empty toothpaste tubes, bottle tops, wrappers, etc., which children were familiar to in urban areas. Prochner et al. (2008) conducted three case studies in semi-rural areas of Canada, India and South Africa and illustrated how the use of materials is connected to indigenous cultural norms and beliefs. It is important to note that such materials were used to supplement rather than replace the standard teaching–learning materials such as manipulatives, puzzles, dominoes, nesting toys and other materials recommended in the ECCE Policy (2013). It is necessary to note that teachers have to spend considerable time collecting and making such teaching–learning aids, which can be an added burden, especially for the Anganwadi workers. Some programmes provided teachers the opportunity to develop these materials during workshops or monthly or weekly meetings.

3.5.1.2. Outdoor Space

Similarly, there were considerable differences in the availability and use of outdoor space. Generally, most rural or tribal centres had adequate space available to conduct outdoor play or gross motor activities outside the classroom. In contrast, most of the urban centres did not have adequate outdoor space, and teachers often had to conduct gross motor activities in the classroom. The learning environment was not restricted to the classroom alone. In some programmes, children were taken for environmental walks or visits to their neighbourhoods, which is an important aspect of activity based approach and compensated for appropriate indoor learning space. For example, an outdoor activity was conducted on teaching colours using large plastic blocks, as the preschool was housed in a small mud hut built by the local villagers.

3.5.2. Sociocultural Environment

The policies on early childhood education in India are anchored in constructivist perspectives (Chawla, 2019) and view the child as an active participant in their environment. According to Rogoff (2003), 'Humans develop through their changing participation in the sociocultural activities of their communities, which also change.' Lev Vygotsky's sociocultural theory of learning is of particular significance as we attempt to understand the rationale for multi-age classrooms and the need to contextualize curriculum. Like Piaget, he believed that children actively construct knowledge (Bodrova & Leong, 2006; Crain, 2016) but strongly emphasized the influence of social interactions rather than engagement with objects. The primary principles of his theory are that children construct knowledge, development cannot be separated from social context, learning can lead to development and language plays a crucial role in mental development. Each of these principles have important bearings on early childhood curricula in the Indian context, given the challenge of diversity and existing inequities in our society. In studying the sociocultural environment, we consider: the teacher–child ratio, importance of play, multilingual and multicultural issues, early literacy and numeracy activities, multiple ages and differentiated teaching.

3.5.2.1. Importance of Play

Every programme emphasized the importance of play and assigned a designated time in the schedule for what was frequently labelled 'free play'. 'Free play is an activity carried out in a protracted period of time in which children choose the activity and thus the playmates. A particularly important part of this is sociodramatic play...' (Prochner et al., 2008, p. 197). Generally, children played on their own in different corners, and some programmes allowed children to choose the corners. This practice may be an example of Montessori's influence on early childhood education in India (Tschurenev, 2021). As in her approach, there is particular emphasis on independence and concentration, free choice and rewards. The teacher's role is to facilitate mastery of developmental tasks by observing, children in their during play activities and engaging in dialogues. In CLR, children arrived early in the morning to select a corner. In SERP, children from Savara and Gond tribes arrived early and stayed late and continued to play after the scheduled time. Their interest and level of engagement affirmed the significance of play in early childhood, as suggested by various theorists including Piaget, Montessori and Vygotsky. However, unlike the Montessori or Vygotskian approach, teachers rarely joined children or tried to provide suggestions to support and expand their play. In response to questions on how children learn, teachers often responded by saying '*Khel khel me sikhte hai*' (learn through play). Administrators and mentors sometimes referred to the use of the play-way method (Prochner, 2002), which reflects contextualization of the pedagogy of using play as a medium of instruction for the Indian society. While teachers in most programmes were aware that young children learn through play, the nuances of this developmental process and how play can be used as a medium of learning were not always clear to them, probably due to the limited training and education which they received. When children were engaged in free play in the corners, teachers rarely spent time interacting with them or joining their play. Many parents in different states demand teaching of reading, writing and arithmetic; however, the data suggests that they are able to appreciate the values of play-based education when organizations explicitly articulate and demonstrate the benefits of this pedagogy through various interactions.

According to Vygotsky, play is essential for promoting higher-order thinking skills in young children (Bodrova & Leong, 2006). It gives them an opportunity to acquire and refine the tools of the mind by strengthening their language, symbolic thinking and self-regulation. Vygotsky proposed that children operate in the zone of proximal distance, stretching their normal boundaries, especially during sociodramatic play. Among the Indian thinkers, Tagore provides a glimpse of the young child's perspectives in sociodramatic play in his childhood memoir, and some of his poems emphasizes the need to give freedom to the child to explore their surroundings, initiate play and enter the world of imagination.

3.5.2.2. Multicultural and Multilingual Issues

Cultural and linguistic diversity in India gives strength to the nation but also poses several challenges as described in Chapter 1. The range of practices indicate that programmes address diversity of language and cultures in a number of ways but do not always have clear guidelines for such practices. The position paper on 'Early Language and Literacy in India' (CECED, 2016, p. 17) clearly states, 'The expectations are not limited to facilitating the transition from the oral to the written cultures. Ideally these settings also carry the responsibility of helping children navigate different oral languages and dialects, often languages and dialects with no scripts and poorly prepared teachers.' In creating a multicultural and multilingual classroom, it is necessary to consider the processes which inform decisions, diversity of parental goals and priorities in different contexts.

Community meetings were held by many of the organizations to capture parental goals and community priorities, which are influenced by the cultural and linguistic heritage. The evidence from the case studies indicates that needs assessment and ongoing dialogues with parents and community members are essential to create a contextually relevant curriculum. These practices are consistent with recommendations in the ECCE Policy (2013), ECCE Curriculum Framework, and DAP (NAEYC, 2020). Both Pratham and Prajayatna launched new centres only after conducting a needs assessment in the communities.

Teachers in early childhood programmes in rural and urban areas used the local dialect or language to converse with children and transact the curriculum and introduced the state language. English was included in some programmes based on requests from parents. For example, teachers primarily communicated and conducted lessons in Marwari at Bodh located in Rajasthan, in tribal languages in SERP, in Garhwali at Seva Nidhi and in Urdu at Prajayatna. Programmes also introduced children to the dominant state language. For example, SERP in Telangana introduced Telegu and English in preschool for tribal children, Prajayatna in Karnataka introduced Kannada and English, while Bodh and Seva Nidhi introduced children to Hindi. However, a uniform approach to introduce the state language could be problematic, especially for communities living close to state borders whose language preferences may be different, as they may need to interact with people from the neighbouring state for livelihood or other activities as described in the study of CLR.

Diversity in developmental priorities was evident is some areas. The practice of using the *doka* (basket) for young infants described in the previous chapter is a case in point. Moreover, in Uttarakhand, the importance of *santulan* (balance) was articulated by parents, teachers and trainers on several occasions. Through discussions, we realized that their primary concern was teaching children to maintain physical balance to avoid accidents in the mountainous terrains. However, this word was also occasionally used to refer to mental balance (*mansik santulan*), which was addressed in the curriculum through activities like *santi khel* (peaceful play). Generally, these were short activities involving songs or slogans and some physical exercise to help children transition or calm them down when they became unruly.

3.5.2.3. Early Literacy and Numeracy Activities

The longitudinal research of the IECEI Study suggests that there is a positive relationship between classroom quality (ECEQAS) and school readiness (SRI) in young children around the age of five years (Kaul & Bhattacharjea, 2019). Moreover, the findings indicate that play-based developmentally appropriate curriculum is related to higher scores on school readiness as compared to a didactic pedagogy.

Although it was not possible to statistically analyse the data collected through SRI from the case studies due to the small sample size, we observed certain trends which support both of the above findings (refer to Table 3.1). The SRI scores are highest for CLR (55) and Bodh (67.5), which according to the case studies had a clear developmental progression in their curriculum and followed an evidence-based pedagogy. The SRI scores of children in both these programmes were much higher even when compared to the longitudinal study. Further, it appears that the language and reasoning and teacher disposition factors contributed to a greater extent to the school-readiness scores. The Gujarat ICDS programme (37.5%) was in the process of making major changes, though a new preschool kit had been introduced however review of the existing curriculum by an expert indicated that it needed improvement. As discussed in various case studies in Part II of the book, compared to literacy, the numeracy aspect was not addressed systematically in many programmes. For Pratham (32.5%), while the

Table 3.1. Comparison of ECEQAS and SRI

Strands	Programmes	ECEQAS of the Best Centre					SRI (%)
		Language & Reasoning Experience %	Fine and Gross Motor Activities %	Creative Activities %	Social Development %	Teacher's Disposition (%)	
Case Studies (Strand C of the IECEI Study)	CLR	85	83	93	64	67	55
	ICDS Gujarat	55	58	57	93	33	37.5
	Bodh	85	33	86	50	33	67.5
	Pratham	85	75	93	93	67	32.5
	Seva Nidhi	75	100	86	64	33	32.5
Longitudinal Study (Strand B of the IECEI Study)	Known practice	—	—	—	—	—	47.8
	Anganwadi	—	—	—	—	—	39.8
	Private preschool	—	—	—	—	—	47.4

ECEQAS scores were high, possibly because they followed a play-based curriculum and the children were observed to be engaged, the corresponding SRI scores were low, which may be attributed to the observations made in the case study that the curriculum emphasized specific domains rather than a holistic approach to learning and lacked clear developmental progression. Although Seva Nidhi (32.5%) had a developmentally appropriate curriculum, all the children who were tested were below five years of age, as children above five years had moved to Grade 1. Moreover, there was scope for improvement in the numeracy aspect. The SRI is designed to test school readiness of children above five years before entry to school. Therefore, the three major observations from this limited quantitative data confirms the findings from the longitudinal study: (a) the importance of play-based age-appropriate curriculum, (b) the need to address developmental progression in the curriculum and (c) language and reasoning aspect of the curriculum along with teacher disposition are key factors in determining school readiness (Refer to Table 3.1). In summary, a push-down curriculum and didactic pedagogy are not just meaningless to young children but also not useful in facilitating their learning and development.

When contextualizing recommendations from central ministries and organizations such as NCERT or NIPCCD, it is not adequate to simply use local materials; it is necessary to create a pedagogy based on the local cultures, and in some settings educators may be challenged to consider multiple cultures. The position paper on 'Early Language and Literacy in India' (CECED, 2016) clearly identifies a set of goals for teaching language and literacy and principles of good pedagogy. The principles are as follows: oral language must be linked to literacy, emphasis on writing, development of multilingual capabilities and focus on a comprehensive model of instruction. Unfortunately, we do not have a parallel comprehensive evidence-based position paper on numeracy for India, but the ECCE Curriculum Framework and Early Learning and Development Standards offer some guidance.

The study of SERP describes an activity in which the teacher narrates a local story of a monkey and the thorn in the form of a dialogue between the various key characters. The curriculum in some programmes was organized by developmental domains, where specific activities were designed to deliberately address specific goals within a single domain. Activities were planned for the following domains: cognition, language, social emotional, gross motor and fine motor and sometimes creativity. This approach was consistent with guidelines offered by NIPCCD and ensured that adequate learning opportunities were planned for each domain; however, the fragmentation of the complex processes of learning and development limits the ability to recognize the interrelatedness across domains and the opportunity to address various domains in a single activity. A spectrum of interesting literacy activities was observed in the various programmes which have been reported in the case studies. These activities primarily focused on print awareness, letter recognition and storytelling. A systematic approach to phonemic awareness was observed in very few centres. Seva Nidhi published a book where teachers wrote down local stories and drew sketches to document oral narratives passed down through generations in Uttarakhand villages.

Children's early numeracy skills help to develop a strong platform for learning more complex operations in arithmetic in the primary grades. Count forward and backward, one-to-one correspondence, understand the cardinal values of each number, explore relationships between adjacent values, demonstrate number sense and meaning of numbers are concepts that children need to master in the early years. The importance of not only teaching numerical skills but also integrating these in other activities to promote generalization was not always evident. Numbers, shapes and spatial relations were observed. But measurements, patterns and predictions were not observed.

There was considerable variation in the numeracy curriculum. While the curricula in CLR and Bodh reflected considerable rigour, the curriculum of Gujarat ICDS was critiqued for the lack of a systematic approach to numeracy concepts in a developmentally appropriate manner. Also, there were certain gaps reflected in many curricula. For example, while all programmes focused on teaching shapes, few of them focused on the concept of patterns, which provides the foundation for complex numerical operations. In promoting cognitive skills, Kaul (2009) suggests sequential progression from identification, naming, matching, sequencing and serration. These early numeracy skills are necessary for scientific thinking, which require children to observe, articulate problems, explore solutions, hypothesize and draw conclusion.

Montessori's concept of sensitive periods and Piaget's cognitive development theory with an emphasis on development can help to strengthen numeracy in the early childhood curriculum (Crain, 2016). Based on her observations, Montessori concluded that children get interested to engage in certain tasks at certain ages and need to have the opportunity to master these skills during those periods. She developed specific materials to encourage mastery of various skills. The preoperational stage described by Piaget corresponds with the preschool years. He proposed that children's thoughts become more organized compared to the sensorimotor stage, and children begin to engage with symbols and internal images, but their ability to engage in logical thinking is still emerging and is different from that of adults and older children. His theory especially helps us to understand the development of mathematical knowledge in preschoolers (Kaul, 2009) and why children lose interest in learning and demonstrate limited ability to engage in mathematical tasks meant for primary school children such as addition and subtraction which involve place value. Moreover the data from ASER Centre (2019) report indicates that children's ability to accomplish cognitive tasks is associated with early language and numeracy skills, which suggests that play-based activities rather than an early focus on content knowledge are more beneficial during this period.

3.5.2.4. Teacher–Child Ratio

The teacher–child ratio is an important factor in determining classroom quality. The ECCE Policy (2013) recommends a ratio of 1:20, while the NEP 2020 (GoI, 2020) suggests 1:30 teacher–child ratio for preschool children. Both of these recommendations are higher compared to the 1:15 ratio suggested by NAEYC (2020) in DAP. The empirical data from this study suggests that it is difficult to conduct lessons and provide adequate attention to children when the ratio exceeds 1:20. Most programmes tried to follow a ratio of 1:15 but struggled to find the necessary resources to maintain this ratio. The study of Nidan presents the difficulties which teachers face when there is a large class. Some programmes addressed this issue in informal ways. In Bodh, the problem of ratio was addressed by recruiting mother teachers, who were older women from the community and were not always literate to support the fellow teacher who conducted the learning activities. Similarly, in Gujarat ICDS, the Anganwadi helper received training on the curriculum and supported the worker in the classroom.

3.5.2.5. Multiple Ages and Differentiated Teaching

Differentiated teaching is an essential strategy for ensuring that all students are engaged and learning age-appropriate content in multi-age classrooms. In this regard, the ECCE Policy (2013) recommends teachers to approach differentiation in three ways: content, process and products. While the first aspect focuses on what the child needs to learn, the second focuses on the nature of activities and the process of conducting the activity to facilitate learning at different ages. Finally, the third aspect underscores the need to have age-appropriate expectations from the children and the kind of product expected from the students. The DAP (NAEYC, 2020) also emphasizes the need to make modifications to ensure that the curriculum is individualized and considers developmental abilities of children.

Differentiated teaching is primarily conducted by separating younger and older children by their age groups, especially for guided activities. The case studies present various examples of differentiated teaching. Researchers observed that teachers divided children into two or sometimes three different groups based on their chronological age. This enabled teachers to interact individually with children and make the lesson more developmentally appropriate for children. Specific concepts related to numeracy and literacy were often addressed in small group activities, where a teacher interacted with children of a particular age. The concepts of zone of proximal distance and scaffolding proposed by Vygotsky influenced the formulation of these activities in the curriculum.

The SERP case study illustrates an example of problems related to conducting numeracy and cognitive activities in large groups. First, children had to wait for a long time for their turn and it was difficult for them to pay attention to the teacher. Second, classroom observations indicated that older children were able to engage with such activities meaningfully, but the younger ones imitated the actions in a mechanical way. Large group activities were not as much of an issue when children were participating in art or fine motor activities, though the opportunity to engage in conversations with the teacher was compromised.

3.6. Summary and Conclusion

The evidence emphasizes the need for dialectic between the national policies and local perspectives, which enable programmes to create a curriculum which is meaningful and sustainable. This is essential to question existing practices and hegemonic practices and create space for innovative practices and indigenous activities. Moreover, it is essential to create praxis between the theoretical perspectives underlying the curriculum, current evidence and local practices to ensure both pedagogical rigour and cultural meaning. There is a need to consciously reflect and revive the education practices and philosophy espoused by Gandhi, Gijubhai Badheka and Tagore, as they were congruent with the notion of place-based education and held the potential to address both SDG 4 and SDG 13. The data indicates that integrated thematic and activity-based approaches give more opportunities to develop contextually relevant meaningful activities to promote development when compared to a domain-based approach. While play-based learning was emphasized in all programmes, teachers needed to develop a more nuanced understanding of the scope and value of play and develop the skills to participate and expand young children's play. The teacher–pupil ratio in most programmes was between 1:15 and 1:20, though the current NEP suggests a 1:30 ratio. Differentiated teaching is crucial to bring quality in multi-age learning environments. Finally, there is a need to develop a position paper with clear guidance for promoting numeracy skills for preschoolers to strengthen the existing curricula.

References

Ansari A. (2017). Multi-grade kindergarten classrooms and children's academic achievement, executive function, and socio-emotional development. *Infant and Child Development*, *26*(6), e2036. https://doi.org/10.1002/icd.2036

Apple, M. W. (1993). *The politics of official knowledge: Does a National Curriculum make sense.* Taylor & Francis.

ASER Centre. (2019). *Early years.* National Findings.

Au, W. W., & Apple, M. W. (2009). The curriculum and the politics of inclusion and exclusion. In S. Mitakidou, E. Tressou, B. B. Swadener, & C. A. Grant (Eds.), *Beyond pedagogies of exclusion in diverse childhood contexts: Critical cultural studies of childhood.* Palgrave Macmillan. https://doi.org/10.1057/9780230622920_7

Bodrova, E., & Leong, D. J. (2006). *Tools of the mind.* Pearson.

Burns, R. B., & Mason D. A. (2002). Class composition and student achievement in elementary schools. *American Educational Research Journal*, *39*(1),207–233. https://doi.org/10.3102/00028312039001207

CECED. (2016). *Early language and literacy in India: A position paper.*

Chaudhary, A. B., & Kaul, V. (2019). What works for school readiness: Understanding quality in preschool education. In V. Kaul & S. Bhattacharjea (Eds.), *Early childhood education and school readiness in India: Quality and diversity.* Springer.

Chawla-Duggan, R. (2016). Pedagogy and quality in Indian slum school settings: A Bernsteinian analysis of visual representations in the Integrated Child Development Service. *Research in Comparative and International Education*, *10*(2), 123–140.

Chawla-Duggan, R. (2019). *The sociology of knowledge: The intended and enacted curriculum* (pp. 143–154). Taylor & Francis.

Crain, W. (2014). *Theories of development: Concepts and applications.* Pearson Education.

Crehan, L. (2018). *Clever lands: The secrets behind the success of world's education superpowers.* Unbound.

Day, M., & Hernandez, D. (2015). *Discovering place-based education in the foothills of the Himalayas* [Occasional Paper Series 33]. Bank Street.

Dunst, C. J., Harter, S., Shields, H., & Bennis, L. (2001). Mapping community based natural learning opportunities. *Young Exceptional Children*, *4*(4), 16–24.

Ghosh, R. (2015). Caught in cross traffic: Rabindranath Tagore and the trials of child education. *Comparative Education Review*, *59*(3), 399–419.

GoI. (2012). *Quality standards for ECCE.* Ministry of Women and Child Development.

GoI. (2013a). *National policy for early childhood care and education (NPECCE).* Ministry of Women and Child Development.

GoI. (2013b). *National early childhood care and education (ECCE) curriculum framework.* Ministry of Women and Child Development.

GoI. (2020). *National policy on education*. Ministry of Education.

GoI. (2021). *Annual report 2020–2021*. Ministry of Women and Child Development. https://wcd.nic.in/sites/default/files/WCD_AR_English%20 final_.pdf

Hutchison, D. (2004). *A natural history of place in education*. Teachers College.

Katz, L. (1995). The benefits of mixed age grouping. *ERIC Digest*, ED 382411.

Kaul, V. (2009). *Early childhood education programme*. NCERT.

Kaul, V., & Bhattacharjea, S. (2019). *Early childhood education and school readiness in India: Quality and diversity*. Springer.

Kaul, V., & Sankar, D. (2016). Early childhood care and education in India. In R. Govinda & M. Sedwal (Eds.). *Elementary education in India*. Oxford University Press.

Macy, M. (2007). Theory and theory-driven practices of activity based intervention. *Journal of Early and Intensive Behaviour Intervention, 4*(3), 561–585. http://dx.doi.org/10.1037/h0100392

Mobile Creches. (2020). *Status of the young child in India*. Routledge.

NAEYC. (2020). *Developmentally appropriate practice*.

O'Donnell, C. R., Tharp, R. G., & Wilson, K. (1992). Activity settings as the unit of analysis: A theoretical basis for community intervention and development. *American Journal of Community Psychology, 21*, 501–520.

Prochner, L. (2002). Preschool and playway in India. *Childhood, 9*, 435–453.

Prochner, L., Cleghorn, A., & Green, N. (2008). Space considerations: Materials in the learning environment in three majority world preschool settings. *International Journal of Early Years Education, 16*(3), 189–201.

Rogoff, B. (2003). *The cultural nature of human development*. Oxford University Press.

Shaheed, M., & Chanchal, R. (2021). Impact of Covid 19 on school education: A study of underprivileged social groups in Haryana. *Social Action, 71*(1), 67–69.

Sobel, D. (2004). *Place-based education: Connecting classroom and communities, closing the achievement gap—The SEER report*. https://www.semanticscholar.org/paper/Place-Based-Education%3A-Connecting-Classrooms-and-Sobel /4211933133bcf79aa24f3090b925eb2cdae03eb2

Tschurenev, J. (2021). Montessori for all? Indian experiments in 'child education', 1920s to 1970s. *Comparative Education*, 1–19. https://doi.org/10.1080/030 50068.2021.1888408.

CHAPTER 4

Early Childhood Education Teachers in India
Professionals or Volunteers?
Venita Kaul and Swati Bawa Sawhney

4.1. Introduction

India's enrolment rate for three- to six-year-old children accessing preschool education is at present relatively significant. Although there is no official database to establish the exact percentage, recent data from a large-scale survey in the rural sector indicates that almost 80 per cent of the four-year-olds were found attending an early childhood education (ECE) centre or a preschool (ASER Centre, 2019). The *India Early Childhood Education Impact Study* (IECEI Study; Kaul et al., 2017)[1] has in the recent past also provided supportive evidence. The IECEI Study had further demonstrated that participation in ECE not only influences children's levels of cognitive readiness at school entry but also has a bearing on the learning outcomes later at the primary school

[1] IECEI Study is the first-of-its-kind longitudinal research in India on 14,000 rural children tracked from the age of 4–8 years (Kaul & Bhattacharjea, 2019).

stage. However, this conclusion comes with a caveat that for the impact to be sustained over time, the quality of ECE offered to children is a significant variable. While *The Lancet* (2017) emphasizes the critical role of quality of early childhood development (ECD) interventions, Yoshikawa and Nieto (2013) have moved this argument further by emphasizing that it is not just 'quality' (which in itself is an amorphous entity) but also 'effectiveness' factors which determine impact. The IECEI Study, in its empirical exploration of the multiple dimensions of quality and effectiveness factors, identified 'teacher quality' as a critical factor of effectiveness of an ECE programme in determining the impact on later outcomes (Kaul et al., 2017).

In this chapter, we explore this teacher dimension further by attempting to deconstruct the profile of an 'ECE teacher' or a 'preschool teacher' in the Indian context from the perspective of professionalism, mindful of the fact that it often reflects not only a disparate status but also a wide diversity of roles and expectations. We use the pronoun 'she' deliberately for the teacher, since it represents the fact that the teacher community at all levels of school education tends to be dominated by women, and this is more true of the preschool stage in particular. This is possibly a reflection of the fact that women tend to be preferred in this role as, 'feminization of teaching is merely seen as the extension of family matters, which are closely related to mothering and nurturing. Consequently, feminization projects another form of domestication for women' (Rahayani, 2010).

This 'feminization' is further evident in the fact that female teachers are also often not easily given due status and career opportunities. In many cases, she is not a regular teacher but a volunteer or is on a contractual position as in the case of Anganwadi workers (AWWs) in India. This anomaly in the status of preschool teachers is perhaps not unique to India, as evident from a similar description in the USA.

> Today, the early care and education teaching workforce ranges from people without a high school degree to people with graduate training. Some teachers get evidence-based in-service training and coaching; others have no access to professional learning opportunities. Some teachers earn a living wage that approaches the median

income in their communities, while others are among the lowest-paid workers in the country. (Phillips et al., 2016)

We examine the extent to which her status and expected job description influence the nature and extent of the preparation she undergoes and how these together contribute to her self-perception of her role as an ECE teacher and thereon the effectiveness of the quality of her service delivery. In this context, we analyse the arrangements and provisions for her preparation in both public and private preschool provisions and review these against the larger backdrop of the state's own conceptualization or positioning of teachers for this stage of education within a 'professionalism vs volunteerism' paradigm framework. While reviewing this dimension systemically, we also explore it from the lens of 'positive deviance' in the context of eight low-cost good practices in early childhood care and education (ECCE), which have been reviewed and documented as a part of the IECEI Study and presented in Part II of this publication and try to identify factors reflected in these practices which could be considered to have contributed to teacher effectiveness. This analysis has ramifications for our concluding recommendations for enhancing the professionalization of the ECCE sector at scale.

4.2. Final Professionalism vs Volunteerism: A Conceptual Dichotomy

To facilitate our analysis of the status and context of ECCE teachers in India with reference to this framework, we begin by first trying to operationally explore how the two concepts, that is, volunteerism and professionalism, have been defined and how these differ. Volunteerism has been described as

a basic expression of human relationships. It is about people's need to participate in their societies and to feel that they matter to others.... The ethos of volunteerism is infused with values such as solidarity, reciprocity, mutual trust, belonging and empowerment, all of which contribute significantly to quality of life. (UN Volunteers, 2020)

Volunteerism is generally considered to be an altruistic activity for which the individual gives his or her own time at one's own will with the intention 'to benefit another person, group or organization'. Volunteering may result in some benefits for the volunteer as well as benefit the person or community which is being served. Often, it is also intended to enable networking and establishing contacts for possible employment.

Professionalism, on the other hand, is defined as 'an ideal to which individuals and occupational groups aspire, in order to distinguish themselves from other workers' (Pratte & Rury, 1991). Grady et al. (2008) describe professionals as persons who are able to exercise their own discretion in decision-making within the scope of their expertise and assume some authority for their own professional development. Brehm et al. (2006) bifurcate professionalism into three distinct categories: (a) professional parameters, (b) professional behaviours and (c) professional responsibilities.

> *Professional parameters:* These focus more on the legal and ethical issues to which a professional must adhere to, such as local, state and federal laws or rules pertaining to the service domain.
> *Professional behaviours:* These 'are observable actions that demonstrate the individual's appropriate behaviours such as: maintaining appropriate relationships with students, parents, and colleagues; modelling of the appearance and attitudes of a professional; and promptness'.
> *Professional responsibilities:* These, for a teacher, may include demonstrating responsibility to the profession or as a professional, to students, to the school district and the community. 'Many of these can be converted into observable and measurable behaviours, which often get converted into checklists for teacher behaviour. Some of these could refer to maintaining appropriate relationships, acceptable appearances and attitudes such as the belief that all students can learn' (Brehm et al., 2006).

More specifically, in the context of ECE, professionalism is seen as 'established professions that are built upon a shared purpose, common identity and agreement on the unique responsibilities and characteristics of their professionals, defined by the profession itself (NAEYC, 2019). According to this definition, 'The four dimensions of professionalism (professional knowledge, competence, commitment to the ethical standard and personal characteristics) work in tandem to make up a qualified, competent, and ethical workforce of early childhood professionals.'

Professionalism is thus multifaceted and therefore difficult to define. Regardless of the lack of a universally accepted definition of professionalism, what is consistent in the relevant literature is that professionals are expected to have specific skills, knowledge and disposition, which they utilize to make sound judgements. To develop these qualities, candidates need to participate in specialized training and field engagement/internships which are unique to their field, to meet the standards to which they are accountable (Brehm et al., 2006).

A third category which emerges is that of 'professional volunteerism', a fusion of the two! A professional volunteer could be someone who decides to devote most of his/her life—as much time as is allotted for any paid labour—to the service of others for little or no compensation. A professional volunteer is willing to give up material comforts and financial stability in order to make the world a better place, even leaving friends and family to pick up and move to unfamiliar areas.

This differentiation and Brehm's framework encourage us to explore where the ECE teacher is located on this binary of professionalism vs volunteerism, as this has important implications for the quality of ECE accessible to children in India. Prior to deep diving into this analysis, we briefly revisit the two major provisions for preschool education in the country, that is, the Integrated Child Development Services (ICDS) and the private preschools already discussed in Chapter 1, and alongside we also draw out lessons from a smaller segment of case studies of non-governmental initiatives which have been introduced in Part II of this book. We examine the ECE workforce in these three sectors with due attention to the structure and nature of provisions, respective profiles of service providers or teachers, and their roles and career provisions from social and historical perspectives.

4.3. Major ECE Provisions in India

4.3.1. The Integrated Child Development Services

The ICDS, perhaps the largest integrated programme for children in the world, is a public programme for integrated ECCE for children below six years of age. It is implemented across all Indian states with financial contribution at an agreed ratio from the federal government. At a habitation level in the ICDS, the ECCE centre known as Anganwadi (or 'courtyard centre' due to its location within a habitation), functions as the 'single-window' service outlet for all six services offered by the ICDS which cater to pregnant women, lactating mothers and children from prenatal to six years of age. The six services include the following:

1. Supplementary nutrition
2. Preschool non-formal education
3. Nutrition and health education
4. Immunization
5. Health check-up
6. Referral services

The six services listed above are indicative of ICDS's adherence to an integrated concept of ECD, with all six services to be delivered from the centre by a single service provider, who is designated as an AWW and is expected to be a local woman from the community with some basic education. The AWW is assisted by a less qualified helper, who is also from the local community. The ICDS is now almost universalized across the country with over 1.37 million integrated child development centres established for children below 6 years of age with 1.28 million AWWs and about 1.2 million Anganwadi helpers manning these centres with the responsibility of delivery of all 6 services (MWCD, 2018). With 5,652 ICDS projects[2] functional in the country comprising 4,533 projects in rural, 759 in tribal and 360 in urban areas (Parker & Willan, 2006), the programme caters more to the rural and tribal sectors as compared to the urban slums. With the principle of

[2] An ICDS project is an administrative unit comprising 100 centres.

self-selection operating, the beneficiaries of this programme are almost in all cases from the lowest strata of the society.

Interestingly, ICDS is commonly perceived and presented solely as a health or nutrition provision, with the ECE or preschool education component underplayed or very often conspicuously absent in public perception, although clearly listed officially as one of the six services. The popular perception of an Anganwadi is that of a 'nutrition center that additionally supports the health department by mobilising children and pregnant women for ante-natal check-ups and immunization' (Parker-Reese & Willan, 2006). It is rarely seen even by the community it caters to as an educational service, as is evident from a large percentage of underage children moving out into primary schools or, where feasible, into pre-primary sections of private schools (Kaul et al., 2017).

4.3.2. Private Preschools

With a shift in political ideology towards a more neoliberal paradigm in India for the last few decades, there has been an exponential expansion of private preschools in India, resulting in the number of preschool teachers in the sector steadily increasing. Data from a reliable source indicates the latest estimation of the percentage of children attending private schools across India as opposed to government provisions to be nearly 50 per cent with 0.45 million privately managed schools reported across the country (GoI, 2019). This possibly does not include a very large number of unregistered preschool-cum-primary schools which are outside the frame of any centralized data management system. With the preschool/primary education sector being completely unregulated, this has allowed for free expansion of private services across rural, urban and even tribal geographies with no requirement of any conformity to norms and standards. However, most private preschools are part of a composite school structure with very few standalone provisions, except as playgroups. About 45.5 per cent of students in private schools pay less than ₹500 per month as fees, suggesting that a majority of the sector is low fee paying or affordable (CSF, 2020).

In terms of demand, a recent survey of rural preschool children in India (ASER Centre, 2019) which tracked enrolment rates in

5-year-olds reported a significant 37.3 per cent of the total enrolment to be in private preschools/schools, 26.7 per cent in government schools and 27.3 per cent in Anganwadis. The IECEI Study which tracked a rural sample of 14,000 4-year-olds also found 23.8 per cent of the sample attending private preschools, although there were state differences (Kaul et al., 2017). The researchers report that

> The private schools observed did not follow a defined curriculum at the preschool stage as there is no such prescription from the state's education boards. Our interactions with school personnel indicated that they had no understanding of appropriate preschool curriculum. Consequently, these preschool classes were a downward extension of primary classes with the curriculum largely focusing on formal teaching of alphabet and numbers. (Kaul et al., 2017)

While the private school sector is not at all a homogeneous category, given that there is a wide range in terms of quality and clientele, the desired emphasis on professionalization and specialized training of teachers for ECCE in this formative stage of education is absent across the sector, albeit in varying degrees. As Alcott et al. (2018) report in the context of the IECEI Study,

> Very few parents visualised the ECE phase as requiring an environment and set of inputs distinct from those provided in primary schools.... In addition, parents interest in goals such as 'good quality teaching' 'focusing on studies' and 'better discipline' help us to understand why so many chose to pay for private provision.

4.3.3. Non-governmental Organizations

A much smaller player in the domain of ECE services is the non-governmental sector which runs creches or Balwadis or small standalone preschools which cater to specific localized communities. While there is no authentic data on the number of such Balwadis or creches, a newspaper reports that while in 2015 there were 23,000 centrally run creches/Balwadis, in 2019, due to decreased funding, these were reduced to just 7,000 centres across the country (Pandit, 2019). Recent restrictions on non-governmental organizations (NGOs) by the government in the context of sources of funding could possibly reduce this number further. As with the private provisions, these are also not a homogenous category, although most operate on a low-cost basis and the quality of education offered is not always evidence based and often minimalist in nature, as in the case of many Anganwadis.

Nonetheless, a few organizations have demonstrated innovative and exemplar practices in ECE. These are generally led by some professionally committed social activists and informed professionals who often also provide technical support to government programmes. Part II of this publication presents case studies of eight such organizations which may be considered exemplar and can offer some learnings for the larger system.

In most cases, these programmes do not adhere to an integrated or holistic design which includes health and nutrition services; instead, these focus solely on the preschool education dimension. As these serve designated poor communities, they tend to draw their teachers also from the same communities, with academic qualifications in most cases being Grade 10 or below. While most NGOs run independent centres, they take on the responsibility of strengthening and supporting the government system, in this case the ICDS. Their strength in most cases lies in their innovative methods of training and mentoring/scaffolding, which compensate for the limitations of poor academic qualifications and training. Learnings and insights for teacher development from these experiences are discussed later in the chapter.

4.4. ECE Teachers in India: A Case of Diverse Expectations

Unlike the category of a 'primary teacher', which may be a known entity universally, there is no corresponding job category of an exclusive 'ECE teacher or preschool teacher' across India. This anomaly is largely context driven for each sector. Typically, in any system, the expected role and functions determine the designation and related profile of respective functionaries. As discussed above, in India, the primary ECE service providers who operate at scale for children below six years of age are the AWWs, under the government-sponsored ICDS programme. The other major service provider is the private sector which has educators designated as teachers but may not necessarily be referred to as ECE teachers. A third category is the NGO sector which offers low-cost programmes of a limited scale, largely catering to specific underprivileged communities. These generally employ local community women, referred to as Balwadi workers, often with limited schooling, but boost up their capability through a range of recurrent training and mentoring measures, as highlighted in the case studies.

Within the ICDS, the concept of ECE is integrated as it is designed as a composite of health, nutrition, early learning and care services. Since preschool education is only one of the six services, the expected role of the service provider in the ICDS is therefore not just that of a 'teacher' but more of a 'multipurpose worker' who can deliver all six required services. In the case of the private sector, the perspective is different. While most schools are composite schools with preschool sections attached to them, the major role of the teacher is to 'teach'. Yet there is no state stipulation regarding any basic requirement of professional training as eligibility for an ECE or preschool teacher, as is there for the primary and higher stages of education. In practice, therefore, there seems to be a systemic dilution and devaluation of the concept and scope of ECE, as reflected in the classrooms, either in the form of a minimalist provision of songs and rhymes to keep children busy or at the other extreme a focus on formal teaching of literacy and numeracy, referred to in literature as the '*schoolification* of ECE' (Kaul et al., 2017). In both cases, these are expected to be carried out with or without minimal training. There is thus limited refection of any understanding of a scientific approach to planning of what is known as a 'developmentally appropriate curriculum' and of the competence to deliver such a curriculum, thus resulting in the quality of preschool education getting compromised (Kaul et al., 2017).

4.5. Emergence of Volunteerism in Social Sector: A Historical Perspective

It is important to understand the genesis of this attitude in the social sector as a whole and the consequent neglect of ECE and its possible implications for quality and teacher professionalism within the ECE sector in India. For this, a comprehensive understanding of the contextual challenges at all levels becomes vital. We identify several factors from a historical perspective which have been responsible for the neglect of ECE or preschool education as a professional programme or provision for young children.

The Indian Constitution (Constitution of India, n.d.) enunciated the government's commitment to ensure education of all children 'upto the age of 14 years', thus including children below 6 years. However, the Right to Education Act (2009), which made basic or elementary education a justiciable right of every Indian child and laid down standards and specifications for its quality, excluded children below six years of age from its ambit, thus failing to include this foundational stage of education as a legitimate right of every Indian child. ECE had till recently not been an integral part of the formal school structure, which in the public education system starts only from Grade 1.[3] As a result, ECE has not only remained completely unregulated but also much less invested in with the conflict of ownership of this subject between the Ministry of Education and Ministry of Women and Child Development (which is the nodal ministry) in the business rules of the government taking a further toll.

This exclusion from the domain of school education and the overall lack of appreciation of the emerging science of ECD and of the related need for ensuring professionalism have reduced the demand for trained teachers. This has also prevented the states from forming an organized cadre of ECE teachers in the country (as is there for the other stages), and this vicious cycle has resulted in a low demand and supply of teacher preparation programmes for this stage of education, thus further contributing to its neglect. There is also a popular belief that any woman, especially one who has been a mother, is suitable to deliver ECE or preschool education and no special training is required—a clear case of feminization of ECE as a domain within the discipline of education.

---

[3] This lacuna has to an extent been corrected by the recent National Education Policy 2020 which has recommended curricular integration in the education of children between three and eight years of age (i.e., three years of preschool and two years of primary schooling) and restructured this stage as the foundational stage within the school structure.

With education being primarily a state responsibility in the federal arrangement, and with the Department of Women and Child Development being the nodal agency for the ICDS which is the main vehicle for ECE in the public domain, there has historically been a complete absence of interest in ECE in the Departments of Education. This is compounded by the fact that as mentioned earlier, the public school structure starts from Grade 1 in the states and, therefore, there is no official cadre created by their governments for teachers of the pre-primary stage.

At the federal level, however, the National Council for Teacher Education (NCTE), the statutory organization of the Government of India for regulation of teacher education for all stages of education in the country, has officially notified an approved curricular structure and standards for a professional undergraduate diploma in ECE. The open and distance education systems, including the National Institute of Open Schooling and Indira Gandhi National Open University, also offer certificate, diploma and advanced diploma programmes in this area. But being an unregulated sub-sector of education, as discussed above, with no stipulated requirement, there is minimal demand for trained teachers or teacher preparation programmes for this stage of education. This phenomenon has contributed to very diverse, inequitable and scarce provisions of teacher education programmes across states and sectors for this stage of education in the country (CECED, 2015). To quote Phillips et al. (2016, p. 139), as compared to other stages of education, 'not surprisingly, the pathways into the early childhood workforce, the opportunities for professional development, and the compensation and other work supports together have been characterized as "perpetuating a cycle of disparity"'.

While in the education sector ECE was neglected since it was not a part of the school structure, in the ICDS context it was clearly indicated as one of the six services in the integrated structure. However, the factors responsible for the low priority to preschool education in the ICDS are perhaps different. These could relate to (a) the emphasis on engaging a local community-based multipurpose worker instead of a trained preschool teacher and (b) greater priority to survival over development/education of the child. We discuss the historical context and basis for this assertion to get a better understanding of this anomaly.

4.5.1. Choice of Local Woman as a Multipurpose Voluntary Worker

Given the requirement in the ICDS of locally delivering six services to the underprivileged families related to health, nutrition and preschool education as an integrated package, the choice of a multipurpose worker is perhaps logical. To further understand the choice for a local community woman as the service provider, we will need to make a historical detour to when India emerged as an independent, socialist democratic nation state and adopted and enacted its Constitution in 1950. Articles 39 and 45 of the Constitution emphasized the state's responsibility in ensuring health, education and general welfare, especially of its children. Initially due to resource constraints and to yet meet this commitment, the Indian government continued in a welfare mode to support voluntary organizations to provide various family welfare services, generally through the Central Social Welfare Board (Khalakdina, 1998). It was only by the Third Five-Year Plan period (1961–1966) that a shift became evident in the government's perception of children as potential beneficiaries themselves, whose range of specific needs are required to be met. The government decided to directly engage in delivery of integrated services for children through a multi-centric Welfare Extension Project (WEF) with a network of Balwadis (children's centres) and mahila mandals (women's groups), run by the CSWB.

Given that the services had to be delivered as per local context and need, it became necessary in this model to identify a local woman volunteer who would be familiar with the community to deliver these services. Given the lower levels of female literacy in several underprivileged communities, a community woman who often did not even have basic education was often identified as the multipurpose service provider for rural and tribal communities. She was given 11 months' training to equip her to deliver 6 multi-sectoral services related to health, nutrition, women's issues and preschool education. This model of a 'community worker' was appreciated at that time, as Baig (1979) states, 'It was Smt Durgabhai Deshmukh who ... understood the need to give voluntary workers status, responsibility and mobility.' Subsequently, in 1975, when the ICDS, modelled on this relatively successful WEF project design, was piloted in 33 administrative blocks of the country, it also identified a local woman from the community as an AWW, but more significantly as a volunteer and not a salaried person, to deliver its 6 multi-sectoral services, maintain records and carry out home visits. While the initial requirement was fixed at secondary-level schooling, in remote contexts where eligible candidates were not locally available, the qualifications were reduced to even semi-literate levels.

By the Fifth Five-Year Plan (1974–1978) of the Government of India, which focused primarily on poverty alleviation and a Minimum Needs Programme, the ICDS was initiated as a pilot in 35 blocks of the country as a decision 'to start a holistic, multi-centric programme with a compact package of services'. The local multipurpose worker as a volunteer remained as a single service provider for all the six services of the Anganwadi with one helper, both considered as honorary work-ers. With the rapid scaling up of the ICDS in the later years after the Eighth Five-Year Plan, the workers received reduced levels of train-ing and supervision as well, and this combination of low academic qualifications and reduced training and support led to an inevitable dilution of the preschool education component across states, albeit with some exceptions.

4.5.2. Low Priority to Preschool Education in ICDS

The context which contributed to the low priority to preschool educa-tion in this integrated model can be further traced back to 1971 when the first census in independent India reflected the persisting situation of poor health and nutrition indicators of women and children, which led to the launch of the ICDS programme of services in 1975. While the programme design included non-formal, preschool education as one of the six services, the bleak health indicators and in particular the distressing infant mortality rate led to 'child survival' being designated as a major priority of the government. This triggered off a debate, which continued till several decades later in the professional fora (to which the first author of this chapter was a witness as a young profes-sional!) on why child survival should be privileged over child develop-ment and learning in terms of the six ICDS services. With the health component of ICDS directly under supervision of the Department of

Health, this priority also led to more concentrated attention to this component. Given this priority, the preschool education component was neither implemented well nor adequately monitored, so that the AWWs also tended to devote less attention to it. As Parker and Willan (2006) describe it, preschool education, although included in the scheme, was 'enmeshed in the child welfare concept' as reflected in its minimalist provision.

4.6. Teaching in Early Childhood in India: Applying the Professionalism Lens

Given this historical context and its implications for the present state of services, we now revert to the professionalism framework discussed earlier in the chapter (Brehm et al., 2006). As mentioned earlier, the Brehm framework defines professionalism in terms of the following three dimensions: (a) professional parameters, (b) professional behaviours and (c) professional responsibilities. We apply this lens to examine the different aspects of the work situation of ECE teachers/multipurpose workers in both public and private spheres and asses that to what extent these serve to promote or undermine professionalism in teachers at this stage of education.

4.6.1. Professional Parameters

We explore this parameter in terms of the nature of state's own stipulations or regulations, legal or official, which have been framed and are being implemented to explore the extent of professionalism in this particular domain of public or private services. These include eligibility requirements for teachers' position, including initial or pre-service training and professional development opportunities while in service.

4.6.1.1. Job Description and Eligibility

NCTE, the regulatory authority of the Government of India for all stages of pre-service teacher education, lays down the basic eligibility conditions and norms for all teacher positions in the country. In the case of preschool education, NCTE, as per its latest notification (dated December 2014), which is no longer in the public domain, has specified the minimum eligibility condition for being recruited as preschool teachers to be Grade 12, with a two-year professional teacher education programme leading to a diploma in preschool education.

We examine this parameter of professionalism in the context of job description and eligibility conditions for both AWWs under the ICDS as well as private preschool teachers.

The position of an AWW, who is expected to deliver preschool education to children between three and six years of age, is completely honorary or, as alternatively described, voluntary in nature. To quote from an official document,

> The Anganwadi Services {under Umbrella Integrated Child Development Services (ICDS) Scheme} envisages the Anganwadi Workers & Helpers as honorary workers from local community who come forward to render their services, on part time basis, in the area of child care and development. Being honorary workers, they are paid monthly honoraria as decided by Government from time to time. (MWCD, 2019)

The appointment of AWWs is done on a temporary basis at the block level in all the states of the country. In the case of private preschool teachers, ECCE being an unregulated sector, these are recruited by individual schools as per their own priorities and are often required to teach both preschool and primary classes, reflecting inadequate sensitivity to age-appropriate learning needs of the younger children, as evident in most cases in the 'schoolification' of the preschool curriculum (Kaul et al., 2017)!

In terms of eligibility to become a teacher, the requirements for the ICDS are not at all aligned with the NCTE stipulation, since it must be conceded that AWWs are not envisioned as teachers but multipurpose volunteers. Again to quote from the document,[4]

> To become an Anganwadi worker, the candidates should be secondary pass from any recognized university or board. Candidates

---

[4] https://www.jagranjosh.com/articles/know-how-to-become-an-anganwadi-worker-eligibility-criteria-selection-process-and-more-1531898994-1

having certificate in public health problems from any recognized University is given preference. The candidate applying for the position should be from the same village he or she is applying and from the same ward in the urban area where she wants to apply.

Interestingly, this official quote clearly privileges the health-related functions over preschool education.

In the case of private preschool teachers, according to a recent report published by Central Square Foundation, teacher salaries and qualifications in private schools tend to be lower than in government schools. However, teacher presence and activity are higher on average in private schools, which are stronger predictors of learning outcomes (Kremer & Muralidharan, 2008; Singh, 2013). Unfortunately, there is a dearth of any reliable database in terms of the academic and professional qualifications of private preschool teachers. However, a comparative analysis from a sample of preschool teachers and AWWs from the IECEI Study (which it is important to emphasize is at best indicative, and not at all representative of the larger reality) demonstrates that in terms of academic qualifications, while AWWs had an equal mix of secondary (Grade 10), senior secondary and less than secondary qualifications, 80 per cent of the private preschool teachers had post-senior secondary qualifications with 50 per cent of the total sample being graduates. Evidently as per this data, private schools do give preference to higher academic qualifications (Singh & Chaudhary, 2019).

This trend of ensuring higher levels of academic qualifications as eligibility for becoming preschool teachers is perhaps consistent with some developed countries such as Japan, Turkey and Korea, which comparatively have the highest qualified preschool teachers with post-secondary education levels (OECD, 2019). Higher academic education among teachers is associated with higher quality of interactions between staff and children, an important indicator of process-based quality in ECCE settings (Manning et al., 2017, p. 8; TALIS, 2018, p. 6).

4.6.1.2. Pre-service Training

In terms of pre-service/initial training, again although the NCTE stipulation is for a two-year diploma in ECCE or preschool education after Grade 12, data on pre-service training from the sample referred to earlier reveals that 100 per cent of the AWWs had no pre-service training. Interestingly, a similar trend was observed in the case of the private preschools[5] also with about 78 per cent teachers with no training qualifications. The positive aspect in the private schools was that the remaining 32 per cent teachers had some kind of professional training including a diploma in elementary education, or a bachelor's degree in education. But none had any initial training which specifically prepared them for preschool education (Singh & Chaudhary, 2019).

International comparisons indicate some good practices in some OECD countries. For instance, in Germany, ECE teachers are typically required to acquire a graduate-level professional degree, which is often 'fulfilled through a vocationally oriented bachelor's equivalent focused on child pedagogy'. The TALIS report (OECD, 2019) confirms this to be the case in approximately 65 per cent of the teachers they covered across countries which reported acquiring this qualification. Only around 4 per cent of teachers report an academically focused bachelor's degree in pedagogy or child pedagogy. In some cases, to become teachers, there is also an additional requirement of having worked in the field for at least two years and completed 'sufficient professional development hours related to pedagogy'.

Across OECD countries, the duration of the initial teacher training varies more in pre-primary education (ISCED 02) than at any other level of education, as it varies from two years for basic certification in Korea and Japan to five years in Austria, Chile, France, Iceland and Italy. All teachers of pre-primary education who enter the profession have a professional degree at bachelor's level in Finland and Australia, as in most other OECD countries too. In some countries, including England, France, Iceland and Italy, initial teacher education of pre-primary teachers is at Master's level (OECD, 2014, Table D6.1a).

According to OECD (2018, p. 6), professional development for ECCE teachers is 'related to both process quality and stronger learning and development for young children'. However, any linear association of educational levels with quality enhancement is not clearly evident in

[5] These are rural preschools from the 'affordable private schools' category (Kaul & Bhattacharjea, 2019); http://doi.org/10.1007/978-981-13-7006-9_1

research. Most studies find a positive correlation between educational attainment and process quality, rather than specific improvements in process quality from one level of staff education to another (e.g., vocational training compared to bachelor's level training).

The fact that in India there is no regulatory compliance of professional qualification of teachers teaching at the preschool level, despite the NCTE regulation, speaks volumes about the health of this sector from a professional perspective. The inequitable distribution of preservice teacher education institutions across states in the country at the preschool education stage further compounds the problem. Even among the programmes which are available, there is wide disparity with some institutions offering certificate programmes ranging from three months' duration to five months and even up to two years! Of the 51 institutions offering diploma in ECE which were surveyed, only 3 had certified recognition from the NCTE (CECED, 2015)!

Crehan (2016, p. 237–261), in her analysis of teacher education provisions in school education in five high-performing countries in Programme for International Student Assessment (PISA) from the perspective of professionalism, identifies four common features across these countries: (a) They are selective about who enters their teacher training programmes. (b) Their teacher training is hosted in respected institutions and last at least for a full year. (c) They confer teacher certification only after successful graduation from the programme and an induction training. (d) They ensure that teachers are mentored in their first few years and remain in close collaboration with experienced colleagues through weekly planning sessions and then they are allowed autonomy to take responsibility for their work. Thus, the emphasis is on mastery, autonomy and relatedness—all of which enhance intrinsic motivation.

4.6.1.3. In-service Training

Professional development may be considered in terms of onsite and offsite induction and in-service training, onsite support and mentoring; access to membership in professional associations and/or professional literature; participation in conferences; etc. If we examine the Indian scenario from this parameter, in the ICDS there is a provision of both induction or job training and refreshers. However, in the private sector, while individual schools, particularly the more elite ones, do organize professional development opportunities for their teachers, there is no such provision generally within what is known as the affordable schools' segment. The training institutions responsible for in-service training like National Institute of Public Cooperation and Child Development and National Council of Educational Research and Training at the national level and their counterparts at the state level in the public sector do not cater to the private school sector. Overall, in the absence of any framework for teacher competence, these trainings when held are also completely unregulated and incidental.

In the ICDS, given the fact that there has traditionally been a low expectation at entry level in terms of academic or professional qualifications for AWWs, an in-service infrastructure has been put in place ever since the inception of the programme for providing induction and in-service training. This is in the form of 498 Anganwadi Workers Training Centres (AWTCs) supported by the government across the country. These with the exception of a few being government owned are mainly in the NGO sector. The government provides them financial support to meet the faculty and training costs. These institutions are mandated to conduct both the induction and refresher trainings of the AWWs and their helpers. The induction training is of 26 days' duration, of which 5 days are earmarked for preschool education. With a benchmark of two years' training set by NCTE, this is clearly at best just an orientation and nothing more! Often the trainers who may meet prescribed qualifications of postgraduation in social science are also themselves not familiar with the field and the current issues in ECE.

Of late, these training centres have also been closed down with the introduction of a web-based Incremental Learning Approach (ILA) under the National Nutrition Mission (POSHAN Abhiyaan), wherein the AWWs are provided orientation/training with the help of 21 training modules, with 1 module introduced every 15 days. An e-ILA software has also now been developed as a comprehensive training and evaluation web-based learning portal for the field workers. This is in addition to ongoing face-to-face ILA. Again, these are supporting multiple Anganwadi services and not confined to preschool education only. There is also no evaluation to date of the effectiveness or impact of these online trainings, especially given the imperative need in preschool education for training to be more 'hands on' and experiential and supplemented with onsite mentoring.

4.6.1.3.1. Impact of In-service Training

There is evidence to suggest that in-service training is associated with better process quality in ECE programmes, as per the OECD (2018) report. Teachers who participated in ongoing professional development activities were observed to 'more likely provide support for language and literacy development among children in their classrooms or play room'. Markussen-Brown et al. (2017) associate this impact with more focus in the training on this content area in many in-service training programmes. In addition, it has been established that professional development activities which use a coaching model or offer a clear feedback component as part of training are more effective in changing staff practices than programmes which lack these individualized aspects (Egert et al., 2018, p. 12; Eurofound, 2015, p. 13). An interesting observation from research is that teachers who may need training the most tend to participate less in professional development activities! Those with a bachelor's degree or equivalent or higher are more likely to participate in professional development opportunities than their colleagues with lower levels of pre-service education (TALIS, 2018). In the ICDS system, the training offered is not voluntary or optional but mandatory, following an official order. So the issue of choice is not relevant.

4.6.2. Professional Behaviours

We consider professional behaviour for the purpose of this analysis operationally in terms of the extent to which the actual classroom behaviour of the teacher is in alignment with what her own beliefs are regarding her role and function, as she may have gleaned from her training, her experience and/or her association with her colleagues or even from other professional sources. Creasy (2015) specifies two broad categories of teachers' beliefs to include 'direct transmission beliefs about learning and instruction and constructivist beliefs about learning and instruction'. These dimensions of these beliefs are well established in educational research at least in Western countries and have also received support elsewhere (Creasy, 2015). Staub and Stern

(2002) further elaborate on these in terms of defining the direct transmission view as one which is guided by the view that a

> teacher's role is to communicate knowledge in a clear and structured way, to explain correct solutions, to give students clear and resolvable problems, and to ensure calm and concentration in the classroom. In contrast, a constructivist view focuses on students not as passive recipients but as active participants in the process of acquiring knowledge.

The teacher's role is therefore seen as one of facilitating enquiry and emphasizing student agency in trying to solve problems rather than teaching solutions. Here, the development of thinking and reasoning processes is stressed more than the acquisition of specific knowledge.

Singh and Chaudhary (2019) reported on a sample survey of teachers in India in which they tried to capture their beliefs about children's learning and examine these with respect to their respective classroom practices. The sample included 378 teachers engaged in preschool and early primary education. Of these, 194 were from private preschools/schools and 175 were from government institutions. Nine were from non-governmental educational programmes. Three main issues on which teachers' beliefs were explored included their views on children's inclination to ask questions in class, use of corporal punishment in class and children making mistakes. The findings revealed contradictions in beliefs and practices. While teachers agreed that children should be encouraged to ask questions in class, the classroom observations indicated that they neither asked children questions nor encouraged them to ask. Similarly, while majority of the teachers believed that corporal punishment in class is not desirable, at least 30 per cent did practise it, especially in the private preschools/schools. With regard to the third aspect, that is, making mistakes in class, while most agreed that it is fine for children to make mistakes and learn from them, more than 50 per cent of the teachers either scolded the children for mistakes or did not react at all to them, thus not considering them as opportunities for furthering children's learning.

The researchers further reported teachers' beliefs regarding the difference between preschool and primary curriculum to be distinct in most cases with the preschool curriculum described as 'play-way' method and the primary as formal teaching of reading and writing. But the classroom observations reported in the IECEI Study across states indicate the preschool practices to be also dominated by formal and didactic teaching (Kaul et al., 2017). This evidence, though definitely not representative of all teachers in the country, does provide a fairly insightful glimpse into the need to strengthen the professional understanding and practices of teachers in early education for greater teacher effectiveness and consistency with classroom practice.

4.6.3. Professional Responsibilities

We examine this aspect of professionalism, that is, professional responsibilities in terms of an expected commitment demonstrated by teachers to upgrade one's professional knowledge; seek professional guidance through membership of professional associations; participate in professional events, workshops, conferences and trainings; and refresh ones knowledge by accessing professional literature.

In terms of professional associations, India has historically had a very active professional association for preschool teachers known as Indian Association for Preschool Education (IAPE), which was established as far back as in 1964. IAPE was established by an eminent group of early childhood professionals at New Delhi and inaugurated at Lady Irwin College in the presence of the first prime minister of India who had a special interest in the health and welfare of children. The IAPE gradually set up branches in several states of the country and had a fairly large and active membership of preschool teachers from all categories of programmes, including NGOs. It was able to create a momentum for preschool education across states. It hosted annual conferences which were well attended and had significant participation of preschool teachers, as the attraction was for them to attend workshops and upgrade their skills. Many active and experienced teachers also conducted workshops and several participated and travelled at their own expense. The leadership was with a group of eminent preschool education experts who also played a major role in advocacy at the policy level for ECE. In the late 1990s, with the 1986 Education Policy changing the nomenclature of preschool education to ECCE and conceptualizing it in a more holistic frame, the association also decided to widen its scope and take on a new form. Over the years, it was reincarnated as the Association for Early Childhood Education and Development (AECED) but in the process lost its national character and momentum and has remained limited geographically to Mumbai and in terms of advocacy and outreach to an annual conference in association with different organizations.

The proliferating private preschool industry has in the meanwhile formed an Early Childhood Association (ECA), which has active membership from preschool chains as well as independent preschools and has branches and membership in many states. As per its website,

> The Early Childhood Association is set up with the vision that all the preschools, balwadis, N.G.O's, children's activity classes, parents, student teachers, media houses, companies that deal with children's products, in short everyone connected to young children can all come together to advocate, discuss, learn and share, connect and bring about a change in the quality of care development and learning in early childhood in India.[6]

The ECA is active in organizing not only professional events, workshops and annual conferences but also conducting training programmes with the mandate to address issues and challenges of the private school system. It plays an important role in developing and providing access to its own publications and literature for upgradation of the member schools/teachers' knowledge and skills.

Thus, an interesting paradox which emerges is that while, on the one hand, in terms of public provisions and national commitment to preschool education this stage of education has been traditionally weaker as compared to other stages of education, on the other hand, in terms of professional responsibilities and professional commitment to sharing and upgrading their experience, knowledge and skills, the preschool teachers at this stage of education have in the past demonstrated greater agency and enthusiasm as compared to the primary teachers.

In terms of availability and access to professional literature for preschool teachers, there is a lacuna in the country, since most scientific

[6] https://eca-aper.org/about-us/

literature is available only in English. There are organizations like Bodh Shiksha Samiti, which ensure that their teachers do get access to some inspirational literature and make critical reading of professional literature an important component of their in-service training. However, in the ICDS and other NGO programmes, the limitations of academic qualifications and skills in most cases precludes the possibility of engaging teachers or AWWs in reading and discussing useful texts and conducting discussions around them.

4.7. What Works for ECE Teachers: Some Lessons from Good Practices

If we reflect on the preceding discussion on the three parameters of professionalism with respect to teaching at the early childhood stage, the overall status does not hold out much promise in terms of professionalization in this sector. The overall picture which emerges is more tilted towards teachers being seen as volunteers rather than professionals across these parameters. However, if we read through the case studies included in Part II of this publication, which are of initiatives undertaken by NGOs in some equally or if not more challenging disadvantaged contexts and include both independent ECE centres run by them and initiatives undertaken to support the ICDS, we do see glimpses of some silver linings. These case studies suggest that there can be multiple possibilities of working with and enabling ECE teachers, including those who cater to underprivileged communities, in more innovative ways which can bring about impact.

Based on an analysis of these case studies, we identify some programmatic principles below, which, if applied to mainstream programmes like the ICDS or the private preschools, can help to realize the vision for high-quality ECE for all children at scale and across diverse socio-geographical contexts in India. These principles/practices have been identified and discussed below as they indicate that the negative impact of lower levels of education at entry level among teachers on the quality of preschool education delivered by them to children can be mitigated to a significant extent through employment of these practices. If incorporated, they can add value to the existing provisions and strategies in the mainstream programmes for curriculum and pedagogical interventions and training.

1. *Setting up model/demonstration centres:* Setting up 'model' centres, within the provisions of the given infrastructure, to physically demonstrate what is considered 'good-quality ECE' practice enables teachers and all other concerned functionaries to themselves understand, experience and develop a collective vision of good-quality ECE and appreciate the feasibility of achieving this in their setting. The Dharni case study demonstrates the significance of this principle as key to its diffusion model beginning with classroom organization and display and moving deeper into the content and quality of classroom processes. The demonstration centres served as the benchmark for quality for all other AWWs and teachers to work towards. The case study documents the impact in terms of quality improvement on the remaining centres through peer learning. The Bodh Shiksha Samiti and Nidan case studies also reflect the importance of experiential learning in model centres as part of the training for teachers in that the latter was mentored by the former and their programmes demonstrated similar processes and classroom environment. Seva Nidhi case study records how the community is closely involved in selection of teachers as they believe that 'Teacher or shikshaks, whatever you may say must want to be with children.... Otherwise why will the children go there?' The community clearly expressed the understanding on their own that teachers need to be trained on 'how children learn and what they should learn'.

2. *Ensuring recurrent and onsite training:* For training to be effective and impactful, it is important to 'prioritize and invest in recurrent and onsite training which leads to deeper levels of capacity strengthening of teachers and supervision' (Bodh Shiksha Samiti). According to a teacher in Bodh,

> Training of teachers in Bodh is not forced. It is two way process between the trainers and students. During the training sessions the actual classroom issues and concerns are also solved and discussed among all the coordinators, fellow teachers and mother teachers. (Fellow teacher, Amagarh centre)

The organization considers training inputs and institutional support as the strongest pillars of their organization and organizes training and workshops involving introspection and reflection on a regular basis with a focus on aspects of teachers' own behaviour and attitude towards the community, children and other human beings as key elements of their training. Training also includes reflective reading and critical analysis of inspirational narratives, for example, the well-known teachers' diary titled *Divya Swapna* by a leading educationist, Gijubhai Badheka.

On a similar note, Nidan, another NGO in Bihar, modelling its approach on that of Bodh Shiksha Samiti, organizes regular training, capacity building and scaffolding with the help of external and internal resource persons. Following a systemic or whole school/ programme approach, Nidan conducts a formal induction training for teachers, supervisors and programme managers, followed by recurrent training for which a pool of master trainers has been especially created.

We make a note of how diversity demands multiple solutions and strategies, as we document the approach adopted by Prajayatna, an NGO in Karnataka, which is more unconventional and decentralized based on the apprenticeship model. On joining the organization, a teacher is given a day's orientation and then placed in another centre for a month in an apprenticeship mode. Further training is thus a continuous ongoing process of close observation, hands-on learning and implicit mentoring into the organization's vision of quality ECE. In Pratham, which unlike the other NGOs operates at scale across various states in the country and follows its own model of training, a six-monthly refresher is provided after the initial training to its community teachers, which is more focused on honing their skills of conducting activities and communication with children and parents. We thus identify multiple models addressing the diversity in the country, but the principle is common, that is, to ensure recurrent and onsite experiential training and not dwell on a series of lectures as commonly seen in many teacher education institutions.

3. *Setting realistic goals for training:* With an emphasis on recurrent training, Dharni emphasizes the importance of setting realistic goals for each training and addressing these through a 'bite-size'

incremental approach 'based on clear principles of effective coaching' for the purpose of deciding, designing and delivering content and expectations which can be expected to lead to step-by-step behaviour change in teacher skills and behaviour in the classrooms. This principle, according to the Dharni project, is particularly important considering the entry level of the AWWs who are not academically very well qualified. The Seva Nidhi case study also records the diversity in levels of teachers even within the same organization, as evident from their classroom practice, and emphasizes the importance of need-based support and mentoring.

4. *Including observation of 'real-time' classroom processes:* Ensuring opportunities (as a part of the training for the AWWs or teachers) to be within actual classrooms with children and observe good practices as well as practise the same on their own is emphasized in most organizations which have been included as 'good practices'. Most conventional training programmes at best offer opportunities for practical activities in simulated situations which do not serve the same purpose as working directly with children. As observed in the case studies, this element of participating directly with children not only sensitizes the trainee teachers or AWWs better but also enhances their understanding about how children learn and enables a positive change in their attitudes towards play and its importance in children's learning.

5. *Providing a strong mentoring and follow-up component to supplement training:* This principle is observed to be key to nurturing and promoting developmentally appropriate practices and improving the quality of ECE in Anganwadis or Balwadis, as reported in the case studies. An important aspect of this feature is that the 'trainers are themselves mentors' and carry out regular follow-up and supervision as well as scaffolding of teachers' competence, thus ensuring and maintaining a feedback loop between training and practice. This is rarely seen in the AWTCs, where the trainers are in most cases disassociated from the field and the training therefore tends to remain theoretical. This feedback loop is evident in most good practices documented, but more particularly in Seva Nidhi, Bodh and Dharni.

Seva Nidhi has a three-tier support system of trainers, mentors and teachers. The trainers are from Seva Nidhi, and the mentors are experienced and well-educated teachers who work with and support the teachers. An essential feature of this mentoring and supportive supervision component across programmes is the significant non-hierarchical relationship between the mentors and teachers, which is conducive for an enabling work environment. As mentioned in the Dharni case study, 'a mentor–mentee relationship, if it focuses on regular communication and "demonstration" of good practice by mentors, within the frame of a non-hierarchical relationship and not through instruction by a "superior"', can prove to be very effective. The basic principles of mentoring documented in the Dharni case study (Part II) including recurrent training and 'mentoring' of the mentors reflect the deep sense of purpose and attention to detail, which was a hallmark of this project and which is evident in the multiple lessons it offers for the larger system.

6. *Emphasis on nurturing and maintaining positive relationships with a common goal and purpose:* Recurrent training and mentoring and opportunities for planned peer interaction provide the space in the programme for building and maintaining positive relationships between the workers/teachers and with the trainers and supervisors and contribute to working collectively towards a common goal or vision. These relationships not only are seen to have a positive impact on the programme and on the supervisors and programme managers but also lead to the AWWs' or teachers' own self-transformation, as reported in the Dharni case study, where the AWWs reported developing a sense of self-worth as a consequence of the training and mentoring as also observed changes in their own attitudes and behaviour. A well-trained and good-performing AWW mentioned that she used to have a foul temper and constant headaches and kept on picking up fights with everyone, but after working with children, those are a 'thing of the past'! Professional development has also been observed to mitigate negative associations between staff stress and their interactions with young children (Jennings & Greenberg, 2009; Sandilos et al., 2018, p. 15).

An overview of these practices/principles reflects an important learning. This is that despite low entry-level academic qualifications, what seems to have worked out for teachers/workers in these projects, and what the larger system needs to consider, is that close onsite mentoring and handholding and recurrent training and follow-up by the same trainers can, to an extent, mitigate the contextual limitations of lack of school education and can contribute to developing teachers' skills and understanding to the extent that it can impact quality of ECE programmes.

4.8. In Conclusion: Moving Forward with the National Education Policy 2020

A clear understanding which emerges from our analysis of the level of professionalism evident in teaching as a profession at the preschool education stage is largely contingent upon the kind of priority, support and provisioning for it demonstrated by the government. This in turn rests on what Drury and Baer (2011) diagnose as an issue of perceiving the domain itself as unprofessional and unscientific with a clear reliance on 'a combination of "expert judgment", "best practices", and "conventional wisdom", which are in turn informed by an ambiguous and inconclusive body of evidence'. Drury and Baer further elaborate that what is required for professionalization is for the discipline to develop a 'coherent, agreed upon knowledge base as in the case of medicine'.

From the above perspective, this disparity and lack of professionalization of the teacher force in ECE is particularly unjustified, given the fact that as compared to other stages of education, this domain or stage of education has a very robust research framework as its foundation. 'It has benefited significantly from the last few decades of very significant research from across disciplines, including from Neuroscience, Child Development and Economics, which have together yielded credible evidence to build up a Science of Early Childhood Development' (Shonkoff & Meisels, 2000).

The persisting hope that ECE will get its due acknowledgement and priority in the country is now gathering steam with the recent launch of the new National Education Policy in India (Ministry of Education, 2020). The policy has given high priority to ECCE as a game changer, in education in the light of its credible and significant research evidence which it has quoted. It has recommended a curricular restructuring in school education structure by extending the preschool education stage of three–six years to up to eight years. It has envisioned this stage as the foundational stage of school education, with a developmentally appropriate incremental curriculum for children from three to eight years of age. This has undoubtedly been a significant policy milestone not only for ECCE but also for the education system as a whole.

The policy has, in terms of ensuring quality and enhancing professionalism in ECE, indicated an immediate as well as medium-term perspective. At an immediate level, the three–five age group is expected to continue to be predominantly taught by the single AWW in the ICDS programme. It is envisaged that she will be able to provide a 'vibrant preschool learning environment' for children for which she will be provided a six-month-long, online training while on the job. This is despite the fact that she continues to be accountable for multiple responsibilities related to the six services of the ICDS of which preschool education is only one service! With the unprecedented experience of COVID-19 not yet behind us, the alternative modes of reaching children through web-based modes or through social media will also be under consideration, but their adaptation for providing ECE through these modes and through parents will need serious analysis and discussion. Again, the option recommended of providing online training to AWWs provides some indication of the government's limited perception of the professional demands of this stage of education. In this context, Sahlberg's (1997) interesting comparison between teachers as professionals and as skilled technicians is relevant, wherein he takes the examples from England and Finland, with the former focusing largely on teaching skills and assessment methods, while Finland emphasizes teacher autonomy and creativity.

However, in the medium-term perspective, the policy does commit to introducing greater professionalism into all stages of teacher education, including that of the foundational stage.

> By 2030, the minimum degree qualification for teaching will be a 4-year integrated B.Ed. degree that teaches a range of knowledge content and pedagogy and includes strong practicum training in the form of student-teaching at local schools.... All such B.Ed. degrees

would be offered only by accredited multidisciplinary higher education institutions offering 4-year integrated B.Ed. programmes. (Ministry of Human Resource Development, 2020)

In this context, the existing standalone teacher education institutions will need to convert to multidisciplinary institutions. A major challenge which may arise in this otherwise welcome professionalization and upgradation of teacher education into institutions of higher learning for all stages including early childhood, could be the further widening of the distance between the theoretical training content and the field-based practice. Emphasis on praxis-based approach and closer linkages with field-based practitioners would help to address this potential gap.

It is hoped that the significant reform in teacher education envisaged in the policy will be commensurate with better career planning and attention to all parameters which define professionalization in the teaching profession. These may include provision in the system for training, onsite support and professional development through professionally trained, field-based and experienced mentors and teacher educators, parity in terms of work conditions and compensation for teachers across stages and opportunities for professional upgradation and career mobility for all teachers in ECE across the country.

References

Alcott, B., Banerji, M., Bhattacharjea, S., Nanda, M., & Ramanujan, P. (2018). One step forward, two steps back: Transitions between home, pre-primary and primary education in rural India. *Compare: A Journal of Comparative and International Education, 50*(5), 482–499.

ASER Centre. (2019). *Annual status of education report (rural): Early years.* http://img.asercentre.org/docs/ASER%202019/ASER2019%20report%20/aser-report2019earlyyearsfinal.pdf

Baig, T. A. (1979). Our Children. New Delhi. GOI, Ministry of information and broadcasting. Publications Division.

Brehm, B., Breen, P., Brown, B., & along, L. (2006). Instructional design and assessment: An interdisciplinary approach to introducing professionalism. *American Journal of Pharmaceutical Education, 70*(4), 1–5.

Constitution of India. (n.d.). Constitution of India, 1950. https://www.constitutionofindia.net/constitution_of_india

CECED. (2015). Preparing teachers for early childhood care and education. https://www.academia.edu/37538673/preparing_teachers_for_early_childhood_care_and_education

Creasy, K. L. (2015). Defining professionalism in teacher education programs. *Journal of Education & Social Policy, 2*(2). http://www.jespnet.com/journals/Vol_2_No_2_June_2015/3.pdf

Crehan, L. (2016). *Cleverlands: The secrets behind the success of the world's education superpowers.* Unbound Publishers.

CSF. (2020). Central Square Foundation, school education In India, data, trends and policies. https://www.centralsquarefoundation.org/wp-content/uploads/2020/09/School-Education-in-India-Data-Trends-and-Policies.pdf

Drury, D, & Baer, J. (2011). *The American Public School teacher: Past, present, and future.* https://eric.ed.gov/?q=drury+2011&id=ED521365

Egert, F., Fukkink, R. G., & Eckhardt, A. G. (2018). Impact of in-service professional development programs for early childhood teachers on quality ratings and child outcomes: A meta-analysis. *Review of Educational Research, 88*(3), 401–433.

Eurofound. (2015). *Early childhood care: Working conditions, training and quality of services—A systematic review.* Publications Office of the European Union.

GoI. (2009). Right to Education Act. https://www.education.gov.in/sites/upload_files/mhrd/files/upload_document/RTI_Model_Rules.pdf

GoI. (2019). *U-DISE.* Department of School Education & Literacy, Ministry of Education.

Grady, M. P., Helbling, K. C., & Lubeck, D. R. (2008). Teacher professionalism since a nation at risk. *Phi Delta Kappan, 89*(8), 603–604, 607.

Jennings, P., & Greenberg, M. (2009). The prosocial classroom: Teacher social and emotional competence in relation to student and classroom outcomes. *Review of Educational Research, 79*(1), 491–525.

Kaul, V., & Bhattacharjea, S. (2019). *Early childhood education and school readiness in India: Quality and diversity.* Springer.

Kaul, V., Bhattacharjea, S., Chaudhary, A. B., Ramanujan, P., Banerji, M., & Nanda, M. (2017). *The India early childhood education impact study.* UNICEF.

Khalakdina, M. (1998). *Early Child Care in India.* International monograph series on early child care (Vol.9). Routledge.

Manning, M., Garvis, S., Fleming, C., & Wong, G. T. W. (2017). The relationship between teacher qualification and the quality of the early childhood care and learning environment: A systematic review. *Campbell Systematic Reviews, 13*(1), 1–82.

Markussen-Brown, S. G., Christopher, F., & Wong, G. T. W. (2017). The effects of language- and literacy-focused professional development on early educators and children: A best-evidence meta-analysis. *Early Childhood Research Quarterly, 38*, 97–115.

Ministry of Education. (2020). National Education Policy. Government of India. https://www.education.gov.in/sites/upload_files/mhrd/files/

NEP_Final_English_0.pdfMWCD. (2017). Integrated Child Development Services (ICDS) manual for district level functionaries. https://darpg.gov.in/sites/default/files/ICDS.pdf

Muralidharan, K. & Kremer, M. (2008). Public-private schools in rural India. In Chakrabarti, R. & Peterson, P (Eds.), *School choice international: Exploring public-private partnerships*. MIT Press Scholarship Online.

MWCD. (2018). *MWCD annual report 2018–19*. https://wcd.nic.in/sites/default/files/WCD%20ENGLISH%202018-19.pdf

MWCD. (2019). *Anganwadi sevikas*. Press Information Bureau.

NAEYC. (2019). *Professional standards and competencies for early childhood education: A position statement adopted November 2019*. USA.

OECD. (2014). *Education at a glance 2014: OECD indicators*. OECD Publishing. http://dx.doi.org/10.1787/eag-2014-en

OECD. (2018). *Teaching and learning international survey 2018 technical report*. https://www.oecd.org/education/talis/TALIS_2018_Technical_Report.pdf

OECD. (2019). Providing quality early childhood education and care: Results from the starting strong survey 2018. TALIS, OECD Publishing. https://doi.org/10.1787/301005d1-en

Pandit, A. (2019, 31 January). Why the number of creches has dropped sharply since 2017? *The Times of India*, New Delhi.

Parker-Rees, R., & Willan, J. (2006). *Early years education: Policy and practice in early education and care* (Vol. 3). Taylor & Francis.

Phillips, D., Austin, L., & Whitebook, M. (2016). The early care and education workforce: The future of children, *26*(2), 139–158. http://www.jstor.org/stable/43940585

Pratte, R., & Rury, J. L. (1991). Teachers, professionalism, and craft. *Teachers College Record*, *93*(1), 59–72. http://www.tcrecord.org

Rahayani, Y. (2010). Feminization of teaching. *Journal of English and Education*, *4*(2), 13.

Sandilos, L. E., Goble, P., Rimm-Kaufman, S. E., & Pianta, R. C. (2018). Does professional development reduce the influence of teacher stress on teacher–child interactions in pre-kindergarten classrooms? *Early Childhood Research Quarterly*, *42*, 280–290.

Sahlberg, P. (1997). *The teacher in the changing school*. WSOY.

Shonkoff J. P. & Meisels, S. J. (Eds.). (2000). *Handbook of Early Childhood Intervention (2nd ed.)*. Cambridge university Press. https://doi.org/10.1017/CBO9780511529320

Singh, S. (2013). Impact of pre school education program of ICDS on children in rural Punjab. *International Journal of Humanities and Social Science Invention*, *3*(8), 25–31.

Singh, S., & Chaudhary, A. B. (2019). Situating teacher's beliefs. In V. Kaul & S. Bhattacharjea (Eds.), *Early childhood education and school readiness in India* (pp. 173–194). Springer.

Staub, F. C., & Stern, E. (2002). The nature of teachers' pedagogical content beliefs matters for students' achievement gains: Quasi-experimental evidence from elementary mathematics. *Journal of Educational Psychology, 94*(2), 344–355.

The Lancet. (2017). Advancing early childhood development: From science to scale.https://marlinprod.literatumonline.com/pbassets/Lancet/stories/series/ecd/Lancet_ECD_Executive_Summary.pdf

UN VOLUNTEERS. (2020, September 22). *The power of volunteerism.* https://www.unv.org/power-volunteerism

Yoshikawa, H., & Nieto, A. (2013). Paradigm shifts and new directions in research on early childhood development programs in low and middle income countries. In P. R. Britto, P. L. Engle, & C. M. Super. (2013). *Handbook of early childhood development research and its impact on global policy* (pp. 487–497). Oxford University Press.

CHAPTER 5

Scaling Up and Contextualizing Early Childhood Education Quality

Negotiating the Paradox

Venita Kaul and Monimalika Day

5.1. Emerging Issues and Challenges

As we come to the conclusion of this research journey, we revisit some of the initial questions raised in Chapter 1 and reflect on these in the context of some significant learning we have gleaned from our analysis of the eight case studies of good practices in early childhood care and education (ECE) for children from marginalized communities, presented in Part II of this volume, and from the critical and thematic analyses of the same in the preceding chapters.

A core question which surfaces at the policy level and which we attempt to respond to in this chapter on the basis of our emergent understanding from this research is: How do we define and describe quality in ECE in India? Can we assume and adopt an international and normative approach in defining ECCE quality, governed by universal child development principles, or do we conceptualize ECCE in the context of India's distinct social reality, marked by challenges of scale, diversity and social inequity? Or do we follow a more prudent 'middle path'?

Further, would this emerging definition of quality stand the test of ensuring optimal intellectual, emotional and physical stimulation and nourishment for all Indian children, in these earliest, most sensitive years of their lives, which the science of early childhood development (ECD) tells us is critical and foundational for their lifelong development and learning? Further, given India's international commitment to the SDGs including SDG 4.2 on ECCE and its national commitment to the National Education Policy 2020 (NEP 2020; Ministry of Education, 2020), how do we meet the committed goal of ensuring high-quality ECCE at scale in a planned manner by the year 2030 and, through this accomplishment, address the widening social equity gap? How can India respond to this enormous challenge which, it must be noted, not only is of national relevance but also has global repercussions, with every fifth child in the world being in India? These questions assume even greater priority today when the social divide is reported to have further widened with the year 2020 almost lost to the COVID-19 pandemic, resulting in an unprecedented economic slowdown, increased social inequality and immeasurable social and economic distress for our children and their families.

We begin this chapter by outlining the emerging paradox which we identify as significant, that is, the imperative on the one hand of scaling up ECE provision for every child universally across the country and on the other, the simultaneous requirement of ensuring that the ECE provisions meet the quality standards laid down for the country for every child, irrespective of diverse contexts. The complexity of this paradox gets enhanced by the need to contextualize interventions by making appropriate adaptations for the diverse socio-geographical contexts across the myriad micro-sociocultural settings within which children are living and growing. These too situated within varied levels of institutional development and governance. Cognizant of this paradox, we move on to deconstruct the concept of 'quality of ECCE' in the Indian context as emerging from our research. We then explore ways to address this paradox of scaling up quality and simultaneously addressing diversity through praxis by reflecting on our thematic analysis of the good practices presented in the preceding chapters in areas of grounded theory building, curriculum and pedagogical development, teacher development, and parent and community engagement. We conclude the chapter with some recommendations for policy and practice.

5.2. Unpacking the Paradox: Policy vs Context

As already discussed in Chapter 1 of this volume, India has accorded its commitment towards the attainment of the SDGs (UN, 2015) including SDG 4 by 2030, which 'aims to ensure inclusive and equitable quality education and promote lifelong learning opportunities for all' and the associated Target 4.2 which commits India to 'at least one year of free and compulsory preprimary education for all children to be delivered by well-trained educators'. In addition, the Government of India has adopted the NEP 2020, which too has in pursuance of this commitment recommended that 'universal provisioning of quality Early childhood development, care and education must be achieved as soon as possible and no later than 2030 to ensure that all students entering grade 1 are school ready' (Ministry of Education, 2020, p. 7). This reflects the policy's and, through it, the government's conviction that prioritizing the early learning continuum 'has the potential to give all young children access, enabling them to participate and flourish in the educational system throughout their lives' (Ministry of Education, 2020, p. 7).

For successful attainment of these international and national commitments by 2030, India needs to reach out with optimal and equitable ECCE facilities to approximately 70 million children in the 3–6 age group across 28 states and 9 union territories, which are at varying levels of development as per the social and economic indicators (Office of the Registrar General & Census Commissioner, 2011). The moot question is: With uneven access to physical, financial and human resources across states and with 1.3 million public-sponsored ECE centres operational across the country, competing with the more affluent and proliferating private preschool segment, how realistic is it to expect each centre in each state to measure up to the specified norms and standards for quality as prescribed by the policy, in terms of teachers' availability and qualifications, physical facilities, learning resources, family support and the overall learning environment? Added to this is a large, intersecting segment of children surviving below the poverty line in the country, for whom, especially in these COVID-19 times, mere subsistence itself may be a struggle and who need more affirmative provisions to narrow, if not eliminate, the social equity gap they are experiencing.

While these are pragmatic concerns, a more academic debate linked to the policy–praxis paradigm relates to the 'normative vs differentiated' approach, especially in the context of international policy conventions such as the SDGs. These international agreements reflect 'an insistence on a certain "universalism" and global standards … so that the discourse on childhood and child rights within India has been further overwhelmed by a hegemonic western centric development and world view, of course couched in the language of global standards' (Raman, 2019, p. 67). This context begs a few key questions: Can there be in essence a common quality vision for ECCE for all children below six years across the global North and South, despite significant variations in countries' developmental status and sociocultural priorities, or should the approach be to 'let a thousand flowers bloom'? Can we envision, even within India, an equitable 'one-size-fits-all' norm for developmental outcomes and quality standards for ECCE across sociocultural contexts for all 70 million children below 6 years of age, which may represent optimal 'quality ECCE for all'? A more probing question which arises is: Is 'childhood' itself not a socially constructed category which varies with changing contexts? If so, can policies be framed with a uniform and global vision for the child as the goal of ECCE, or does it need to be differentiated as per the local context (Kaul & Dogra, 2018)? And then, as we reflect on the implications of this reality, certain complexities emerge. While strategies to achieve the goals may be contextualized to accommodate the 'local' in preference to the 'global', can the goals still not remain normative or universal? And, if differentiated, who decides the goals and for whom and, more importantly, can these even, though varied, still adhere to the nation's commitment towards social equity, equality and social justice (Kaul & Dogra, 2018)?

If we address these vital questions through an economic prism, situating it in a market-driven, neoliberal ideological context, we cannot ignore the fact that the poorest and the most underprivileged also have aspirations for their children, similar to those ahead of them in the hierarchy. Education is thus viewed by all stakeholders as a visible pathway for narrowing the gap of social equity and upward mobility. Applied to education, and within it to ECCE,

> Education at its core does emerge as a normative enterprise in any democratic society. It is a public good that is driven by fundamental social values as well as the imperatives of social justice and these values and imperatives powerfully shape every dimension of educational theory. (Snauwaert, 2012)

This becomes even more pertinent in the neoliberal sociopolitical environment today in India, where, as a fallout of globalization, liberalization and opening up of the economies, on the one hand, and parallel emphasis on rights-based social policies advocated by civil society, on the other, there is an emphasis on uniformity, universalization and standardization to address social equity, with little encouragement at the policy level for a 'thousand flowers to bloom!'

5.3. Deconstructing Quality in ECCE

Any measures to address the above challenges thus require arriving at a clear understanding of what is the core of any good-quality ECCE provision which is non-negotiable and critical for impact and yet contextually relevant. Research consistently demonstrates the need for early childhood provision to be of the highest quality to ensure maximum benefits, particularly for disadvantaged children (Mathers & Ereky-Stevens, 2018, p. 506). Children who have had access to good-to-excellent provisions do better across a wide range of outcomes as compared to their peers in mediocre or poor provision (Loeb et al., 2004). Low-quality provisions, on the other hand, result in few or even negative effects (Mathers & Ereky-Stevens, 2018, p. 506).

These observations resonate completely with our own longitudinal research findings, which clearly demonstrate significantly positive association of ECCE quality with school-readiness levels at the age of five years and learning levels in the primary grades (Kaul et al., 2017). The study also indicates positive impact of a developmentally appropriate curriculum as opposed to a didactic, academic curriculum which was associated with reverse outcomes. While the policy documents and National Curriculum Frameworks for ECCE at the national level have consistently recommended employment of developmentally appropriate curricula and a constructivist pedagogy, the dominant practice as discussed in Chapter 1 continues to be to adopt an academic, didactic and downward extension of the primary grade curriculum at the preschool level across most provisions, public and private. Chawla-Duggan (2016) captures this dynamic effectively in an interpretation of her observations in Anganwadis in Mumbai, where despite the policy emphasis on a child-centred pedagogy, 'Knowledge of children's learning relies on a behaviorist perspective where pedagogical relationships are hierarchical and mostly privilege a vertical unidirectional relation of communication, more adult than child initiated using Bernstein's structure of pedagogical relations.'

Definitions of quality conventionally agree on two broad dimensions, that is, process quality and structural quality. Process quality describes the nature of children's actual experiences within early childhood settings, primarily related to the pedagogical practices employed by the staff. Structural quality, on the other hand, includes features such as adult–child ratios, staff characteristics, group sizes, and structures and characteristics of physical space (Mathers & Erecky-Stevens, 2018). Bernstein (2001) places emphasis on how children learn from their family members through participation in various routine activities and also from direct instruction of important skills by the adults. He describes these as 'visible' and 'invisible' contexts of learning, which within his framework are aligned to and a factor of the extent of relative control and direction available to both, the adults and the children, in any learning situation.

In terms of process quality, therefore, some key elements include warm and responsive relationships which children establish with adults who care for them and with their peers. Such interactions support young children to develop the secure attachment essential for supporting their development later in life (Ahnert et al., 2004). Additionally, children need a supportive environment for their emerging language, physical, cognitive, social and communication skills. There is research to suggest that while volume of speech which children have directed towards them matters, the quality of talk is also important (Schneidman et al., 2013). Crehan (2016) in her analysis of what matters in ECCE in the context of Programme for International Student Assessment (PISA) performance at the age of 15 years emphasizes social and pre-academic skills through rich environments and child-initiated, playful learning before the age of 6 years, rather than expectations of specific academic outcomes from children. Structural aspects of quality are determined by provisions, enabling each of the four aspects listed above that is, features such as adult child ratio, staff characteristics, group sizes and structure and characteristics of physical space.

Given the concerns about the persistence of behaviouristic pedagogy and emphasis on academic rather than developmental outcomes, it becomes necessary to identify some core elements which would qualify an ECCE provision to be rated of high quality. In Chapter 2 of this volume, we have attempted to deep dive into our own research findings to glean out the emergent theory on quality in ECCE to arrive at this core. Two major principles which emerge from the analysis of the eight case studies are: First, to develop good-quality early childhood education (ECE) programmes, it is essential to construct 'praxis' of the existing theories, research and local needs of children, families and the communities. Second, and in continuation of the above, to scale up good practices, it is necessary to consider not just the curriculum but also the entire ecology of the programme to address the paradox of standardization vs contextualization and sustainability. A good example in India is that of an adaptation of the Montessori Method in Kosbad district for tribal children in terms of feasibility, affordability and local relevance by a well-known educationist and social reformer, Tarabai Modak, who had received direct training from Maria Montessori (Tschurenev, 2021). This programme was a precursor to the establishment of the national programme for children, ICDS, in 1975.

The emerging evidence from the research, analysed in greater detail in Chapter 2, indicates that in conceptualizing and scaling up quality of early childhood programmes in a country with great diversity, like India, the following four quality factors are significant and non-negotiable (Day & Parlakian, 2003):

- A relationship-based, developmentally appropriate and contextualized curriculum
- The critical role of the teacher and an enabling and seamless support system for teachers' preparation, mentoring and professional development
- A contextually relevant, multicultural, multilingual curriculum responsive to the local needs
- Close connections of the ECCE programme with families and community members which would ensure both engaging and enabling relationships based on an axis of cultural reciprocity

Each of these aspects lends itself to local conceptualization and/or adaptations while also being aligned to the broader policy goals and frameworks, at both international and national levels, thus offering an optimal balance between the global and the local priorities and resources. The case studies of good practices included in Part II of this volume and their thematic analyses in Chapters 2, 3 and 4 provide some leads into how these dilemmas or paradoxical expectations can be negotiated for ECE without compromising on goals of social equity and social justice. We discuss these emerging leads as broad principles for designing high-quality ECE environments for children.

5.4. Emerging Principles for Improving and Scaling Up ECCE Quality: Lessons from the Field

5.4.1. Negotiating a Consensus on What Is 'High Quality' in ECCE at the Levels of Both Microsystems and Mesosystems Is Key to Quality Reform

As discussed earlier, a major challenge in ECCE is inadequate sensitivity and understanding among most stakeholders regarding the content and pedagogy of what a developmentally appropriate curriculum is and its significance for children's learning and development.

While both the NEP 2020 and prior to that the National Policy on Early Childhood Care and Education (2013) along with the National Curriculum Framework (2014) have recommended a developmentally appropriate play-based curriculum for the three to six/eight years age group, the concern is that the 'intended' curriculum as prescribed in the policy and the 'enacted' curriculum as actually practised in pre-schools/Anganwadis are rarely aligned (Chawla-Duggan, 2016). The prescribed curriculum in all policy documents is informed by theoretical understanding and principles of constructivist and developmentally appropriate practice in ECE, with a focus on play and experiential learning and holistic development of the child. It negates the practice of formal teaching of the three Rs at the early childhood stage.

As opposed to that, the IECEI Study reveals that across the country, parents privilege learning of alphabet and number and academic learning in a structured mode, with little appreciation of play-based, developmentally appropriate and child-initiated learning, as they have not received any orientation regarding what this pedagogy is and what its benefits are and have also not had any exposure to such pedagogical practices. The Anganwadi workers (AWWs) and teachers across public and private provisions are in most cases untrained or inadequately trained and thus also not exposed to play-based pedagogy. Even in cases where they are trained, they do not develop adequate conviction and tend to succumb easily to parental pressures for visible outcomes. As a result, as the IECEI Study clearly demonstrates, formal teaching tends to be the dominant pedagogical approach across private preschools and across many Anganwadis (Kaul et al., 2017).

Our analysis of the case studies of the good practices, on the other hand, indicates a much higher incidence of developmentally appropriate curricular practices across the eight projects. Our further probing into this positive finding indicates that across seven of the eight practices, although in varying degrees, a consistent feature of these programmes was the planned strategy to involve the parents and local community, that is, the child's mesosystem, from the initial stages of the programme with a view to develop a consensus with them on what the curriculum will be for their children and why it is important for them. This indicates a comprehensive strategy involving all stakeholders and acknowledgement of the role of parents and family members with a clear focus or intent to develop a supportive environment for the reform or good practice to be introduced for children.

From an ecological perspective (Bronfenbrenner, 1979), these interactions strengthen the mesosystem, that is, the connection between two microsystems in which the child participates, the preschool and the home. Day et al. (2010) demonstrate that teachers are able to create multicultural classrooms by systematically implementing the four steps of cultural reciprocity proposed by Harry et al. (1999), which included self-awareness of the practitioner, getting to know and understand the families' perspectives, explicitly explaining the educational practices followed by the school and creating the space to share power and collaborate with the families. Many of these steps were evident in the structure and scope of these good practices.

Examples abound, such as the NGO Prajayatna's case study reports a dialogue with parents during the planning phase itself to understand local challenges and parents' priorities and conceptualize a programme which is responsive to these and yet meets the policy prescriptions of a high-quality ECCE programme. As an outcome of the dialogue, some of the women's cooperatives, though few in number, succeeded in operating the preschools on their own. In both Prajayatna and SERP programmes, the content and curriculum were negotiated with the parents and community so that in the former, oral exposure to three languages was introduced for children on parents' request, while in the latter the developmentally appropriate curriculum and pedagogy was adapted to music and rhythm and games to appeal to the tribal community.

Features such as inviting community ownership of the preschools through community's contribution of land as a precondition, engagement of mother teachers from the community to create awareness among parents regarding value of developmentally appropriate curriculum for preschoolers, use of street plays and other modes of outreach for the local community, as well as employment of hands-on demonstration of desired curriculum with children in classrooms have all been reportedly employed by Bodh Shiksha Samiti to develop this consensus within the microsystems and mesosystems, that is, among parents and teachers at the local and block levels, to ensure a collective vision for what high quality 'looks like' in ECE.

Seva Nidhi's case study demonstrates the adoption of a place-based curriculum with a focus on helping children to know their immediate surroundings; understand environmental issues through observation, exploration, stories, group discussions and songs; and address social problems such as caste and gender discrimination by eating together. There was significant emphasis on use of low-cost local materials, local stories and activities and on learning by doing.

On the other hand, as an example of 'negative relevance', we identify the case of Dharni project, where in the absence of this initial effort to reach out to the community and take the community along, the sustainability of the otherwise excellent pedagogical intervention was compromised, since the parents and community had scarce appreciation of it.

The larger lesson we draw from this analysis is that this effort at consensus building and creating a conducive environment for reform in quality, beginning from the level of a child's microsystem, requires a twofold effort: (a) to enhance the understanding of parents and community regarding the value of play for children's learning and development and thereby appreciate and support a high-quality developmentally appropriate ECCE curriculum for children and (b) to invest in professional development of all caregivers, teachers and all levels of personnel involved with a view to enhance their knowledge, skills and attitudes regarding developmentally appropriate content and pedagogy while also enabling and sensitizing them to imbibe the essence of cultural reciprocity in the context of engaging with parents and community through a process grounded in principles of mutual respect, collaboration and reciprocity (Day & Parlakian, 2003). This is also imperative from the perspective of enabling teachers to be able to develop adequate understanding and insights into the nature and content of a developmentally appropriate curriculum so as to be able to contextualize it locally as per the needs and contexts of the children in their respective programmes, thus reducing the gap between the policy recommendation and the practice on the ground.

5.4.2. Treat Early Childhood Educators as Professionals: The Need to Educate, Enable and Empower

Our longitudinal research (Kaul et al., 2017) has identified the 'teacher' within the microsystem of the child as the most significant variable impacting the quality of any ECE provision. However, our research also indicates that in the larger system, whether we see in the Anganwadis or in the private preschools, this factor is severely compromised (refer to Chapter 4 for a detailed analysis). While in the Anganwadis the 'teacher' is not even a salaried person but a multipurpose volunteer with inadequate training in ECCE, in the private provisions, especially in the affordable school sector, the preschool teachers are at the lowest rung of the hierarchy and have also in most cases received no specific training in ECCE. The honoraria or salaries offered to both categories are also much below the accepted levels.

However, our analysis reveals that all eight projects demonstrated a clear acknowledgement of the crucial role of the teacher and the need to invest significantly on teacher training and development through a supportive mechanism. If we further consider each of the three actions—educating, enabling and empowering the teacher—these characterize the overall approach adopted by most of the good practices towards their teachers in acknowledgement of their significant contribution to the quality of the ECCE they are offering.

This approach or strategy was observed across most of the good practices reviewed in the form of creating a capacity-building system which seamlessly integrates induction and in-service training with mentoring and monitoring. This cyclic system was possible since the trainers were themselves monitors as well as mentors, thus creating and facilitating a natural feedback mechanism through this process. This cyclic process often led to a process of reflective dialogue with the teachers to appreciate their gains and resolve doubts or gaps, if any, and together set specific goals and plan strategies to address the same. This approach was very distinct and methodically employed in Dharni, Bodh and Nidan projects. In Bodh Shiksha Samiti, a stratified approach was employed, wherein monthly cluster-level meetings for teachers were followed by weekly circle-level meetings by the lead teachers. Given the limited academic levels of the teachers and limited opportunities for engaging in literary activities, Bodh teachers were encouraged to read well-known biographies of educationists and reflect and write about their own classroom experiences. This system of capacity building was seen to work very well in addressing the needs of teachers even in cases where the entry-level academic qualifications were not very high, as it was seen to lead to the teachers' growth and transformation. In some organizations, like Prajayatna, new recruits were required to work in a preschool for a month before they received the induction training. Moreover, classroom demonstrations were used during the actual training sessions. Seva Nidhi also demonstrated a thoughtful integrated capacity-building system with training, mentoring and supervision closely interconnected. After conducting training sessions, trainers in between trainings visited the Balwadis to observe the impact of the training and identify areas which needed improvement. The *margdarshikas* (mentors) were local women who had experience of running Balwadis and had graduate-level education. They were responsible for monitoring and mentoring 10 centres each. The lead trainers and mentors collaborated with the local NGOs for monitoring the centres. Two aspects which stand out are the priority to not only higher-level academic qualifications with both trainers and mentors being graduates but also direct field experience privileging not only know-how but also 'do-how', again very distinct from the regular system.

In Dharni, regular mentoring was a key support mechanism for the teachers, and the process of mentoring and training was given significant attention as documented in the case study. To quote from Chapter 2,

> Mentors did not only provide critical feedback on classroom activities but also created a safe nurturing relationship with the mentee and were there to listen to the various challenges women experienced in other aspects of their lives.... They were described by many teachers as a philosopher and guide. The dialogues they had with the teachers were perceived as emancipatory, as they could confide with the mentor and discuss various dilemmas they encountered ... the nature of these relationships was often very different from some of the oppressive interactions they encountered in their families and communities in a society which is fragmented by gender discrimination.

This systematic approach is completely unlike the mainstream programmes, wherein the training is offsite, if at all, with a different set of trainers, and there is negligible follow-up or interface of the trainers with the field. The impact of the respective approaches is very visible in the differential quality of the ECE programmes on the ground. While these processes led to 'educating' and 'enabling' the teachers to play their roles more effectively, the trust placed in the teachers by the management to take their own decisions and the freedom to innovate were also reported by teachers to lead to self-transformation in them, as becoming more confident and positive people in their professional and personal lives.

Crehan (2018) in her insightful analysis of high-performing education systems in the world concludes that what teachers need if they are to be treated as professionals is mastery, autonomy and relatedness with mentors and peers, all of which will enhance their intrinsic motivation. This resonates with our conclusions too, since she also emphasizes rigour in training, and ensuring newly recruited teachers have a reduced workload and more time with mentors 'and have opportunities to be pedagogically supported and learn from one another'. It is also important to make teaching as a career or profession respected and valued in the society for which, according to it, appropriate and attractive compensation and work conditions are important.

5.4.3. Address the Gap between Intended and Enacted Curriculum through Praxis: Ensure Developmentally and Contextually Appropriate Content and Pedagogy

As mentioned earlier, our quantitative research strand yielded the finding that the dominant curricular approach in Anganwadis and preschools is one of 'schoolification', with a focus on formal teaching of the three Rs as the 'enacted' curriculum as opposed to the 'intended' curriculum as per the policy which is more progressive and developmentally appropriate. The quantitative analysis also indicated significantly higher levels of cognitive readiness scores in children exposed to developmentally appropriate curriculum as compared to those exposed to formal teaching while controlling for family contexts. Formal teaching was found to be statistically associated negatively with performance on cognitive readiness scores (Chaudhary & Kaul, 2019). Overall scores on cognitive readiness were also low across the sample of 14,000 5-year-olds, and this was attributed to the developmentally inappropriate curricular practices in ECE (Kaul et al., 2017).

One of the good practices included in this volume (as well as included in the sample for the quantitative strand of the study), that is, Bodh Shiksha Samiti, demonstrated very high scores on the observation-based quality assessment scale, with a strong focus on developmentally appropriate curricular practices. A further in-depth analysis of their practices with children from underprivileged families in comparison to those of children from a better socio-economic category indicated that these curricular practices had the potential to even contribute to closing the social equity gap. The sample size was admittedly small but the direction of the result revealing.

Other than Bodh Shiksha Samiti and Nidan which was mentored by Bodh, among the eight case studies included in this volume, Dharni project was another excellent curricular model, with a very systematic and well-designed cognitive play-based curriculum within a developmentally appropriate framework. A good blend of free choice play in activity corners was seen along with play-based guided activities for language and cognitive development, with children from tribal communities. The sample drawn from its centres also demonstrated relatively high scores on cognitive readiness. Crehan (2018) in her analysis of high-performing education systems in the world (where students obtained the top position in PISA at the age of 15 years) not only identifies ECE as an important component across the systems but also makes a clear recommendation that countries should 'enhance children's social and pre-academic skills through rich environments and playful learning before age six rather than requiring specific academic outcomes from them'.

The analysis of the curricular and teacher support practices in the Dharni project indicates several features which may be treated as lessons for the larger system. At the microsystem level, emphasis had been placed in each Anganwadi on ensuring a visible experience for all who visited the Anganwadi of the nature of the desired classroom setting and organization, in terms of activity corners for free play, small and large circles drawn on the ground with chalk for large and small group activities, and a print-rich environment with books' corners and through hanging labels, indicating windows, doors, etc., to create an emergent literacy environment. As the project director, Zakiya Kurrien, emphasized, 'Seeing is believing.' A visual experience of the child-friendly classroom and children's enthusiastic response to it in terms of their involvement in activities is itself an extremely effective way to convince parents and teachers about the value of this pedagogy.

The systematic thought and planning which informs the design of recurrent training, follow-up and mentoring by the mentors (for which the mentors also receive recurrent training) is also a contributing factor. The emphasis on a 'bite-size' incremental approach to design each training module to facilitate easy assimilation by teachers, the non-hierarchical relationship between mentors and teachers/AWWs (which was seen across most of the eight projects) and an appreciation-cum-demonstration approach by mentors of gently nudging the teachers towards further improvement rather than any open criticism were very enabling and supportive mentoring processes observed in the project, with an underlying effort to build relationships. This approach in a way served as a model for teachers too so that a similar supportive and congenial interpersonal relationship was observed between the AWWs and the children who had in terms of Bernstein's framework the freedom to express themselves, to interact with the teacher and, through child-initiated and peer-initiated activities, to learn from each other in a joyful learning environment.

Across the eight practices reviewed in the research, there were distinct variations in terms of priorities and strengths. While Dharni and Bodh had a clearer focus on the constructivist, cognitively oriented and child-centred pedagogy, the other six programmes were not at the same level. Interestingly, Nidan, which was mentored by Bodh, was also not able to reach the mentoring organization's level, indicating the need for longer-term scaffolding and mentoring at the institutional level and the need to provide time and space for this growth trajectory of every institution, which cannot respond adequately to just one shot training as is routinely observed in the larger system. For instance, while researchers were able to observe various good practices in early literacy in most sites, the same was however not true for early numeracy. Two of the case studies—SERP and Gujarat ICDS—reported specific concerns related to the pedagogy for early numeracy in the curriculum and classroom practices, again reflecting a diversity and unevenness even within this sample.

5.4.4. Bringing Community, Home and Preschool Together: A Productive Partnership for Children's Development by Strengthening the Mesosystem

The NPE 2020 conceptualizes ECE as a provision for holistic development of the child, which includes care, health and early learning, in acknowledgement of the interdependence of these aspects of human development. WHO's Nurturing Care Framework (2018) also advocates for a holistic approach to early childhood provisions, which include responsive care, health, nutrition, opportunities for early learning, and safety and security. Further, the quantitative strand of our research (Kaul et al., 2017) demonstrates that children's cognitive readiness at the age of 5+ years is positively associated with mother's education level and the early learning environment in the family. Given this policy and research context, ECE programmes need to address the holistic development of every child, and that can be accomplished in a wholesome way only if ECE in the preschool can be sensitive to and complemented by care and early learning opportunities at home, which are consistent with each other.

In this context, closer engagement with the community aimed at the community developing a sense of ownership of the programme and simultaneously a collaborative partnership with the parents become important mandates for every preschool programme. The COVID-19 pandemic which has stretched across the year 2020 and is continuing into 2021 has also demonstrated the important role parents can play to supplement the Anganwadi's or preschool's efforts to provide learning opportunities to children, by bringing the home and preschool closer to each other, and this partnership needs to be sustained and strengthened. The case studies provide several examples of how this home–Anganwadi/preschool linkage is not only possible but also an important factor in ensuring that every child receives holistic care and education which is foundational for the child's lifelong development.

The Seva Nidhi programme was initiated as a response to a demand from local women to cater to their children's education. Significantly, the organization's approach was to mobilize the villagers to be involved in addressing the issues of development, reflected in several aspects of the programme, including starting of the Balwadis, selection of teachers, timing of the centre, family participation and engagement with women's groups as well as collaboration with local NGOs. Thus, Balwadi was conceptualized not only as an entry point to address the learning needs of children but also as 'a platform designed to bring villagers together to work on various environmental and social issues to build cohesive rural communities'. The SERP project which catered to a tribal community invited parents' involvement right from the beginning from the stage of mobilization, followed by planning and implementation and finally sustainability.

SERP succeeded in establishing a community-based model of Balwadi programme in which the parents and local community not only participated but were also a part of the decision-making, monitoring and supervision. The model was one of parent empowerment and partnership, with parents being given responsibilities such as each parent being required to take responsibility for three children to ensure they attend the preschool. Two parents attended the Balwadi every day for an hour by rotation to help out, and every Saturday, the parents were required to come to the Balwadi to observe what children were learning. Interestingly, every parent was asked to save ₹100 every month for their child/children! The Balwadis had become an integral part of the lives of this tribal community. The Nidan project is another good example which catered to the Dalit community and involved parents integrally into the functioning of the Balwadis. The Pratham model, which is an urban model, ran Balwadis which were 'embedded in a network of other community programmes which address related issues and augment the services provided'. The Balwadi teachers were identified by the local mothers' groups.

Most of the projects included as good practices in this volume demonstrate a strong parents–Balwadi connect and place significant value on involving the parents and encouraging them to take responsibility and interest in their children's learning. The COVID-19 experience has also been an awakening experience from the perspective of the phenomenon of home–preschool divide. With the compulsion to ensure children's continuity in 'learning', which was getting disrupted due to school closure, the parents were approached to take over the responsibility, with teachers providing the inputs through technology. This experience has not only brought the home and preschool/school closer to each other but also revealed the acute digital divide with majority of parents in the country not being able to provide the children with the required access to technological devices. There have been alternative modes adopted to reach the homes through social media, small group interactions, etc., but the realization of the important role of parenting as the microsystem of the child has undoubtedly come to stay.

5.4.4.1. Creating a Multilingual Environment

A significant aspect of connecting with the community is to ensure inclusion of all children, irrespective of language, caste, religion, gender and other social factors. Given India's language diversity, multilinguality can be not only a vital resource but also a major challenge for any learning situation. The Dharni project, again in a tribal belt, adopted Hindi as the language of interaction on request of the parents, since it is privileged in that area over Marathi which is the regional language, because of the geographical proximity with Madhya Pradesh. But alongside, the project also identified stories in Korku, the tribal language, and prepared little storybooks in the Hindi script but in the tribal language to introduce early literacy experiences to the children with material which was meaningful for them.

5.4.5. Systemic Quality Improvement in ECCE Calls for a Catalyst Outside the Government/Implementing Agency

India has almost universalized access to ECCE through the ICDS in the public sector and an exponentially expanding private sector, with almost 80 per cent three- to six-year-olds participating in an ECCE provision (ASER Centre, 2018). However, a large number of children graduating from the Anganwadis or preschools demonstrate very low levels of 'cognitive readiness' at the age of 5+ years on entry to Grade 1 as demonstrated in the quantitative and longitudinal strand of our research (Kaul et al., 2017). The research attributes this deficit to the developmentally inappropriate and rote-based curricular practices in the centres. We explored this dimension further for a more nuanced and granular understanding of quality in ECCE, especially for children from marginalized communities through an analysis of the eight case studies of good practices.

We observed that of the eight practices, seven were led by different NGOs and one was led by a private trust, albeit in diverse models. While some like Seva Nidhi, Bodh, Prajayatna, Pratham and Nidan had independent Balwadis run by the respective organizations, Dharni and the Gujarat public–private partnership project were actually focused on mediating with quality interventions in the mainstream ICDS run by the state governments. We thus not only see an endorsement of Lewis's (2001) categorization of the role of non-governmental or private trust's in terms of (a) the service delivery role and (b) the catalyst role but also perceive an overlap in the two. As he elaborates,

> One form of catalyst is the non governmental organisation that aims to bring about change through advocacy and seeking influence, another is the agency that partners with organisations including government, private sector, donors other nongovernmental organisations and aims to innovate and apply new solutions to developmental problems. (Lewis, 2001)

Some organizations such as Bodh and Pratham straddled both kinds of roles, as they worked with the ICDS system in various states and/or provided expertise to the system for quality improvement based on the demonstration of their good practices in their independent endeavours.[1]

With the governments running provisions or programmes for children at scale, the focus is more on routine implementation with little inclination or capacity to pause, review and recast or to contextualize. The design is also 'one size fits all' to be scaled up. This leads to the

---

[1] Prajayatna also provided support to ICDS but after the study.

quality of the system remaining static and tends to even deteriorate at times. However, the case studies demonstrate the catalytic role of an 'outside agency', be it a trust or an NGO, such as the Bhansali Trust in Gujarat, in helping to contextualize the design and content of the ECE component of the ICDS and introduce measures for quality improvement.

It is seen that the governments also thus tend to demonstrate a dependence on partnership with non-governmental entities or other partners to address or lead any quality reforms which the system may require from them. The case studies also demonstrate the role these agencies outside the system can play to motivate not necessarily by taking over the management but by the demonstration of good practice or by providing technical assistance, for instance, from mother NGOs to other smaller NGOs to take the reform forward. For example, Nidan NGO was trained and technically guided by Bodh Shiksha Samiti in Rajasthan and carried the good practices into Bihar. While this could be seen as a case of mother organization mentoring a smaller one, an alternative mode of extending influence was in the case observed later of the West Bengal ICDS strengthening programme which drew several lessons from the Dharni experience of the diffusion model of quality expansion of Anganwadis. The larger lesson one can draw from the case studies is that one mode of addressing and resolving the paradox of negotiating scale vs diversity is for the government programmes to work at scale but simultaneously facilitate and mobilize the catalytic role of technical, funding and implementation partners and other potential partners towards helping the government to address the challenge of contextual relevance of the provision while meeting the prescribed quality standards, thus negotiating both the goals concurrently.

5.5. Ecology of a Preschool: An Emerging Proposition for Constructing and Scaling Up Good Practices

The challenge of scaling up and sustainability of good practices, given economic, social and institutional diversity across the country, can best be addressed by rooting any planned initiative for ECCE firmly in a strengthened, well-resourced and engaged community context. This is necessary to create a sense of ownership and investment in ensuring its success, sustainability and expansion and for providing support as and when required to withstand risks due to disruptions in financing from sources external to the programme or from other political and institutional interferences.

The emerging lessons from the field, therefore, point in no uncertain terms to the need to perceive a preschool/Anganwadi/Balwadi not as a centre which is physically and socially isolated but as a central part of an ecosystem which surrounds it and impacts its scope, functioning and quality of its provisions in an interactive mode. Drawing from these lessons and from Bronfenbrenner's ecological Systems theory (1979), we propose the following ecological model (see Figure 5.1) as a guidance for comprehensive planning and implementation of an effective preschool education programme for children, particularly from the margins.

5.5.1. Proposing an Emerging Socioecological Model for an Effective Preschool

The ecosystem of a preschool education programme which needs to be addressed for an effective and impactful provision of high quality would include the following levels:

Microsystem: This would include the preschool itself, the teacher, the classroom organization, the curriculum and the child's home.

Mesosystem: Reaching out to and strengthening connections with the family in support of the preschool would be considered the mesosystem.

Exosystem: The local panchayat, mahila mandals, village leaders, local related institutions such as the primary school or the ICDS system would form this layer of support and engagement.

Chronosystem: This could include any episodic event such as changing priorities of funding agencies and government, and pandemic situations like COVID-19, which would require advance preparedness where possible in mitigating measures.

Macrosystem: This could include the policy environment such as National Policy on ECCE 2013, NPE 2020, National

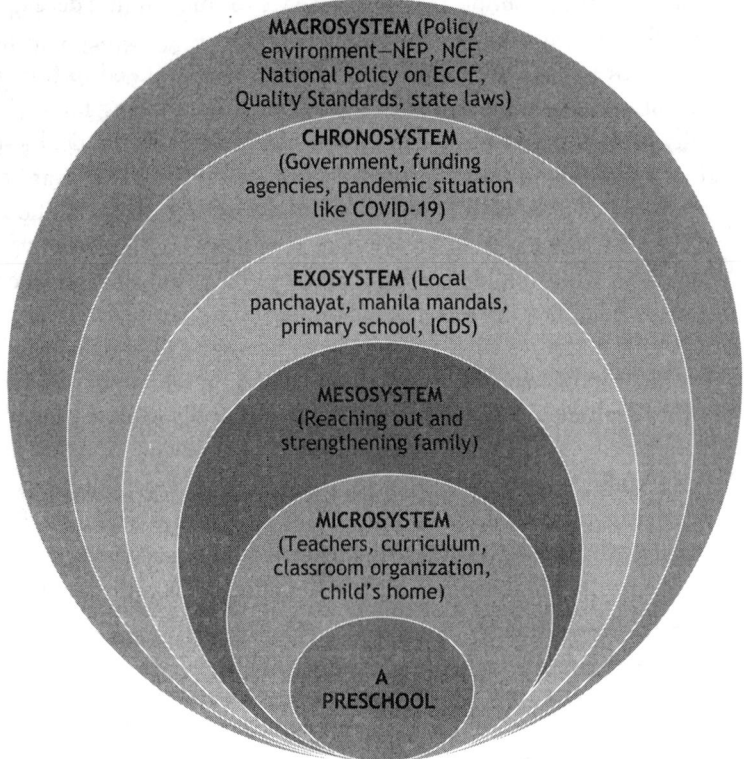

Figure 5.1. *Socio-ecological Model of a Preschool*

Curriculum Framework and Quality Standards and state laws, rules and regulations.

The critical levels are the microsystems and mesosystems which, in an interactive mode, determine the quality of a preschool programme. These need to be specifically addressed in any planning for a preschool of high quality.

5.6. Recommendations

India is committed both internationally and nationally to reach all the children below six years of age with ECCE, with at least one year of high-quality preschool education for three- to six-year-olds by 2030.

Alongside, there is ample research evidence to confirm that developmentally and contextually appropriate content and pedagogy sets the benchmark for quality in preschool education as opposed to formal teaching and has the potential to contribute to narrowing the social equity gap. In this context, the lessons emerging from the field also provide some significant operational guidance on the way forward to address the challenge of scaling up and universalizing early childhood provisions while ensuring appropriate sensitivity to the diversity of contexts in which children are growing up. Based on this guidance, we make the following recommendations:

1. The proposed socio-ecological model of a preschool may be further examined and empirically and theoretically explored for the purpose of refinement and validation as a framework for designing and scaling up preschool education programmes for children below six years of age. This could be considered in ways which provide adequate space to negotiate the tension between addressing multiple realities and conforming to the national recommendations.

2. ICDS being the main vehicle in the public domain to reach all the children, its existing normative approach and 'one-size-fits-all' design needs to be reviewed and made flexible to allow for decentralized planning, local contextualization and need-based adaptation within the given programmatic framework. Given the need for a catalyst to initiate/oversee the contextualization, the programme may be opened up to invite local partnerships with nongovernmental or non-profit organizations, trusts or public–private partnerships (as in the Gujarat project) for model demonstrations with provision for training and evaluation to ensure a high-quality and contextually relevant preschool education provision which meets prescribed quality standards.

3. A communication strategy at all levels of implementation, national and subnational, may be devised and employed to create a favourable environment for appreciation, acceptance and implementation of developmentally appropriate content and pedagogy for children below eight years of age with clear indicators of success, as per NEP 2020. It would be important in this context to additionally develop in all stakeholders a nuanced

understanding of the value of play for children's learning and development.

4. With the teacher emerging as a crucial factor for high-quality ECE programmes, a professional development strategy for teachers may be developed which interlinks the different components of professional development, that is, induction training, recurrent training, onsite mentoring, supportive supervision and reflective sessions and linked to compensation as an integrated whole to enable early childhood teachers to develop adequate understanding and expertise and be treated and compensated as 'professionals'.

5. Multi-site qualitative researches may be encouraged and supported to further explore the dimensions of diversity in social contexts and the phenomenon of 'multiple childhoods' and to study the implications of this diversity for setting process and structural quality standards which have inherent flexibility to adhere to contextual variations at subnational and substate levels.

References

Ahnert, L., Gunnar, M. R., Lamb, M. E., & Barthel, M. (2004). Transition to child care: Associations with infant-mother attachment, infant negative emotion, and cortisol elevations. *Society for Research in Child Development, 75*(3), 639–50. https://doi.org/10.1111/j.1467-8624.2004.00698.x

ASER Centre. (2020, January 14). Annual status of education report (rural) 2019, 'early years'. http://img.asercentre.org/docs/ASER%202019/ASER2019%20report%20/aserreport2019earlyyearsfinal.pdf

Bronfenbrenner, U. (1979). *The ecology of human development: Experiments by nature and design.* Harvard University Press.

Chaudhry, A. B., & Kaul, V. (2019). What works for school readiness? Understanding quality in preschool education. In V. Kaul & S. Bhattacharjea (Eds), *Early childhood education and school readiness in India: Quality and diversity.* Springer.

Crehan, L. (2018). *Clever lands* (pp. 239–242). Clays.

David, L. (2011). *Non government organisations: Management and development.* Routledge.

Day, M., Demulder, E. K., & Stibling, S. M. (2010). Using the process of cultural reciprocity to create multicultural classrooms. In Salili, F. & Hoosain, R. (Eds.). *Democracy and multicultural education.* (Research in Multicultural Education and International Perspectives). Information Age Publishing.

Day, M., & Parlakian, R. (2003). *How culture shapes social-emotional development: Implications for practice in infant-family programs.* Zero to Three.

Duggan, R. C. (2016). Pedagogy and quality in indian slum settings: A bernstein analysis of visual representation in the integrated child development service. *Research in Comparative and International Education, 11*(3), 298–321. SAGE Journals. https://doi.org/10.1177/1745499916663575

Harry, B., Kalyanpur, M., & Day, M. (1999). *Building cultural reciprocity with families: Case studies in special education.* Brookes Publishing Co.

Kaul, V., Bhattacharjea, S., Chaudhry, A. B., & Ramanujan, P., Banerji, M., & Nanda, M. (2017). *The India early childhood education impact study.* UNICEF.

Kaul, V., & Dogra, M. (2019). Social policy and research interface: Challenges and prospects. In T. S. Saraswathi, S. Menon, & A. Madan (Eds.), *Childhoods in India* (p. 67). Routledge.

Lewis, D. (2001). *The management of non-governmental development organizations: An introduction.* Routledge.

Loeb, S., Fuller, B., Kagan, S. L. & Carrol, B. (2004). Child care in poor communities: Early learning effects of type, quality and stability. *Society for Research in Child Development, 75*(1), 47–65. https://doi.org/10.1111/j.1467-8624.2004.00653.x

Mathers, S., & Stevens, K. E. (2018). Quality of early childhood education and care for children under three: Sound foundations. In Miller, L., Cameron, C., Dalli, C., & Barbour, N (Eds.). *The sage handbook of early childhood policy* (p. 504). London.

Ministry of Education. (2020). *National education policy.* Government of India.

Ministry of Women and Child Development. (2013). *National policy on early childhood care and education.* Government of India.

Ministry of Women and Child Development. (2014). *National curriculum framework for early childhood care and education.* Government of India.

Office of the Registrar General & Census Commissioner. (2011), Census of India. Ministry of Home Affairs, Government of India.

Raman, V. (2019). India's children and the brave new world. In T. S. Saraswathi, S. Menon, & A. Madan (Eds.), *Childhoods in India* (p. 67). Routledge.

Shneidman, L. A., Arroyo, M. E., Levine, S. C, & Susan, G. M. (2013). What counts as effective input for word learning? *Journal of Child Language, 40*(3),672–686. https://doi.org/10.1017/S0305000912000141

Snauwaert, D. T. (2012). The importance of philosophy for education in a democratic society. *Journal of Peace Education and Social Justice, 6*(2), 73–84.

Tschurenev, J. (2021). Montessori for all? Indian experiments in 'child education', 1920s–1970s. *Comparative Education, 57*(3), 322–340. https://doi.org/10.10 80/03050068.2021.1888408

United Nations. (2015). *Sustainable Development Goals.* https://sdgs.un.org/goals

World Health Organization. (2018). *Nurturing care for early childhood development.*

Part II

Quality Preschool Programmes for Children in the Margins

CHAPTER 6

Place-based Education in Himalayan Villages

**Monimalika Day and
Swati Bawa Sawhney**

'*Pahar mei bahut mehnat karni padti hai. Bachche ke liye to pahar mei zindagi barbad hai*' (Focus group). (One has to work very hard in the mountains. (Thus, a child's life is completely destroyed.)

The director explained, 'In these sort of places, *jaise bakri ko bandhte hain waise bachcho ko bandhke* (children were tied up like goats), women had to go out for work.' The Balwadi programme of Uttarakhand Seva Nidhi–Paryavaran Siksha Sansthan (USNPSS) began at the request of village women in the mid-1980s. The organization was started as a public charitable trust in 1967 and was appointed as the nodal agency by the Ministry of Human Resource Development (MHRD), Government of India, in 1987 to launch environmental education programmes, considering the fragile ecology of the Central Himalayas. The organization was registered as a non-profit organization in the same year and Dr Lalit Pandey became the director. They focused primarily on education, environment and energy, women's empowerment and gender issues, health issues related to water and sanitation, and livelihood. The various programmes on environmental education, women's empowerment and preschools were anchored in the main principles of place-based education. Although the organization did not use this phrase to describe their work, they reviewed our reports and agreed with our interpretation.

When the organization approached women to initiate an adult literacy programme, they responded by saying, '*Hamara ab kuch nahi hoga, hamare bachchon ke liye kuch karo*' (Nanda, 2001, p. 1). (Nothing will change in our lives, but do something for our children.) The organization responded to such requests from various villages by developing a Balwadi programme based on Gandhian principles. Radha Behan from the Laxmi Ashram in Kausani and other Gandhian workers in the region played a crucial role in conceptualizing the programme and the two trainers, played an active role in pioneering the programme in remote villages through partnerships with Community Based Organizations (CBO).[1] From the beginning, the Balwadi programme was conceptualized not just to address the academic needs of young children but also as a platform designed to bring the villagers together to work on various environmental and social issues, with an intent to build cohesive rural communities.

The rise and fall in the number of preschool centres reveal the influence of the macro environment on preschool programmes for marginalized children. In 1987, two Balwadis were started at the request of village women. The programme expanded exponentially, and in 2001 there were nearly 355 Balwadis operated by the organization. However, in 2012, the numbers dwindled to 22, and some of them were struggling. While the spirit of the programme remained the same, significant changes such as expansion of Anganwadis and priorities of funders affected the sustainability of the programme. Using our lens of early childhood education, we were able to capture great variety in the quality of preschool centres and teachers, which provides insights on salient features related to quality in preschool. During our visit in 2012, the Balwadi programme was limited to only three districts: Dania, Shama and Ritholi. We selected two centres

[1] www.sevanidhi.org

in Dania and Shama based on the criterion for sample selection with guidance from the director. They were selected based on geographical context and teachers' experience of working at the Balwadi. However, we visited three more centres, one in Dania and two in Shama, to explore variations in quality. We begin by presenting the geographical and social problems in these mountains, the need for childcare and some unique childcare practices.

6.1. Challenges Faced by Young Children and Women in the Himalayan Villages

The unique fragile ecology of this region poses special challenges for early childhood programmes. Some centres in Shama were located in the last few villages before the Himalayan ranges, begin their steep ascent near the Pindari Glacier. The breathtaking beauty of these mountains, with pine forests and the azure blue sky, was often interrupted by patches of brown, due to deforestation. There were serious environmental concerns in these areas, and Seva Nidhi worked ardently on these issues through their education and women's empowerment programmes.

A village consisted of a small group of houses perched on a hill top or on a gentle slope. The smaller hamlets often referred to as *toks* had as few as 15–20 families. Many families owned some agricultural land and cattle. Generally, women were primarily responsible for both agricultural work and household chores. We visited a village where about 15 families lived. The Balwadi had to be closed, as the number of children fell below 10, and a mini Anganwadi had opened. It is expensive to run preschools in every village. However, a centre generally cannot cater to more than one village, as they may be located 2–3 km away, and negotiating the narrow paths through difficult terrains is especially formidable for young preschoolers. In another village called Tiketa, Seva Nidhi continued to operate a Balwadi, even though the number of children was less than 15. It was located on a plateau, but the hill was extremely steep and dangerous. The trainers and mentors had to climb nimbly using all four limbs for monitoring visits, as a slip could be absolutely fatal. One of the trainers described the risk in the following words: '*Girne se, ek tukre bhi nahi milenge.*' (If one falls, it is unlikely that even a piece will be found.)

While Tiketa is an extreme case, negotiating these foothills in general is not an easy job. We have both grown up and lived in the plains; for us, a 2-km or 3-km walk was an exhaustive exercise, climbing up or down a hill, or negotiating narrow pathways. We observed that parents or grandparents often carried children in their lap or in a *doka* (basket). During one of the focus group discussions with parents in Shama, a mother said that she stopped sending her four-year-old son to the Anganwadi, as he had to cross a *gadera* (a crevice between two adjacent hills) and began to have nightmares. She had enrolled him in the Anganwadi, as his cousin attended the adjacent primary school and the two children walked together. She then moved him to the Balwadi which was a 5-minute walk from their home. During our conversations with teachers, we learned that many of them had experienced fractures due to accidents in the hills.

The situation becomes much worse during monsoons when it rains incessantly for long hours or even for days. Such downpours are sometimes followed by landslides, which seriously disrupt the daily routines. Some villagers said that they needed to close the Balwadis during the monsoon season for a few weeks or months. In Ritculla, a village in the Liti district, we learned that officers from Dehradun visited a neighbouring village in the month of June and advised villagers to vacate immediately due to risk of a serious landslide.

Women in these regions have an extremely difficult life. Most able-bodied men had migrated to the plains to find employment, a phenomenon locally referred to as *palain*. Life was difficult for women and they worked from dawn to dusk, collecting wood, tending to the crops, cutting grass and gathering fodder for the cattle, followed by cooking and cleaning. We often saw women dangerously perched on a tree to collect leaves or cutting grass on a steep slope. Sometimes, women had to travel great distances during the day and night to fetch water. Moreover, there are serious gender biases which add significantly to their hardship. We observed that adolescent girls were often involved in household chores or agricultural work, but boys played cricket after school. The absence of men across all villages affects the quality of life for both women and children. These issues have to be considered in developing early childhood programmes in such regions.

6.2. Use of *Doka* and Need for Childcare

There is a critical need for good childcare programmes for young children in the Himalayan villages. When mothers came to drop their children to the Balwadi, some of them started to run right after dropping the child, to make good use of the four hours available to them. We observed that children as young as two years of age often attended the Balwadi, especially when their siblings attended the programme. The teachers responded warmly to these children, but they often interrupted learning activities. The following quote from a mother explains the challenge of childcare:

> *Jaha jate hai waha le jate hai ... khet mei ... hum toh 2 bahnein thehri ... ek kaam karti hai or dusri bachho ko sambhalti hai ... unki bhua dekhti hai ... aur agar koi nahi hota to ghar mei band kar dete hai ... 3 saal dala, 4th saal mei nikal diya ... sab 3 saal rakhte hai....* (Focus group discussion with mothers)

> (We take the child wherever we go ... to the fields. We are just two sisters. One works on the field and the other manages the child.... Sometimes the aunt watches.... When no one is available then we tie them at home.... For 3 years they are kept at home and then in the 4th year they are out.)

During a focus group discussion, we learned about a childcare practice unique to some parts of Uttarakhand, such as Shama. Babies and young children were swaddled in cloth and kept in baskets commonly referred to as *doka* or *tokri* (basket) for long hours, especially when the mother worked on the fields or the forests and was outside the home. During a focus group meeting, a mother who had just returned from the fields said in a very agitated manner:

> *'Hum bachcho ko jhula bana ke rakhte hai ... ta ki maa ko jaane ko fursat milti hai ... do teen saal tak tokri mei raakh kar, kaam karte hai ...*

pahar mei bahut mehnat karni padti hai ... bachche ke liye toh pahar mei jindagi barbaad hai. (Focus group discussion with mothers)

(We have to put the child in a swing ... so the mother has the opportunity to go.... For 2–3 years we keep (the child) in the basket and work.... One has to work very hard in the mountains.... Childhood is destroyed in the mountains.)

We were confused when we first heard about the *doka*, as we did not quite understand why a child would be left on a swing. To help us understand this unique practice, members from the local NGO took us to three families who were using the *doka*. There were two kinds of *dokas*. Babies below six months of age were kept in a small basket on a bed, as their movements were limited. When children became mobile, they were placed in a basket hung from the ceiling like a swing and connected to a pulley. Interestingly, the room in which the basket was kept was warm compared to other parts of the house. The doors and windows were shut, and very little light entered the room. The following quote explains the purpose of the two *dokas*:

Tokri me ... jo Balwadi jaate hai ... toh unko bhi dalte hain aur jo Anganwadi jaate hai unko bhi dalte hain aur jo chhote bachche hote hain ... jo na Balwadi jaate hain na Anganwadi jaate hain, unke liye chhoti tokri hoti hai. Do prakar ki tokri hain ... jab bachche bade hote hain to badi tokri me dalte hain, jab bache chhote hote hain to chhoti wali tokri hoti hain.

(In the basket ... those who go to Balwadis ... they are also placed and those who go to Anganwadis they are also placed. And those who do not go to Balwadis or Anganwadis, for them there is a small basket. There are two kinds of baskets ... when children are big they are put in the big basket, when children are small they are put in the smaller basket.)

Although we had read about such practices, we were intrigued for a number of reasons. The current research in child development empha-sizes the importance of stimulation, especially for infants. It seemed that the *doka* restricted children's ability to explore their environment. However, when we observed young children in the Balwadis, we did not notice any patterns of developmental delay. A local female politician recalled being in the *doka* till six years of age and described it as a comforting experience. A more nuanced qualitative enquiry of this phenomenon is needed to understand the cultural meaning of this childcare practice and its implication for development.

6.3. Description of the Balwadis

The preschool programme was launched to provide education to children between the ages of three and five years in remote villages of Uttarakhand. It was initially funded by MHRD and later by Tata Trust and expanded rapidly in the first decade. The main office of Seva Nidhi was located in Almora. The two early childhood trainers were responsible for monitoring and mentoring the Balwadi programme and reported directly to the director (refer to figure 6.1). They collaborated with small local NGOs to reach remote areas and provide quality services. In addition to training and developing the curriculum, the two trainers mentored the *margdarshikas* (mentors) and the *shikshikas* (teachers). Seva Nidhi deliberately chose to use the word *shikshika* to emphasize the role of the teacher as the main responsibility. Each Balwadi was run in a Balwadi Bhawan (building). A minimum of 15 children were required to launch or continue operation of a centre. The village community was expected to take an active role in setting up the Balwadi and running the programme.

The *shikshika* was primarily responsible for the education (*shiksha*) of children. In addition, she was expected to play a lead role in bringing villagers together to address various social issues. The teachers were mentored by *margdarshikas* as well as the two early childhood trainers and coordinators of the programme. The *margdarshikas* were local village women who visited each centre once a month to supervise the *shikshika* and scaffold their learning. The mentors were supervised by the trainers. Seva Nidhi collaborated with small NGOs in different parts of Uttarakhand to scale up, contextualize services and promote empowerment of local people. The local NGO monitored the day-to-day operations and distributed payment to employees through small grants obtained from Seva Nidhi and were also involved in other projects. The two trainers maintained the collaboration and visited the field for mentoring and monitoring.

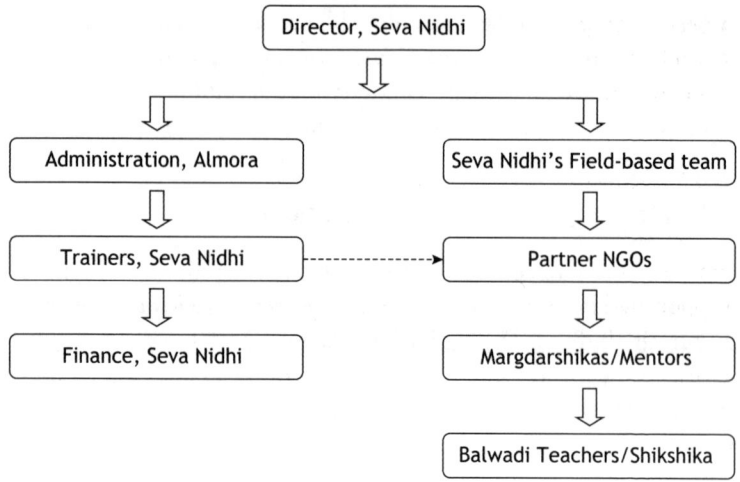

Figure 6.1. *Organizational Structure of Seva Nidhi*

The curriculum for the Balwadi programme was inspired by the work of Gijubhai Badheka. This was evident in the use of local activities and materials. The curriculum and implementation guidelines were developed by Seva Nidhi. The data on Early Childhood Education Quality Assessment Scale (ECEQAS) revealed that on most parameters, the Balwadi in Shama performed better compared to the Balwadi in Dania. Interestingly, the teacher at Shama was new and had been working for about three months. She rigorously followed the prescribed routine and activities. The teacher at Dania had been with the organization for 22 years. She talked much about joyful learning, but her activities were not always connected to specific learning goals, and she often had down time and filled them with songs and dances.

6.4. A Community-based Programme

As mentioned earlier, the imagination of the Balwadi was based on the ideas of various Gandhian workers. While the programme was developed in response to the requests from village women, the founders envisaged it as a platform to mobilize the villagers to address issues of development. This intent of the organization was reflected in several aspects of the programme, including how Balwadi centres were started, selection of teachers, timing, family participation, engagement with women's groups and collaboration with local NGOs.

6.4.1. Starting a Preschool

A Balwadi was started only when villagers agreed that such a programme was needed and accepted the responsibility to monitor and support it. The local panchayat (a village council) allowed Seva Nidhi to run the Balwadi in the panchayat bhavan (building). In other villages, community members came together to construct the building. Some villagers donated land or materials for the building. Others contributed through *shramdaan* (contribution of labour). During a focus group discussion, an old woman recalled how the construction of the preschool brought the villagers together:

> *Pehle kisi logo ne jagah di … shram dan mei … Mahilao ne bhi pursho ne bhi … khali dande mei chapar banaya tha … phir har saal badal mei dikat hoti thi … phir inhone pathar dho ke wahi par balbhavan banaya … phir block se demand kar kay ek building banwai.*

> (First, some people gave their land … then the donation of labour … both women and men participated … we attached canvases on poles … every year there was a problem during the rains … then they carried rocks and built the preschool building … then we placed our demands at the block level and got the building constructed.)

Another woman narrated how the beginning of the Balwadi affected other aspects of village life, including the ecology:

> *Jungle se pehle Balwadi aiye, phir mahila mangal dal, jungle katne paar pratibandh lagaya, jungle bhi bandh kiya, sab kuch shram daan se kiya…. Bal bhavan bana … usse samay 40–45 bachche the.*

> (The Balwadi came even before [our work on] the forests, then the women's group, we stopped cutting the forest, then we put a fence around the forest, did everything with donation of labour … built the preschool building … there were 40–45 children at that time.)

6.4.2. Selection of *Shikshika* (Teacher)

The villagers worked closely with Seva Nidhi to select the teacher. She was usually a young local woman above 18 years of age, who had some formal schooling. The teacher could be from the same village or from a neighbouring village. Seva Nidhi sometimes preferred to hire a person from the neighbouring villages because the teacher was expected to mobilize the community. It was sometimes difficult for a woman from the same village to do so as she was viewed as a daughter by the community.

6.4.3. Timings of the Preschool

All Balwadis operated for four hours, but the timings were determined by the villagers. During our visit in the month of April, the centre in Dasili was on winter schedule (10:00 AM to 2:00 PM), agricultural work had already started due to arrival of the spring rains and the attendance was poor as parents went to the fields at dawn and took the children with them. The timings were changed to 8:00 AM to 12:00 PM on the following week to synchronize better with parents' need for childcare. A mother explained the importance of Balwadi during a group discussion:

> *Agar hamme apni Balwadi majboot banani hai ... toh hamme apne bach-cho ke bare mei khud bhi sochna padega ... ab anpadho ka zamana nahi hai ... bena pade kuch nahi hoga pehla se shuruwati shiksha dena padega.*

> (If we wish to make our Balwadi strong, then we must also think about our children. It is no longer a period for illiterates. Without education, nothing will happen. We need to begin with early education.)

6.4.4. Family Participation in the Classroom

We observed that parents and grandparents dropped in unannounced and participated in some of the classroom activities. They mostly came on their way back from the fields and remained in the periphery of the classroom. Some of them participated in the songs and encouraged the children to recite various poems or slogans (*naras*). The teachers generally continued with their lessons and were not flustered by such informal visits. In Shama, a grandmother regularly sat outside the centre to ensure that children remained safe if they stepped out of the room to go to the toilet, as the building was on a small hill.

6.4.5. Mahila Mandal Dal (Women's Group)

In addition, to running the Balwadi programme, the teachers were expected to convene a monthly meeting for the village women with support from their respective mentors and the local NGO. The women's group was organized in four tiers, the Uttarakhand Mahila Mandal Dal, the Mahila Mandal Dal (400–450 villages), the regional parishad (20 villages) and the local Mahila Mandal Parishad at the village level. Various trainings, workshops and *goshtis* (discussion meetings) were organized to discuss the early childhood programme. Initially, parents demanded opportunities for reading and writing, but during our visit, most of them were aware of the importance of play and mentioned that young children learn through play (*'khel khel me'*). The discussions were not limited to the Balwadi but encompassed a variety of topics which concerned the village women. These dialogues often motivated community members to initiate actions on personal hygiene of children, sanitation, deforestation, alcoholism, etc. A mentor explained that problems of the Balwadi was solved with the women's group:

> *Balwadi me jitni bhi samasyae aati hai, Balwadi aur mahila sangathan milke samadhan karti hai…. Ab jese kahi kahi par sauch ka gadda (toilet) nahi hota hai, bachcho ko bahar jane mei pareshani hoti hai, toh gadda tyre ka banate hai, aur parda laga diya.* (Mentor)

> (When there is any problem in the Balwadi, the Mahila Mandal Dal and the Balwadi together solve the issue. For example, if there is no toilet, children have to go outside, a hole is dug in the ground and curtains are hung.)

6.4.6. Balmela (Children's Fair)

The Balmela was an annual event, an important mechanism to engage the community and make them aware of the significance of preschool education. We observed a Balmela during our visit to Dania. It was a very festive occasion, characteristic of a mela. A large multi-coloured tent was set up in the grounds of the local NGO, which was built on Gandhian principles and collaborated with Seva Nidhi to operate the Balwadis. A small stage was constructed for the children to perform. Music boomed from the sound boxes and attracted the passing children and adults to the event. The students and the teachers from 10 Balwadis demonstrated various activities—songs, dances, poems and skits—which were part of their curriculum. Some elderly women of the Mahila Mandal Dal spoke about the importance of early childhood education and fondly shared stories about various Balwadis. Nearly 100 people attended the gathering, and many villagers had walked several kilometres for the event. This appeared to be an effective way to engage villagers in a dialogue on preschool education.

6.5. Role of a Teacher Is Critical

Seva Nidhi selected, trained and mentored teachers carefully, as they recognized the vital role which teachers play in facilitating children's learning. The director explained, 'Teacher or *shikshika* whatever you may say "must want to be with children"; otherwise, why will the children go there?' Our observations at different Balwadis suggest that some teachers were able to conduct meaningful and engaging learning activities even when the infrastructure was poor. Members of the village community agreed with this view. They emphasized on the need to train teachers appropriately, so they understand 'how children learn' and know 'what should be taught to children'. We deliberately visited five centres, interviewed teachers and conducted a focus group meeting with them to understand variations in quality. Using our lens of early childhood education, we categorized one of them as average, two as above average and two as below average, based on their ability to engage children and conduct activities with definite learning objectives. We explore the two extreme categories constructed to highlight the differences.

6.5.1. Teachers Whose Performance Was Above Average

We examined the pedagogy of these practitioners from a critical perspective and identified six strategies used by them.

6.5.1.1. Differentiated Teaching

At the Chill Balwadi, we found that children were engrossed in an activity in which they were placing stones on the edges of the drawing or shapes given to them. This activity was called *seema gyan* (knowing the limits). When enquired about the reasons for giving different shapes to children, Meena explained that she modified the task based on their age. Below is a quote from the participant observation:

> She draws a simple picture on the floor and asks a child to fill it up with stone chips. For an older child (4 years), she draws a 9 and asks him to arrange stone chips on the outline. For a 5 year old, she traces the *swar* (letter) A in Hindi. The girl next to him is younger. Meena draws a circle and encourages the child to simply put the pebbles inside the circle. She verbally prompts her by saying '*bharo sab bharo*' (fill it up).

During the interview, the teacher explained, '*Group bana dete hain umar ke hisab se*' (make groups based on their age). The mentor added that having a helper in the class really helps to facilitate differentiated teaching.

6.5.1.2. Following Children's Interests

The two teachers, who excelled in the classroom, spoke about discussing the routine with children and modifying the activities based on their interests. One of them stressed that children should not be forced to join class activities. She said,

> *Ek do bachche hai jo nahi karna chahte hain to unko fir jese kitabe di jati hain thodi der padne ko… ya thode khilone de diye bachcho ko or … toh usko matlab uski ruchi anusar kam diya….*

> (One or two children do not want to do the activities. We give them books to read or toys … so giving the child work based on their interest.)

6.5.1.3. Disciplining through Positive Guidance

Meena said that she makes an effort to explain expectations in a polite way at the beginning of the day. She tries not to intervene when children have conflicts but sometimes that is not possible. She also tries to divert their attention, for example, *'Ye Suraj hai, abhi vo jyada hi shaitani kar raha tha, toh usko kaha ke kitab le aa or likh isko baithke or vo thodi der mei kitab likhne mei magan ho gaya fir.'* (This is Suraj. He was mischievous today, so told him to get a book, write something and in a little while he was absorbed in it.) Many teachers mentioned *shanti khel* (activities that bring peace), which was part of the curriculum and was designed to calm children down.

6.5.1.4. Relating the Lesson to Children's Immediate Experiences

At the Chill Balwadi, we observed a storytelling session, in which the teacher had created a story about local animals and their food habits. It was the story of a deer and things it ate. She introduced the picture chart and asked children to identify the characters of the story. She emphasized on the use of the local language. She highlighted the relevance of selecting stories related to children's local environment.

Questions she posed were such that the answers were not available in the story but required children to reflect on what they observed in their surroundings.

6.5.1.5. Planning New and Thematic Activities

We visited five Balwadis in order to maximize our chances of documenting good classroom practices. We paid a surprise visit to a Balwadi in Dana Bhanar and had the opportunity to observe an excellent thematic lesson conducted by the teacher. The activity was *paryavaran bhraman* (nature walk) for which the teacher Nanda had done some rigorous planning. She referred to the use of *purv* diary (before) and *pashchat* diary (after), a requirement from the organization to engage teachers in planning and reflection.

She had made a number of paper boats. She took the bag of boats and led children to a nearby pond, constructed for rain water harvesting. It was about knee deep for adults. She made the children to sit around the pond and gave safety instructions. She began by singing *'nao chali nao chali'* (the boat moves) and released a few boats in the water. She helped each child to release a boat in the water and encouraged them to wait for their turn. She pointed out that some boats were sinking while others were floating. She also sang *'machli jal ki rani hai'* (the fish is the queen of the water) with action. The children were very excited and keenly observed the boats. She then threw pebbles in the water and pointed out to the circles formed. Some children repeated her action and carefully observed the ripples in the water.

Next, she moved the children closer to the Balwadi and drew a circle to represent the pond. With the help of the trainer, she engaged the children in a game where the alligator chased the children when they entered the pond. The children had great fun but also had difficulty following instructions at this time. Finally, she took the children to a small patch of garden, just outside the centre, where she had planted saplings of local crops such as corn, bajra (millet) and rajma (kidney beans). She pointed to the plants and named them. The children pulled out a few saplings out of curiosity. Nanda laughed at them and gently demonstrated how to touch the plants and also instructed them not to trample upon them.

Through this lesson, Nanda motivated young children to closely observe the objects in their environment to learn concepts such as floating and sinking, recognize the shape of circle, sing songs related to the activity, engage in a pretend play and recognize local crops. This integrated activity which addressed a large number of learning objectives strongly impressed us.

6.5.1.6. Vision of the Teacher

Finally, Nanda seemed to be very connected to her students and had high aspirations for them. She was gentle but also demanded engagement.

> *Abhi to mai bachchon ko aur jyada forward banana chahti hun, taki kisi ko dekh kar unhe jhep na ho aur karyakramo me wo ruchi le, aisa karne ko sochti hun … jo kaaam karna hai toh karna hai.*

(I wish to make the children, confident to move forward, so they are not afraid of anyone. They should take interest in the activities. Whatever has to be done has to be done.)

6.5.2. Teachers Who Struggled

Out of the five, two teachers struggled to keep children engaged in the classroom activities. They primarily followed the prescribed routine but lacked insight on the purpose of the activities. We did not observe them engaging in differentiated teaching and they seemed to have limited understanding of children's development.

> *Following the prescribed routine:* The teacher in Dania mentioned that they needed to conduct activities based on age, but we did not observe her doing so in the three days we spent in her classroom. Both teachers adhered to the routine but seemed to lack a nuanced understanding of children's abilities and the ways they could engage students. Activities such as counting, shapes, numbers and classification were conducted by repeating instructions rather than through play. Lessons were often completed quickly. Although children were happy, sometimes it was chaotic.
>
> *Difficulty in disciplining children:* In Dania, the activities were completed quickly and then the down time was filled with songs, dance, poems and slogans, which were not connected to any specific learning goals. Some of the children tended to wander and leave the classroom as they were probably getting bored. Another teacher rhetorically kept saying, '*Sabash*' (well done). It seemed that she had not fully understood the concept of positive guidance addressed in the training session. On one occasion, she said, '*Nahi karoge to kya hoga?*' (What will happen if you don't do it?), a young three-year-old promptly replied, '*Maar parega*' (you will get a beating)!

6.5.3. Gender Experiences of Teachers and Their Transformation

Gender discrimination continues to be a serious concern in this region. Many teachers talked about low expectation of parents from their daughters. Parents were reluctant to educate girls beyond Grade 7 as they would need to travel to the local high school, 4–5 km away. In addition to concerns for safety, they treated boys and girls differently. For example, Meena was an excellent teacher who had some physical disabilities. Her parents initially refused to write the property in her name and only did so after several dialogues with the trainers.

Some parents were reluctant to allow their daughters to become Balwadi teachers; they were especially concerned about sending the girls to Almora for training. Many of the teachers had never left their village. The trainers and mentors visited the homes of the educators, established relationships with them and sometimes succeeded in changing perspectives through critical dialogues. Seva Nidhi allowed family members to accompany the teachers and stay with them during the in-house trainings in Almora. Sometimes, parents left after a few days after reviewing the arrangements at the training centre. During a 10-day training which we attended, a mother-in-law stayed in the dormitory, caring for a young infant belonging to a teacher.

Seva Nidhi encouraged the teachers to discover their potentials through training, individual mentoring and journal writing. The in-house training provided an opportunity for the teachers to be away from their villages, experience themselves in different ways and form friendships. The trainers and mentors played a critical role in transforming the perspectives and lives of the teachers. They focused on developing trustworthy relationships with the teachers, where they could safely discuss their dilemmas.

Meena, a confident outspoken teacher, shared that she remained upstairs in the women's dormitory for an entire week during her first training. Nanda, the best teacher we met, said that she had to leave school after completing Grade 7 and was married. In spite of stiff resistance from her in-laws, Nanda decided to join the Balwadi. At the time of our visit, she had completed Grade 12 through open school and was registering for her bachelor's degree. Once again she faced much criticism from the village women. The villagers said, '*BA karke inter karke, khad hi toh pakana hai ... ghas hi to katna hai*' (After BA and intermediate, you will still be preparing the dung and cutting the grass). Nanda and Meena's narratives illustrate the gender oppression which teachers experience, but the Balwadi programme provided an avenue for growth and transformation.

The nurturing relationships with the trainers and mentors gave teachers the courage to pursue their dreams, especially in education. A publication of Seva Nidhi from 2001 claimed that out of the 1,500 teachers who had received training, more than 60 per cent had moved to increase their educational qualifications. Our own interactions with several teachers affirmed that out of the 22 teachers, 11 were working on completing their inter-college (Grade 12) through open school. One of the trainers felt that teachers' ability to understand children's development increased as they engaged in college- or university-level education.

6.6. Capacity Building through Training, Monitoring and Mentoring

Recognizing the importance of teachers, Seva Nidhi designed a thoughtful, integrated capacity-building system. Training, mentoring and supervision were closely connected. After conducting training sessions, the trainers visited the Balwadis to observe the impact of the training and identify areas which needed improvement. The areas and challenges faced by the Balwadi workers were addressed in the subsequent training sessions. It is important to note that this approach is very different from what is practised in Anganwadi training centres.

The training in Almora gave teachers an opportunity to be away from their homes, focus on the content, discover their own potential and relate to other teachers. Initially, trainings were conducted for two weeks twice a year, but women found it difficult to stay away from their homes for such long periods. Therefore, it was reduced to a 10-day annual training. The mentors attended the training session with the teachers to ensure that they were aware of the issues discussed during the training. They attempted to address the concerns expressed by the teachers during mentoring. The teachers had great confidence on the trainers and the mentors, as they were well versed with issues in the field. We observed the last three days of the annual training programme for Balwadi teachers. The 22 teachers and 2 mentors lived in the dormitory during the 10-day training. We lived in the guest rooms but spent the entire day with the teachers. The day began with prayers and then breakfast. The training sessions were long (8:00 AM–5:00 PM) but were thoughtfully planned to engage the teachers in a variety of activities, both indoors and outdoors.

There were opportunities for guided reading and discussion on various aspects of the curriculum. There was emphasis on reflections from each day, and the schedule of the following day was modified accordingly. Three principles appeared to influence the training sessions: an activity-based approach, a relationship-based approach and emphasis on literacy. Different approaches to conducting activities such as storytelling were demonstrated by the trainers or mentors. Following these demonstrations, the trainees practised some of the activities. There was great emphasis on 'learning by doing'.

The two trainers grew up in the villages in Dania, one had a master's degree and the other had a bachelor's degree. They were well versed with local issues and greatly respected by the teachers. Anita, a widow who faced several challenges, said, '*Woh to hamare liye Bhagwan hai*' (They are Gods for us). When a trainer protested, she argued saying, '*Jo saach hai wo to mai bolungi chahe aapko bhala laage ya bura laage*' (I will speak the truth, whether you like it or not). The trainees were required to write reflective narratives and notes on various activities, which were reviewed by the trainers. It was pointed out that teachers had very limited opportunities to engage in literacy activities in their villages, which affected their ability to teach.

The *margdarshikas* were local women who had experience of running Balwadis and had graduate-level education. They were responsible for monitoring and mentoring 10 centres each. The lead trainers and mentors collaborated with the local NGOs for monitoring centres. A mentor explained, '*Shikshikao ko main madat is parkar se karti hu … Balwadi me aaie … phir total gatividhiyo ke bare me bataya … poorv–paschat diary, register upastithi wala*' (This is how I help teachers … visit the Balwadi … discuss all the activities … review pre- and post-activity diaries and the attendance register). The mentors were supposed to visit each Balwadi once a month but sometimes only succeeded in visiting after two months due to difficulties in travelling. Sometimes they had to stay the night in remote villages to complete their tasks, with help from the local women's group.

6.7. Curriculum

Gandhian workers in the region, especially from the Laxmi Ashram in Kausani, envisaged the Balwadis as a platform for engaging villagers in rural development. Therefore, there was a focus on helping children to know their immediate surroundings and understand environmental issues through observation, exploration, stories, group discussions and songs. A specific aspect of the curriculum was dedicated to environmental education (*paryavaran shiksha*). Efforts were made to address other social problems of the villages such as caste and gender discrimination. Although the Balwadis did not serve food, children were required to bring food from home for *nashta* (snack), an integral part of the routine, during which children of all caste shared food and ate together, with support from the teacher. The curriculum was inspired by Gijubhai Badheka, a pioneer in conceptualizing education based on Gandhian principles and contextualizing the Montessori approach for rural areas. There was significant emphasis on use of low-cost local materials, local stories, activities and on learning by doing.

When asked how children learn, teachers promptly replied, '*khel khel me*' (through play). The curriculum was developed centrally by the trainers, with careful attention to address the five domains (language, cognitive, social–emotional, physical and creative). They also developed the curriculum for Uttarakhand Anganwadis known as Rimjhim. Since the unit of focus was activities rather than domains, this provided an opportunity to address more than one developmental domains during most lessons. It seemed that the approach was consistent with activity-based learning, though this phrase was not used by participants. They identified eight types of activities, from which teachers could select to plan their daily schedule. They are as follows:

1. *Bhasa gyan* (language)
2. *Anka gyan* (mathematics)
3. *Kahani* (stories)
4. *Khel* (games)
5. *Bhavgeet* and *kavita* (songs with expressions and poems)
6. *Samanya gyan* (common sense or daily experiences)
7. *Paryavaran shiksha* (environment)
8. *Prayogatmak karya* (activities related to daily life which promote logical/scientific thinking)

The trainers focused on *saarvangeen vikas* or holistic development and categorized activities such as *kahani* and *bhavgeet* (stories and songs), *baatcheet* (discussion), *baalkarya* (children's activities) and games to maintain a balance between attention given to different domains. According to the trainers, literacy activities were designed to promote vocabulary, memorization, movement and self-esteem. Children were given the opportunities to listen, remember and recount the sequence of events. During *baatcheet*, children were engaged in conversations on their daily experiences related to themes. During *baalkarya*, children were encouraged to label objects in their surrounding and use them in creative ways. There were four types of games: *bahar ke khel* (outdoor games), *andar ke khel* (indoor games), *parichay khel* (games related to identity and socialization) and *shanti khel* (activities which help to calm children).

6.7.1. Use of Local Materials in Classrooms

Each Balwadi received some teaching–learning materials procured centrally such as books, puzzles, nesting toys and crayons. However, there was great emphasis on getting to know the local environment and use of low-cost local materials to promote environmental awareness. During their nature walk, children were encouraged to collect twigs, sticks, leaves, etc. The teachers brought different types of seeds, plants, recycled materials such as cloth from tailors shops, papers, etc. During trainings, a session was dedicated to developing teaching–learning materials. All classrooms had a dolls' corner, reading corner and an area for fine manipulative activities. Children's work was displayed in both big and small classrooms.

During a focus group discussion, mothers complained about the teacher–child ratio in the classroom:

Ek shikshika se kuch nahi hota hai aur bhi shikshika rakhna chaihye … karib karib … 20–25, 30 bachcho ke liye.

(One teacher cannot do anything, more teachers need to be recruited … there are about 20–25, for nearly 30 children.)

Teachers were encouraged to develop or narrate local stories. The NGO published a book of local stories with pictures written by preschool teachers. Further, we observed use of cultural artefacts to conduct certain preschool activities. For example, the brass bell is considered auspicious in this region and is seen frequently in temples and entrances to buildings and hung from the rear view mirror of cars. We observed a listening activity using a small brass bell. The entire class sat in a circle and closed their eyes. One child held the bell carefully and tip-toed behind the children. Others listened with great attention and clapped as soon as there was a sound from the bell. It was then given to the nearest child. This activity promoted listening skills and maintaining equilibrium of the body. Trainers and teachers often referred to the importance of maintaining *santulan* (balance or equilibrium), which is an essential skill to survive in the mountainous terrains.

6.8. Closure of Balwadis and Lessons on Sustainability

The programme expanded rapidly in the 1990s but suffered a setback between 2006 and 2012. This happened primarily for two reasons: expansion of Anganwadis and private preschools and lack of funds. The number of Anganwadis increased rapidly in the first decade of the 21st century. Some villagers argued that both programmes should remain as they had different effects: the Anganwadi provided food but the Balwadi brought education and promoted rural development. During our second visit, we purposely visited three villages in Shama where the Balwadis had closed. In one of them, the Balwadi was closed during the monsoon months and a mini Anganwadi was opened during this period. The number of children in the Balwadi fell below five, and it became difficult to sustain.

In another village, the women reported that the closure of the Balwadi weakened the women's group, slowed down the efforts to protect the forests and led to increase in alcoholism and violence against women. A village leader pointed out that the Balwadi teacher was accountable to the villagers, but the Anganwadi worker did not acknowledge them and rarely spent time in the community. However, the NGO felt that they should not duplicate services by running Balwadis in villages, where the Anganwadi centres are opened. In the 1990s, the Balwadis were funded by MHRD but as the Anganwadis expanded, the funding was discontinued. Simultaneously, many of the major funding agencies such as the Tatas changed their priorities, as they decided to spend more resources on advocacy programmes and less on service delivery. Other funders preferred to support programmes in states which had poor macro indicators, and Uttarakhand was not a priority.

6.9. Concluding Thoughts

We learned much from our two visits to the Seva Nidhi Balwadis. The unique child-rearing practice of using the *doka* prompted us to question current perspectives on infant stimulation and the need to understand development in the context. The variations in the five Balwadis gave us the opportunity to explore quality in early childhood education. By observing a range of practices, we were able to get clarity on key issues which contributed to quality. Very clearly, the quality of the teacher emerged as a crucial factor in determining quality. The organization developed a well-integrated, relationship-based approach to build the capacity of the teachers and promote their growth. The nature of relationship trainers and mentors developed with teachers, led to their transformation, gave them the courage to address gender biases and motivated them to pursue education. The lack of funds certainly affected the sustainability of the programme. However, according to the villagers, the Balwadis could not be replaced by the Anganwadis, as there were key differences in the nature of engagement with the communities and accountability to the local people.

Reference

Nanda, M. (2001). *The Balwadi: Binding the Himalayan village* [Unpublished report]. USNPSS. http://sevanidhi.org/publications/The_Balwadi.pdf

CHAPTER 7

Community-managed Balwadi-cum-Creches in Tribal Communities

Usha Abrol and Ratnamala Vallury

I like to work with children and make them learn and develop. I wished to be a teacher; hence, I have taken up this job. MMS committee members identified me as a qualified teacher. I understood their faith in me. I got motivated and wished to try my best to teach and make children learn. I also have good relationship with the parents and community members of this village. (Teacher of Ghanpur Balwadi)

Developing appropriate services for tribal populations poses an important dilemma for many government and non-governmental institutions in various states. The providers struggle to create culturally meaningful programmes for the population in the presence of hegemonic structures of the mainstream institutions. Experts in the field of education have especially struggled to bring education to the tribal areas without interfering with the existing culture of the tribal society. This is especially difficult, as teaching and learning are cultural processes which need to be anchored in the local culture to be meaningful for both students and their families. The Society for

Elimination of Rural Poverty (SERP[1]) in Andhra Pradesh succeeded in developing a community-based Balwadi programme, where villagers not only participated but were also responsible for the decision-making, monitoring and supervision of these programmes. This case study presents a compelling model of a community-based preschool programme developed through partnership with self-help groups (SHGs), non-governmental organizations (NGOs) and, to some extent, the Integrated Child Development Services (ICDS). The villages were small in size, everyone knew one another and the children were looked after by the entire community.

7.1. Background

Kopuvalasa village nestled in the hills of Seetampet in Srikakulam district is a poet's dream with serene surroundings and scenic locations. The tribal hamlet of some 45 families of Savara tribe is a homogenous close-knit community, where people live together like a joint family. As we approached the village, we were welcomed by a chorus of children's voices singing '*Balwadi pillalu very good pillalu*' accompanied with the rhythmic sound of khanjira. As we entered the hut from where the music came, we saw a group of 12 children between two and six years of age engaged in various activities closely supervised by a young teacher. This was a Balwadi centre operated by SERP, the only preschool in the village.

In India, many tribal areas have remained isolated due to difficult geographical approach and their unique cultural heritage. These economically marginalized tribal areas were often out of the ambit of government programmes due to the small habitations and difficult geographical access. The tribal population in some regions still lag behind their rural and urban counterparts in their access to services such as education and healthcare. A number of development programmes were initiated in tribal areas by the state government; the acceptance of such initiatives among the tribal populations was relatively poor, primarily due to cultural incongruence. Some of these

[1] https://www.serp.ap.gov.in/SHGAP/

programmes failed to understand and respond to the needs and expectations of the tribal people. One of the reasons is that the bureaucracy in the government, is sometimes not very successful in engaging villagers in the decision-making process and the implementation of the programmes.

However, the SERP Balwadis brought a ray of hope to the people in these remote tribal villages and fuelled their aspirations to educate their children. These Balwadis present a model of early childhood education, which is designed to meet the needs of local people, and take into consideration the local culture and ethos of the group. Due to the contextualization, cultural responsiveness and emphasis on empowerment of the community, these Balwadis quickly gained popularity among the villagers from the Savara tribe and served as a model for replication in other areas.

7.2. Replication and Rapid Expansion of the Programme

The manner in which the Balwadi programme of SERP expanded reflects their popularity among the Savara and Gond tribes. A systemic approach to alleviate poverty was initiated by the Government of Andhra Pradesh around 2001. The SERP was set up to conceptualize, implement and monitor these programmes. The main agenda of SERP was to bring empowerment by strengthening grass-roots structures for the poor and marginalized. Towards this purpose, grass-roots structures of community-managed institutions such as SHGs of women and Mahila Samakhya were mobilized. A community-managed model of Balwadis developed by an NGO—Sodhana in Cheepurupalli—was considered to be suitable for the Balwadi programme of SERP. This model provided a vibrant learning environment for young children, prepared them for schooling and prevented dropouts. A carefully constructed curriculum facilitated learning through play, which gained popularity in the tribal villages.

Learning from the success of these Balwadis, SERP supported a few selected Mandal Mahila Samakhyas (MMSs) at Golconda and Devarapalli in Vizag district to run 37 ECCE centres as a pilot.

The response was overwhelming, and many more MMSs came forward demanding similar centres in their areas. Meanwhile, the MMS members of Seetampet who visited the Balwadis of Sodhana in Cheepurupalli expressed the desire to replicate that model in Seetampet. The Balwadi programme of Seetampet taluk where we visited was launched in 2008.

This was followed by a rapid expansion, as the centres were replicated in four talukas (Sirpur, Jainoor, Utnoor and Indervelly) of Adilabad district where SERP supported local MMSs. By May 2009, some 209 Balwadis were functioning.

Around 2011, SERP was supporting the MMS in 40 mandals in 10 districts of the state. During 2010 and 2011, a total of 1,373 centres were operational (Sodhana: 1,031 centres enrolling 17,500 children and Centre for Development and Research [CDR]: 342 centres enrolling 5,487 children—community-Managed educational services, SERP, Hyderabad).

The philosophy of the Balwadi programme was inspired by the SERP's vision to empower families in poverty through quality education, social acceptance and good health. To promote empowerment, SERP believed that it was necessary to engage civil society groups. Therefore, the local women of the SHGs were involved in identifying the location, enrolling children and making necessary logistic arrangements for setting up a centre. The collaboration with the two resource agencies—Sodhana and CDR—helped to ensure the academic rigour and the lessons they had learned from years of work with tribal communities in that area. Thus, the main objective of the Balwadi programme was to provide meaningful, enjoyable preschool experience to promote their overall development and prepare children for later schooling so as to reduce school dropout rate.

7.3. Preschools in Two Tribal Communities

The data for this case study was collected from two centres located in Kopuvalasa village in Seetampet taluk, Srikakulam district, and Ghanpur in Utnoor taluk, Adilabad district. Kopuvalasa and Ghanpur villages were exclusively inhabited by the Savara and Gond people, respectively. The villages were inhabited by small number of families. The main occupation of the people was agriculture. Some had their own land; the others worked as labourers under National Rural Employment Guarantee Scheme. In both villages, all the children between the ages of three and five years were attending the Balwadis. The older children attended the nearby primary school. The villages were small, and there was a sense of cohesion in the community as families knew one another and were socially connected through many day-to-day activities.

The villages were located in the hills amid beautiful and scenic surroundings. There was no shortage of water. The electric connection was available, though the supply was erratic. Some households owned a television set. Almost everyone owned cows, which appeared to be healthy. The surroundings were clean, as was the general appearance of women and children. However, we noted that sometimes villagers wore torn clothes, probably indicative of the poverty they experienced. Both the villages were located at about 8–10 km from the main road. The approach was through mud roads in a hilly terrain, and no public transport was available. Although many programmes were being implemented by the Rural Development Department, the villages remained behind urban communities in their access to facilities such as roads, transport and electricity. Data collection began with participant observations at the centres. Focus group discussions were conducted in both the villages with families of the children attending the two centres, cluster coordinators and other office-bearers of the SHGs. Interviews were conducted with the MMS president, the district coordinator and two cluster coordinators. Classroom observations were conducted using Early Childhood Education Quality Assessment Scale (ECEQAS). In addition, the school-readiness instrument (SRI) and adaptive behaviour scale (ABS) were administered to three students from each centre.

7.4. Description of Balwadis

The Balwadis under SERP provided services to children between the ages of three and six years. The centres were based on a holistic approach to child development; therefore, the centres functioned both as childcare centres and preschools. Nutrition was not an integral part of the Balwadi programme. However, food was distributed to Balwadi children and pregnant and nursing mothers under the ICDS programme. The local public health centre (PHC) took care of immunizations. The Auxiliary nurse midwife (ANM) or the doctor occasionally came to the Balwadi for health check-up and care of sick children. The preschool programme was envisaged as a joyful learning environment for tribal children to ensure smooth transition from preschool to primary school.

7.4.1. A Day in the Balwadi at Kopuvalasa, Seetampet

The Balwadi was a hut-like structure with around 4 ft high walls and a thatched roof. The space between the wall and the roof was deliberately left open to allow air and sunlight into the room. The wall was painted black and was being used as a blackboard by children for writing and drawing. The preschool equipment and toys were kept in a tin box, as there was no storage of space. Children had access to the materials and took them out of the box when needed. There were charts of fruits, animals, alphabets and numbers on the walls but were not used during our observations. The floor was cemented and clean. Children sat on the floor and often wrote on the floor with chalk. The Balwadi was located in the middle of the village and was safe, quiet and ideal for learning. There was enough outdoor space for play with a temporary enclosure, but children did not go out to play very often because of the heat. The teacher reported that children played cricket and football when the weather was more pleasant. There were no toilets; therefore, children went out to relieve themselves to a specified place near the Balwadi.

The teacher began the day with a prayer at 9:30 AM. This was followed by a round of introduction, where 12 children identified themselves by saying their own names, the name of the school and village. The teacher sang with the children while standing in a circle and modelling actions which matched the verses. She played a khanjira (tambourine), and children repeated the lines after her with great enthusiasm and joy. They sang '*Potti bava*, 'A for Apple', '*Banthi Banthi Edi Na Banthi*' in a rhythmic way.

Next, the teacher initiated a literacy activity, where she adapted the game of musical chair to introduce the Telegu letters 'Ea' and 'Eaa' through a song: Telugu letters '"Ea" *Egudu digudu Ellamma*' and '"Eaa" *Eaanugu meeda rupayi edava kunda kurchundi....*' Once again, children were asked to repeat the verses after her. Before shifting to the next activity, the teacher used various energizers such as jumping and clapping. Children were refreshed and started shouting the Balawadi slogan '*Chalamanchi pillalu Balabadi pillalu...*' when they were ready.

During the story session, children were seated around the teacher in a circle, and several choices were presented to the students. This is a common pedagogical practice which motivates children to engage in dialogue with each other. Furthermore, she also sought their opinion by asking them whether she should tell the story orally or by drawing pictures with a chalk piece. Children chose the latter. She then asked which story they would like to hear. Majority of the children requested the 'monkey–thorn'. The children heard the story in silence and paid full attention. It is interesting to note that she narrated the story in the form of a dialogue between the monkey and other characters such as the cobbler, wood cutter, a child and an old lady and, in the process, made the story come alive. While telling the story with actions, she was drawing the related scenes on the floor with a piece of chalk. In between, she posed questions and children were eager to respond. Occasionally, she used English words and asked the children to repeat after her. After completing the story session, she asked the children to clap and jump for some time, a strategy which helped the children to get energized and transition to the next activity.

In the following activity, she engaged the students in identification of letters and numbers on the board. She began with a fun game of number by singing a song, where the teacher asked, 'How many of you?' (*Enthamandi meeru entha mandi?*) and the children answered, 'Whatever number you say' (*Chepinantha mandi*). The teacher called out a number and children had to form a group quickly corresponding to that number. Sometimes she referred to the number indirectly by saying 'days in a week' or 'number of fingers in a hand' which prompted children to think and engage in quick discussions with peers before choosing a number. Children who could not be part of a group had to leave. The game continued until one child remained in the end. The children who had to leave the group began to play with puzzles, building blocks and other materials as per the teacher's instructions.

For clay modelling, the teacher divided the children into groups and gave them clay to make things of their choice. Children were very excited and brought the models they created to us and the teacher. She often appreciated the children's efforts. A group of older children made letters and numbers, while others made toys. It was observed that some girls made bowls and kitchen material, while boys prepared weapons and tools, suggesting that the gender roles they had observed were influencing their play. This was an opportunity for the teacher to discuss gender issues; however, she did not address it. A break of 10 minutes was given during which some children wrote on the blackboard, while others relaxed sitting silently gazing at the surroundings.

In the next session, the teacher wrote letters on the blackboard and gave dictation to children on letters. Few children were writing on the blackboard which was at their height, others on slates. This was followed by a lesson on early numeracy concepts such as long–short, fat–thin and big–small by drawing the pictures on the blackboard.

At 12:30 PM, the children were given a lunch break. The food grains were provided under the ICDS programme. The Anganwadi helper cooked and served the food to children which they enjoyed.

After lunch, the teacher gave them an opportunity to draw. All children above three years of age were allotted some space on the floor in the class. The teacher guided them by posing questions regarding their interests and offered a few suggestions. The day ended with free play, where children had the opportunity to choose between puzzles, blocks and other play materials stored in a box which was accessible to children. Although the Balwadi closed at 4:00 PM, some children continued to play.

Personal hygiene of children was a concern in this village. We observed children putting materials in their mouth, running nose and eating snacks they brought from home without washing hands. The district programme manager (DPM) of Seetampet and members of the community also acknowledged the issue and said that they were making various efforts to address the problem.

Our observation suggests that children were engaged in age-appropriate activities throughout the day. The teacher was a local woman who was fluent in the local language and had clearly succeeded in establishing a strong relationship with the children. However, there were various materials in the classroom which were not used, as the teacher did not know how to use them, for example, basketball, hula hoop, stick puppets and some Montessori material.

7.4.2. A Day at Ghanpur Balwadi

Ghanpur village was about 8 km from the main road and 14 km from Utnoor, the taluk headquarters. Close to 115 families lived in the village, and their primary occupation was agriculture. Most of the villagers were engaged in growing crops such as cotton and maize. There were 15 children between the ages of three and six years in the Balwadi. The Balwadi was located in the centre of the village in a pucca (concrete) building with a spacious room, store room and veranda. The building belonged to the ICDS department, so both the Anganwadi and the SERP Balwadi operated from the same premise. While food and health services were provided under ICDS, the preschool activities were the sole responsibility of the Balwadi under SERP. There was enough outdoor space for play with a slide and a jungle gym, but no fence. The toilet was in a dilapidated condition and was therefore not used. The Balwadi worker, Anganwadi worker and ICDS helper were present during our visit. There was no helper for the SERP programme, so the teacher worked alone most of the times.

The Balwadi was clean, well organized and equipped with charts, alphabets and number cut-outs. The teaching materials prepared by the teacher, during her training, were displayed on the walls, focusing on various concepts.

We spent a day at the Ghanpur Balwadi to get a glimpse of teaching and learning process. Most children arrived at the centre on their own by 9 AM. Some were accompanied by a parent. Unlike the Balwadi in Seetampet, children appeared neat and clean and carried handkerchiefs in their pockets. There were a total of 15 children between the ages of three and six years.

Like the Balwadi in Seetampet, the day began with a prayer during which all the children closed their eyes, followed by a numeracy lesson on teaching of the first three numbers: 1, 2 and 3. The cut-outs of 1–10 were displayed on the wall in a systematic way. First, only the integers of 1–10 numbers were displayed on the cut-outs. Second, pictures of objects were presented, for example, four tomatoes. Finally, both integers and the corresponding number of objects were presented. Each child was asked to say and point to the first three integers for all three displays. While older children were able to do the task successfully, the younger ones appeared to be confused, which indicates that the activity was probably too challenging for the younger children. This was followed by a game and a song on numbers to further reinforce the concepts. This was followed by telling a story. After telling the story, the teacher asked each child to repeat it. Only the older children could do this, which again indicated that there was a need to modify the activities for younger children. However, the teacher conducted the class with enthusiasm and most children were engaged.

Next, the teacher dictated some letters in Telugu and children wrote them on the floor with chalk. A series of activities were conducted focusing on first three letters and numbers in Telugu and English. In between the activities, the children were given a toilet break for which they used the open space outside. We noticed that a village woman came and sat in the Balwadi, carefully observing the activities. Later we learned that she was the president of the village-level organization

At 12:30 PM, children were dispersed for one-hour break for their lunch following a prayer. There was no supply of food on that day from the mini Anganwadi and, therefore, children were sent to their respective houses for lunch. However, we were informed that whenever food is supplied under the ICDS programme, it is cooked by the ICDS helper and served to the children at the Balwadi itself. This was confirmed by our observations on the next day. A systemic collaboration between the Balwadi and the mini Anganwadi, was missing.

All the children came back after one hour and sat in their respective places. In the post-lunch session, the teacher organized a craft activity in which she helped children to make flags. She cut small square pieces of a newspaper sheet and asked the children to bring small twigs. The teacher then put some glue on each piece of paper and asked them to roll the paper around the stick to complete the flag. She helped the younger ones. It was an interesting activity, in which the children participated with great enthusiasm. Craft activities seemed to be a regular feature of the Balwadi programme, as children's drawings, clay work and saplings in small pots were displayed in the classroom. It is important to note that art activities are much valued in the Gond tribe. Some of the products created by children were given to the parents. The children then played an alphabet game to reinforce their concepts of letters.

The teacher gave them half an hour for outdoor play while she kept a watch on the children. Towards the end of the day, she took children out of the Balwadi in a group to visit various houses. After they returned, they talked about what they had observed. It was an interesting activity, which provided scope to engage children in a dialogue regarding what they had observed. By 4:00 PM, most children left for their homes, but some of them continued to play.

From the observations, it seemed that the teacher did not always modify activities based on the children, as she gave the same activities to younger and older children. It was evident that especially younger children struggled to make sense of some of the numeracy and literacy activities. There were many toys in the store, but those were not given to children. On our persuasion the next day, the toys were given and children were very happy to play with them. There was no division of responsibility between Anganwadi worker (AWW) and Balwadi teacher. The helper of the Anganwadi did not help the teacher. Therefore, she ran the show single-handedly. The AWW had received a school-readiness kit but did not even open it.

7.5. Curriculum

A centralized curriculum was planned for all Balwadis operated by SERP by the two resource agencies Sodhana and CDR with detailed description of games, poems and other activities. According to the director of Sodhana, the curriculum was planned based on classroom observations of the trainers. The topics were divided into smaller units and concepts were reinforced in different ways through games and rhymes, using teaching aids. Coordinators ensured that concepts presented during training sessions were implemented in classrooms. They not only guided the teacher but also demonstrated the activities when needed. Each cluster coordinator conducted two meetings with teachers every month. During these meetings, a monthly action plan was prepared in discussion with the teachers. However, the daily schedule was prepared by the teacher the previous evening, using a standardized format. The curriculum consisted of games, rhymes, reading and writing of the first three Telugu letters (number of letters increased every month). The goal was to introduce children to all letters before February of the next year. Similarly, English letters and numbers were introduced in a step-by-step manner. The entire academic programme was designed keeping in mind the local culture of the Savara and Gond tribes. Art activities were greatly valued and were an integral part of the lives in both these groups. Singing, dancing and music were essential parts of the Balwadi programme. The teachers communicated fluently in the tribal language. A handbook was available to the Balwadi teachers, which had a large collection of games, stories, action songs and creative activities relevant to the local tribal culture. The teachers were trained using these, with the overall objective of teaching the three Rs of reading, writing and arithmetic. The coordinators prepared monthly assessment reports for all the Balwadis under their jurisdiction, which included evidence of improvement in the learning outcomes. These reports were presented to the MMSs and the community.

The Balwadi teachers were trained exclusively by the two NGOs—CDR and Sodhana. The master trainers and coordinators were trained by a state-level resource agency, Andhra Mahila Sabha, in Hyderabad. The teachers received a foundation course of 16 days. This was followed by a two-day monthly training, which focused on review and planning. Training was primarily skill based and focused on various methods of teaching children followed by vigorous practice. While aspects such as infrastructure, enrolment of children and regularity were looked after by the MMS members and school committee, the responsibility of supervising curriculum-related aspects was with the cluster coordinators. Each cluster coordinator was responsible for 10 Balwadis.

7.5.1. Classroom Pedagogy

There was considerable congruence between the content of the training and the classroom transactions. The time table given was being followed closely. The children were reading and writing alphabets and numbers on the blackboard and floor. However, the early literacy skills such as tracing the letters and matching numbers with objects were implemented more systematically in the Ghanpur Balwadi compared to Kopuvalasa.

Children had free access to play materials in the first Balwadi. Both centres had adequate space for play. Although same activities were organized for both younger and older children, the younger ones were given more attention and not pressurized for formal reading and writing. Children were encouraged to draw frequently on floor as well as on papers. Their drawings depicted their surroundings such as food and crops. Among the Savara tribe, there is a close connection with nature which is often evident in their drawings on the mud walls.

By and large, a joyful learning environment prevailed, with lively conversations and energetic play among the children. In the first centre at Kopuvalasa, the maximum time was spent on formal reading and writing and 'routine' activities such as prayer, break and play, followed by 'rhymes and songs'. At the Ghanpur centre, the maximum time spent on activities was on formal reading, writing, rhymes, songs, pre number concepts, guided conversation and routine activities. The ECEQAS scores revealed that maximum time was spent on formal teaching of letters and numbers; however, it was conducted through a play-based approach. The activities organized gave opportunities to children to 'wait for their turn', 'learn by rote memory', 'play and work with other children', 'think and answer' and 'express curiosity' in that order. Majority of the activities were conducted using oral instructions using chalk, blackboard, floor, charts and dominos.

In both the centres, all the children were involved and most of the activities were organized in groups. Although the teachers reached out to the younger children, they still could not complete some of the numeracy and literacy activities. On enquiring, the teacher said that if she gave different activities to younger children, they did not like it and wanted to do the same thing. The teacher at Ghanpur Balwadi said, 'I teach them slowly and do not pressurize them.'

One or two children did not participate in activities, but the teacher left them alone as she believed that they would join when they were ready. There was a lot of flexibility and permissiveness. She permitted all children to draw what they wanted. They could take out any material from the suitcase (storage) and explore. Children communicated freely with the teacher in their local language. Children also engaged freely with other children and sometimes shared things with their friends.

In addition to the ongoing informal assessment by the teacher and the cluster coordinators, formal assessment was conducted once a year by the training centre. The items in the assessment sheet included the following:

• Joining the dots and writing the letters
• Ticking the correct answer
• Matching the pictures by counting
• Matching the similar pictures
• Writing the corresponding letter to the given picture

The SRI scores showed that only two children scored above 50 per cent. The children from Ghanpur Balwadi performed better than the Kopuvalasa Balwadi children. This could be due to the greater emphasis on teaching of early literacy concepts in Ghanpur Balwadi. This was consistent with our observations in the two classrooms. Learning is intricately connected with social–emotional skills. Eight children were assessed on the ABS. The children performed well in several domains, including socialization (6–8 out of 10), self-help skills (7–9) and communication (7–10). On emotional adjustment, except for 2, all others scored between 6 and 10. The findings were consistent with what was reported by community members in various conversations. They noted that children had become more confident and independent after attending the Balwadis. The observation notes further confirmed that children were confident in their interactions and not shy of strangers.

7.6. Partnership between SERP, Community and the NGOs

The Balwadi programme under SERP had three main stakeholders: officials from SERP, community/Mandal Samakhya and training institutions (Figure 7.1). The programme had the unique distinction of these streams working in a parallel manner. While general administration was looked after by one DPM who was responsible for the administration of programmes in the entire district, the academic aspects of the programme such as curriculum, classroom transactions, teaching–learning material, training of teachers and supervision were the responsibility of the two resource agencies—Sodhana and CDR— each of them responsible for a few districts. The agencies supervised the programme with the help of coordinators who monitored the implementation of the academic aspects of the programme. The third and most critical stakeholders were the community groups: MMSs, village-level organizations and parents were involved in the selection of Balwadis, recruitment of teachers and monitoring and providing support to the Balwadi teachers.

7.7. Programme Management

The organizational structure of SERP at the district level was as follows (see Figure 7.2):

> *District programme manager:* The DPM is a government employee in charge of all the rural development programmes at the district level including Balwadis.
> *Coordinators (2):* There were two coordinators—academic and administrative—at district level.
> *Cluster coordinators:* The districts were divided into clusters and 1 coordinator was recruited for a cluster of 10.
> *Balwadi teacher:* The teacher was the frontline worker, who worked directly with children and their families.

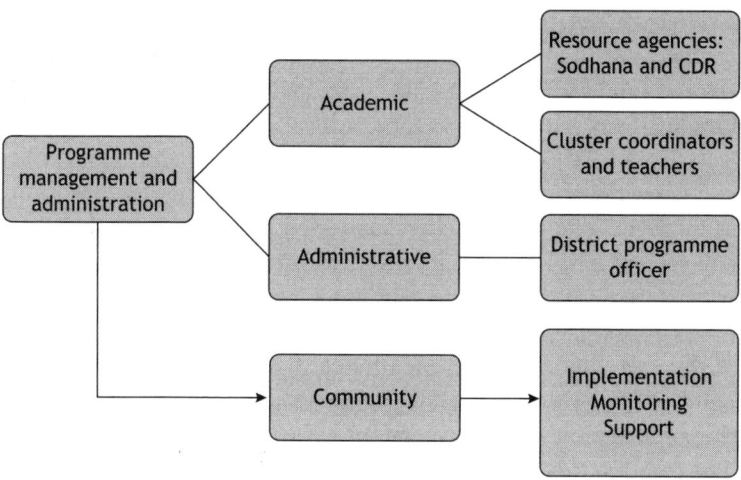

Figure 7.1. *Partnerships in SERP Balwadis*

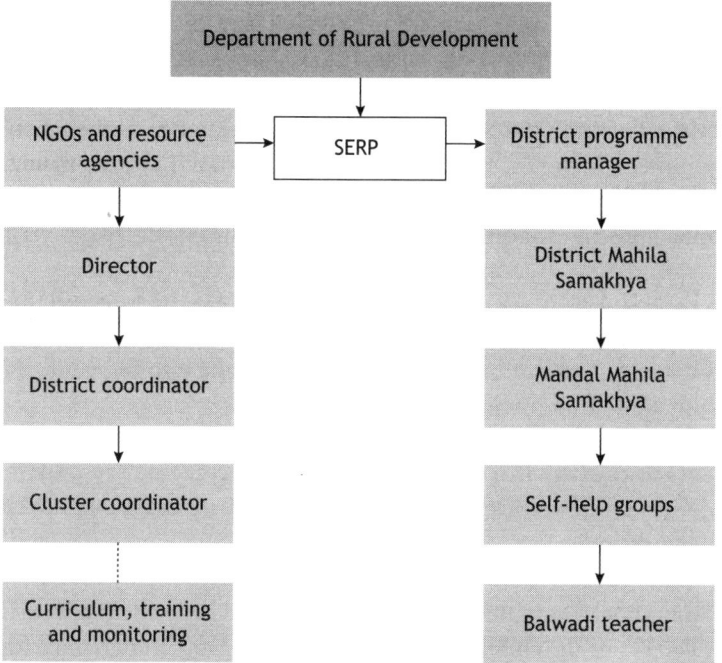

Figure 7.2. *Organizational Chart of SERP*

The MMS took the responsibility for the recruitment of the Balwadi teacher. When there was a vacancy, people were informed through circulars and by word of mouth. Candidates needed to have passed Grade 10 and had to appear for a written examination. All teachers were from local communities belonging to Savara and Gond tribes and knew the tribal languages. Both men and women were working as teachers. The local teachers expressed satisfaction, as they were able to find employment close to their family; as a result, retention rates were high. However, there was greater turnover among male teachers compared to females, as they were more likely to move out of the area. Some teachers mentioned that continuous support and handholding from the resource agencies and MMS combined with the appreciation from the community motivated them to stay on. The coordinators and cluster coordinators were employed by the two resource agencies. Most employees appeared motivated and worked in a harmonious way.

7.8. Parents' Involvement

An important feature of this case study was the parent empowerment model reflected in the constitution and the expectations of the school committee comprising of parents from each Balwadi. The rules framed by the MMS and the DPM for the parents were clearly anchored in democratic values and were displayed in all classrooms:

- Each and every committee member should take the responsibility of at least three children to come to school regularly.
- Every day, parents of two children should take turn to be present for an hour in the school during school hours.
- Every Saturday, all the parents are to be present for the exhibition of creative activities done by the children.
- Every week, stories, conversation and songs are to be told by the grandparents.
- 'Badipaduga' (school festival) should be organized every month by the school committee members. Parents should also attend this fest.
- Parents of the children should save at least ₹100 every month for their children.

The interviews with selected parents revealed that they deeply cared about their children's education. They reported that there were no private schools in the village, and they could not afford to pay the tuition fees and transportation cost for private schools in the nearby village. Their primary goal was to ensure that the children receive good education and become proficient in reading and writing in both Telegu and English and develop strong numeracy skills. They wanted their children to become confident. Parents also wanted the Balwadi to imbibe good values in children like respect for elders. They felt assured regarding the safety and security of the children as they went out to work. The teachers reported that parents took home the artwork of children and knew the poems and songs taught to the children. Thus, the Balwadis had become an integral part of the life of tribal communities in these villages. The parents were satisfied with the programme and were ready to extend any help.

7.9. Community-managed Services

A unique feature of this programme was that each Balwadi was started and operated by the local tribal communities. Their engagement was observed at two levels:

- Women from the SHGs were engaged at the village level.
- MMSs were engaged at the block level.

The Balwadis were started based on the demand from a community and with the involvement of MMSs, village-level organizations and SHGs. This engagement of the community-based platforms created a lot of goodwill and helped to mobilize the local community to engage in different ways with the Balwadi programme. The village people were engaged in constructing the Balwadi centres and in monitoring the operation of the programme and provided support to the teachers. The community members contributed material, labour, modifications and maintenance of the buildings. The village-level organization president in Ghanpur was a very active local leader who visited the Balwadi regularly and played an important role in mobilizing local people. The focus group discussions organized with village communities at

Kopuvalasa and Ghanpur reflected a high level of satisfaction among the communities. Below is a list of benefits reported by the members:

- Children were safe in parents' absence.
- Even grandparents could go to work.
- Children were learning reading, writing and numbers in Telugu as well as in English.
- Children were happy singing, dancing and playing.
- They were confident, not shy.
- They were clean and independent.
- They adjusted well in the primary school; earlier, they were not going to the primary school.

Mothers of children attending the Balwadis proudly presented the slogans composed by them during the focus group discussion in Ghanpur village:

- We are the mothers of Balwadi children (*Balwadi pillalu Balwadi tallalu*).
- Balwadi mothers, very good mothers (*Balwadi tallalu chala manchi tallalu*).
- Mothers are sending their children to school (*Balwadi pillalani balbadki pampudam*).

7.9.1. Role of MMSs and SHGs

The tribal MMS played a critical role in starting and monitoring the Balwadi programme of SERP. Ownership of a programme comes only when the power for decision-making is vested in the people for whom the programme is designed. Important decisions such as identification of a place, building of Balwadi and recruitment of teachers were taken by the MMS in consultation with the community.

The Balwadi programme in Seetampet was started by the MMS. While interacting with local people, it was learned that they needed someone to take care of their children when parents went to the forest for work. They also aspired to educate their children as they themselves were uneducated. The need was discussed with the DPM who explained the concept of Balwadi and sent them to Cheepurupalli to see some model Balwadis being run by an NGO called Sodhana. This visit was essential and provided further impetus for their demand to develop similar Balwadis at Seetampet for the Savara tribe. The MMS conducted a survey of the villages, explained the concept to the people and applied to SERP for Balwadis. The Panchsutra (five-point agenda) for MMS members reveals the nature of their engagement:

- The members will ensure that all children in three–six years of age group are enrolled in the Balwadi.
- One member of the MMS should visit the Balwadi frequently, at least once a month.
- Parents of all the children should save a minimum of ₹50 with the MMS for the education of their children.
- Every month end, there should be a meeting of parents and community members with the teacher and MMS members to assess Balwadi activities.
- The local elderly people should come and tell stories and songs to the children in the Balwadi whenever they have free time.

The MMS members took a keen interest in the preschool programme. They monitored the operation of the Balwadis through the village-level organizations and the cluster coordinator (CCs). Events such as illness of a child or visit of an outsider were reported to the MMS.

7.9.2. Badipaduga: A Community Event to Review the Balwadi Programme

Andhra Pradesh had a unique system of publicly reviewing the performance of all the programmes of the village once in a month on last Saturday of the month at the village level between 6:00 and 8:00 PM, in which both programme functionaries and the local community participated. The Balwadi programme was also reviewed in this event during which the work samples of the children were displayed. The teacher presented a report on the activities conducted by her during the month. The children demonstrated some of their learning by performing songs, rhymes and games. The primary agenda of the event was accountability, but a congenial festival-like atmosphere was created.

Parents took pride in their children's performance and felt more connected with the Balwadis. The teachers' salary was released after the children's performance at the Badipaduga. This is a unique system of community monitoring which instils a sense of accountability among the staff but is organized in a way which is culturally meaningful.

7.10. Concluding Thoughts

This case study highlights the values of collaboration between different stakeholders and the problems associated with duplication of early childhood services. The Balwadi programme was in operation for five years and appeared promising. The SERP Balwadis demonstrated the value of operating an early childhood programme, supported by structures such as MMSs and SHGs associated with the rural development programme and the civil society. The engagement of structures like the SHGs for involving the village community and monitoring was very effective. Furthermore, it illustrates that the academic component could be addressed by local NGOs through training and mentoring. It is important to realize that Balwadis and Anganwadis need continuous monitoring and mentoring, following their training to create good-quality programmes. The demand-driven approach of SERP, followed by close coordination between the various stakeholders, was critical for the success of the programme. The role of two resource agencies, Sodhana and CDR, in developing curriculum, training material, continuous training and mentoring contributed a lot to the quality of SERP Balwadis. While a curriculum was in place, activities were not always modified based on children's ages, which is important for learning.

Under the ICDS programme, there is a provision for providing mini Anganwadis in areas where access is difficult and the number of children is small. Both the Balwadis studied had such mini Anganwadis. Children had their food under the special nutrition programme of ICDS under the supervision of the AWWs and the helper also organized other activities such as conducting survey, coordinating health check-up, and immunization and care of pregnant women with the health department. The SERP Balwadis conducted preschool activities with a Balwadi worker dedicated to it. The Balwadis were in demand in these areas, as the preschool service in the ICDS did not receive adequate attention. Wherever a building for the Anganwadi was available, it was used for the Balwadi as in case of Ghanpur. In places where such a building was not available, the local people made one with their own resources and labour like in Seetampet. A major reason for the success of SERP Balwadis is the accountability of the teacher to the local community, whereas the AWW are not accountable to the communities they serve but only to the government officers. The two programmes were implemented by two different departments: Anganwadis by the Department of Women and Child Development and Balwadis by the Rural Development Department. At the departmental level, there was an understanding that the SERP Balwadis will be started only in the areas where there were no Anganwadis, but in practice this was not followed. When enquired about the issue, the senior officials mentioned barriers in communication between the two departments. It was also reported that there was no emphasis on teaching–learning in the Anganwadi, but the local people wanted education for their children. So the Balwadis were started on popular demand. It was observed that the AWW and ICDS helper did not participate in the activities of the Balwadi or support the teacher in conducting preschool activities. The Anganwadi centre had a lot of teaching aids and play materials, but it was kept under lock and key. The nature of interactions between the ICDS functionaries and the children was very different from that of SERP Balwadi. The latter was more friendly and kind to the children. It is interesting to note that all three, the AWWs, helper, and Balwadi teacher, were local people and yet their engagement with children was rather different, probably due to differences in institutional values, culture and training.

The Balwadi programme of SERP was a new and evolving programme. The DPMs who had been associated with the programme since the beginning were aware of the constraints. Some of the challenges reported by the DPMs were as follows:

- Problems in convergence between Anganwadis and Balwadis
- Lack of awareness about health, nutrition and hygiene in the community

- Continuity of nutrition programme in the Balwadis as supply under ICDS was erratic
- Conducting age-specific activities for younger and older children

On the whole, the SERP Balwadis was a promising model which could be tried out in other tribal areas. The structures for promoting community empowerment and the involvement of technical institutions were essential parts of this model. The concept of community monitoring (Badipaduga) was unique to Andhra Pradesh and Telangana, and a similar mechanism for ensuring accountability can enhance the quality of the early childhood programme.

CHAPTER 8

Relationship-based Programme for Semi-urban Communities

Nandita Chaudhary and Shashi Shukla

All children between 3 to 5 years should get rich human environment, an environment that facilitates holistic development. Every child has a right to a supporting environment and education. (Director, Bodh Shiksha Samiti)

Bodh Shiksha Samiti, a registered non-profit organization, was established in 1987, following a rather unique partnership in Gokulpuri, an urban slum community of Jaipur, Rajasthan, to provide education to children from disadvantaged groups. In the initial years, as they attempted to provide primary education to the children from various marginalized groups, they often had difficulty in fulfilling this goal, as most children were busy taking care of their younger siblings; those who attended the programme brought them along. Therefore, Bodh decided to start early childhood care and education (ECCE) centres to take care of the younger siblings of the primary school students. With some contribution from the Director, Bodh made a long-term commitment to address the needs of these young children. However, ECCE soon became a priority for the organization, as the administrators noted that the preschool programme known as Shala Poorv motivated children to join primary school and more importantly prevented dropouts. Thus, Bodh realized that ECCE was an important step in levelling the playing field and an avenue to facilitate community development. The coordinator of Amagarh centre stated:

> It was never only about the classroom and the children, although that was the central location of the programme, the community and larger society was always in perspective. And bringing the children in the schools on a democratic platform by providing them with good education, was an essential aim.

They developed a research-based pedagogy in consultation with experts and by reflecting on their own experiences. It expanded to engage in teacher education and curriculum development and established itself as a resource agency, which reached out to like-minded organizations across the country. As stated in the website of the institution, *The goal of the organization is to participate in the formation of an egalitarian, progressive and enlightened society by contributing in the process of evolution of a system providing equitable, quality education and development for all children.*[1] *The primary objectives were as follows*[2]:

- To provide conceptual framework, content and method of quality care and education and also ensure equitable access to it for all children
- To support 'hard to reach' communities in raising integrated community schools for their children's holistic development and appropriate education
- To build partnerships with government systems to mainstream and institutionalize tested and validated innovations
- To work with common interest groups and networks for wider policy advocacy and action
- To help establish and manage institutions that provide theoretical and practical support to like-minded people and initiatives/ organizations

[1] http://bodhindia.org/
[2] http://www.bodh.org/

In Bodh, it was believed that every child needed to attend a pre-school in order to succeed in the primary school. The coordinators of both the preschools which were studied stated that they observed a significant difference between the performances of children who entered the primary school after having attended preschool compared to those who entered directly. This view was further supported by the programme coordinator, who stated,

> *Preschool apney aap main ek bohot bada component hai. Zyada dikkat bachcho ke saath aati hai jab wo seedha primary main aatey hai. Primary school main aaney walo ki bohot si difficulties, behavioural difficulties ya adjustment ki problems hai ya retention ki problems hai. Wo bi tabhi rule out hote hai jab preschool se un ka introduction hojaye.*

> (Preschool is a big component in itself. It is difficult to work with children who come to primary directly. Those who come to the primary school have behaviour issues, adjustment problems, retention problems. These issues are ruled out when they come through preschool.)

A critical dimension of Bodh's approach to community service was the efforts to develop partnerships with other NGOs and individuals who shared their philosophy. The Bodhshalas or schools were developed through collaborative efforts of multiple stakeholders, including communities, local governments (rural and urban), Central and state governments, teachers, academics, experts and institutions. The organization took a life-span approach and developed programmes for children of different ages: preschool, elementary, secondary and senior secondary and vocational education. However, they are not just standalone programmes, but there are also interesting synergies between different programmes discussed later in the chapter.

The organogram (Figure 8.1) depicts two main arms: the administrative and the field personnel. The administration for Bodhshalas was headed by the director and joint director, who were responsible for supervision of other programmes, in addition to ECCE. The ECCE coordinator was in charge of the entire early childhood programme and acted as a liaison with the field personnel. A centre coordinator

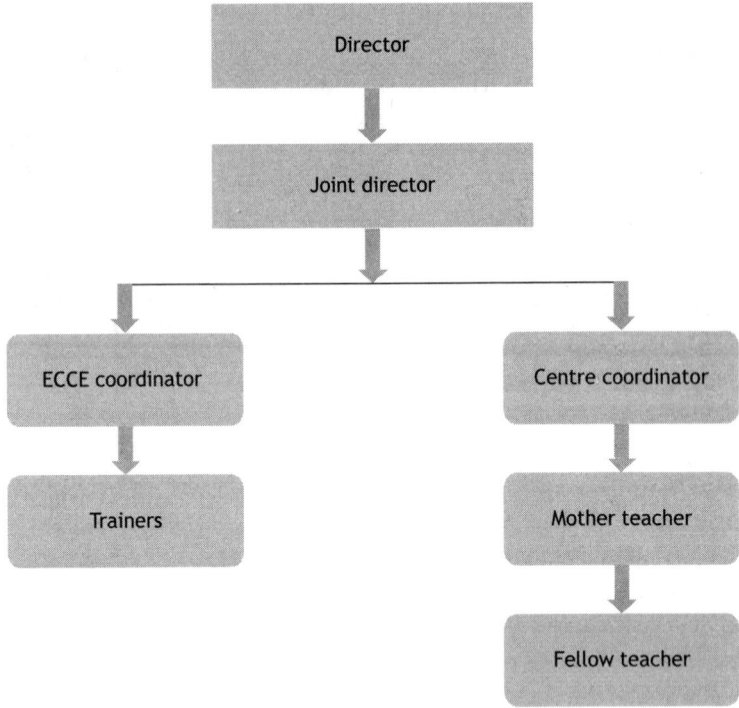

Figure 8.1. *Structure of the Programme*

was present at each site and was responsible for monitoring and supervision. Two important positions were created by Bodh for teaching and liaison with the community. They were the mother teachers and fellow teachers.

Bodh mother teachers usually taught the 4+ age children, while the fellow teachers taught the 5+ age group. Mother teachers were older women from the community who were primarily responsible for facilitating the transition of the child from home to the school environment. Most of them were illiterate. The fellow teachers were young women who were primarily responsible for teaching, admission of children to their centres, visiting families to encourage enrolment and leading the 'sampark' programme to remain connected with parents.

8.1. Profile of the Community

We began the study by identifying key informants who had a nuanced understanding of the preschool programme. There were a total of six Bodhshalas in the urban slums of Jaipur during the time of this study. We consulted the early childhood centre coordinator and selected two centres: one which was considered to demonstrate good practices and the other which was facing specific challenges. The two preschool centres chosen for the case study were located in Nagtalai and Amagarh bastis. These centres were operated at the Bodhshalas for three hours (Monday–Saturday). They were both located on the foothills east of Jaipur near the Delhi–Jaipur highway in Transport Nagar of Rajasthan. To understand the extent of ownership and impact of the programme, we interacted with parents of the children attending the Bodhshalas, teachers, centre coordinators, programme officers, the director, community members, retired mother teachers and other people associated with the organization.

8.1.1. Nagtalai

This region was spread out on two low hills and a small adjoining area, situated near the Nagtalai drain. The community consisted of migrants from different parts of North India, who came in search of work as this place earlier had many brick kilns. According to a survey conducted by Bodh in 2012, the small basti (colony) of Nagtalai had only 512 houses (population 3,109). A majority of the residents (60.09%) were Muslims. The rest were Hindus in unreserved category, OBC, SC and ST. The small, pucca (concrete), single-storey houses with tinned roofs usually had two rooms and a toilet. Many houses on the foothills were rented by the owners who preferred to live higher up. Majority of them had water supply, although we were told that it was unauthorized. Most families owned various modern gadgets such as television, coolers and two wheelers. Stone polishing was the primary occupation for men. Others were employed as daily labourers, in small shops or as drivers in nearby areas. The women were engaged in polishing stones and saree decoration.

Nagtalai basti had no other school, private or government. All schools were located at a distance of about 1–3 km. There were two Anganwadis in Nagtalai and one madrasa operated by one of the mosques. In the basti, there were two temples and two mosques. While the basti had three private clinics, there were no government hospital. There were two manufacturing plants for wrappers of snacks in the vicinity, and only a handful of women from the community were employed by these units.

8.1.2. Amagarh

Unlike Nagtalai, Amagarh basti's population had come from various parts of Rajasthan. Initially, people had migrated for work, considering the vicinity to the highway, with the hope of finding employment or starting a small business. Most of the houses in this community were pucca houses with a toilet. They were small, and the area varied from a maximum of 150 sq. ft to a minimum of 40 sq. ft. About 713 families lived in the 600 houses built close to each other along narrow lanes.

Similar to Nagtalai, there were single-storey houses usually which had a maximum of two rooms and a toilet, though no bathroom. Almost every household had a water connection. Most families possessed various gadgets, including coolers, television and cable connection. Some joint families lived in a single house, and each family unit resided in a room. The men were mostly engaged in polishing stones. Some were daily wage workers, while others worked as drivers or helped in the shops. We observed that most women were usually busy with household chores, and some were involved in decorating sarees with pearls and sequins. A few of them also helped in stone polishing. Amagarh basti had one private school and one NGO-run school, Prayas. In the catchment area of Bodhshala, there was no government school or Anganwadi. The nearest government school and Anganwadi were located at a distance of about 700 m from the community. There were several private clinics but no government hospital. There was a mosque in Amagarh, and the entire population of this community was Muslim. A madrasa was run in the mosque. The Bodhshala was located just opposite the mosque.

8.2. A Day in the Child's Life

The children in Amagarh basti started their day by getting ready for Bodhshala. In the morning, enthusiastic children were seen walking to the centre. Some of them reached the centre before the teachers arrived. Others were brought by their parents. Children not enrolled in the centre were seen playing with their peers and cousins or trailing behind adults. When the preschool ended, the children returned home with their elder siblings, peers or by themselves. Some were picked up by their parents. Once at home, they were seen in the basti lanes playing various games. Some of them tagged along with their parents to visit nearby places. Children were mostly seen playing outside their homes. Some of them visited the shops that their fathers owned.

In Amagarh, around 3:00 PM, all children (both boys and girls) above four years of age went to the mosque to read 'Sipara' from Quran and learn Urdu. They spent at least one hour in the mosque. Children below four years of age studied 'Sipara' at home or at a neighbour's house. After coming back from the mosque, the children again played in the lanes. Around 7:00 PM, they would go home to be with the family, eat dinner and sleep around 8:00 PM. The children in Nagtalai were mostly Hindu; they had a similar routine except for visiting the mosque. We saw them playing in the lanes or in neighbourhood houses. Some children watched TV at home. Most of them entered the house in the evening to be with the family, eat dinner and sleep. We learned that in both the communities, caregivers discussed with children about the activities of the day, usually in the evenings.

8.3. Shala Poorv: The Preschool Centres

The Bodhshala in Amagarh was situated on the ground floor of a double-storey building. Only one classroom was available for the two groups (4+ and 5+) of children. They utilized other facilities such as drinking water and washroom from the main primary school. Classroom space seemed sufficient to accommodate 44 students (22 in each group). Further, there was adequate storage space in the classroom for keeping teaching–learning materials (TLMs) and children's belongings. Children's work was displayed on the walls and on a display board in the classroom. There were two blackboards in the class, one for each group of children. However, the ventilation and lighting could have been better.

The centre in Nagtalai was started in 1989. The Bodhshala for younger children was located at the base of the hill, while the one for higher classes was located on the top. Classes were conducted in three rooms, with one room for the staff. The front room was large and was used for the higher classes. The two rooms behind were utilized for the preschool. The room for the staff was small and had some cupboards for storage of records and other materials. Compared to Amagarh, the classrooms were smaller, a bit untidy, with inadequate ventilation and lighting. Due to limited space, classes were conducted in shifts. In the morning, the ECCE children came to the Bodhshala from 8:00 to 11:00 AM, and in the afternoon it was used for the primary classes. The Nagtalai centre also had another small building nearby, where the elementary classes were conducted. This system of multiple classes was a recent phenomenon, since the preschool was earlier conducted in a small building nearby. In the Nagtalai centre, a range of materials were available such as blocks, net boards, buttons, abacus slates, chalks, puzzles, matchsticks, rubber pipes and beads, which they used to explain concepts. In the 5+ age class, the material was being used based on the activity. The 4+ age group was settling, so the teacher used TLMs to facilitate play. She laid down big rectangular blocks and asked the children to walk on them.

8.4. Curriculum

The curriculum framework at Bodh represents the institutional approach and pedagogy. The framework has been based on guidelines and key references such as National Curriculum Framework (2005), National Council of Educational Research and Training (NCERT) and the Rajasthan State Board-prescribed syllabi. Bodh took help from NCERT publications and the expertise of Professor Venita Kaul in the development of their ECCE curriculum. They also visited several preschools in other parts of the country, especially Gujarat and Mumbai, before developing their own curriculum. The members believed that the curriculum should be practice based and should be evaluated periodically. It should follow an iterative process of teach, practise and evaluate.

Emphasis was given on key areas of child development: cognitive, language, physical, socio-emotional, creative and aesthetic. Teachers prepared daily teaching plans along with the consolidated monthly plans, keeping in mind children's experiences in their communities and their needs. These were reviewed and finalized through special workshops with the coordinators and academic support teams. Promising practices were shared at various forums and replicated across multiple schools. We were told that the organization tried to move away from existing hierarchies in the society; therefore, principals or head masters in Bodhshalas came together with teachers to make decisions collectively through dialogues.

The pedagogy at Bodh evolved from an iterative process of conceptualization, implementation and reflection. The Bodhshalas or community schools played a particularly important role as platforms for experimentation and consolidation of ideas. A multi-level approach of teaching was followed, as children were grouped based on their pace of learning. The groups were flexible and children were allowed to change groups as they mastered certain skills and concepts. Teachers and children sat together in a circle. They encouraged children to ask questions, comment and participate in discussions. In Bodhshalas, a class was not expected to be quiet and orderly; children were encouraged to interact freely and voice their opinions. Punishment of children was strongly discouraged. However, the teacher–pupil ratio was rather high, that is, 1:30.

Bodh has been engaged in developing and adapting TLMs and other resources based on cognitive principles and contextual requirements. Over the years, a significant pool including games, puzzles, songs, cards, worksheets and charts wase developed using locally available materials. Many of these have also been modified based on classroom use and feedback from communities. There has been a special focus on utilizing TLMs in building language, literacy and numeracy skills in children. Games and other such activities are utilized in explaining concepts as well as enhancing developmental skills such as concentration, balance and eye–hand coordination.

Both Bodhshalas had adequate and wide varieties of materials for all the students, such as beads, net boards, buttons, shape equipment and colour equipment. All children had slates on which they could write, draw or play games. A lot of materials were available focusing on language and literacy, for example, charts, worksheets related to different topics, flash cards, masks and puppets were used to promote language and literacy. For instance, a teacher gave students worksheets with a parrot drawn on it. She first asked the students to identify the bird and then facilitated a discussion on the features. Children were then asked to colour the bird and the worksheet was displayed when completed.

The day began with everyone (children and teachers) sweeping the floor and laying the mats for sitting. The teachers asked children to sit in a square layout or against the wall. The duration of each activity varied from 30 to 40 minutes. Children were first engaged in singing rhymes (with or without music); then they moved on to other activities. The 4+ age group played with blocks, puzzles, brick blocks, number blocks and other materials. The 5+ age group was engaged in early numeracy activities such as shape recognition or pattern making. The teachers also conducted language activities and discussed animals and birds. Following which, children were asked to complete worksheets on that topic. These activities were followed by free play, where children were asked to choose the materials and activities. We observed children drawing on slates or on the floor. The day ended with a rhyme or a story or with outdoor play. While the sessions were conducted with great enthusiasm by the teachers, we felt that children needed more opportunities to talk and present their views.

8.5. Contextualized Teaching

TLMs used during the classroom processes were both designed and planned keeping in mind the resources available locally. Concrete low-cost material was taken from the surrounding areas, such as matchsticks, rubber sticks, pebbles, locally available chalk sticks and clay utensils, and used to make shapes by children. All the recorded songs and poems were in local language, that is, Hindi and Marwari. Concepts were introduced by considering items which are familiar to children, for example, Hindi–Marwari rhymes and relating shapes with locally available things like circle with 'rasgulla', triangle with 'samosa' and rectangle with 'brick'. Bodh values the local knowledge and use of local materials in the curriculum. Local materials such as matchsticks, slates and posters of local fruits and birds were used as TLM, the floor was used as drawing board. Children were taught about their environment using pictures of familiar animals, birds, food and activities. Mother tongue was used as the language of instruction and interaction. The teachers gave most of the TLM for free play to the 4+ age children and the 5+ age children were encouraged to move beyond exploration and engage in sorting, making patterns, etc. When children were asked to draw something on the floor, some of them drew 'samosa', 'doll' and 'gusalkhana' (bathroom), and others sketched various shapes. The children had free access to the material during the activity time and were praised by the teachers for their efforts.

Teachers often used children's home language for communicating. For instance, the teacher labelled objects using their Hindi–Marwari names so that children could understand easily. The Muslim children were allowed to wear their caps and visit the mosque for their prayers. This respect and acceptance of the local language, culture and religious practice must have contributed significantly to the popularity and acceptance of the early childhood centres.

8.6. Regular Assessment

For the 4+ age group, the teachers monitored the activities they performed during the class, whether it was a language, gross motor or fine motor activity. For the 5+ age children, the same schedule was followed till the children completed six months in the group. Then the children were introduced to Hindi letters (khel board words—*kup, nal, ajgar*), numbers (1–6) and various shapes. The children were then given worksheet and were tested for their knowledge of words, letters and shapes they knew by exercises such as matching, counting and copying. The teachers taught children for three weeks and repeated whatever was taught in the fourth week of the month and then took the test. According to the performance on the worksheets, the teachers planned their next month's activities, thus connecting assessment and curriculum.

The evaluation took place according to the activities of children, which were divided into three–four levels. However, the performance levels were relative to the performance of children in the particular group, and there was no absolute criterion for each level. The best performance of the children was taken as Level 4, and the others were ranked accordingly. A file was maintained for every child, which contained worksheets and evidence of other tasks completed. This file was used by teachers to review children's progress and identify their learning styles.

8.7. Warm Responsive Environment in the Classrooms

In spite of various challenges, teachers gave attention to individual children and created a warm nurturing environment where children felt secure to explore and learn. This was evident in the interactions between teachers and children and also between the teachers. The classroom environment in Nagtalai was observed during the starting of a new academic session, and new children were admitted each day. Some were shouting, others were crying, a few were lost in their own world. Parents kept walking into the class with their young children whom they wanted to admit into the class. There was no mother teacher in this centre. The teachers were struggling to maintain order in the classroom. They tried to use various games and stories to help children settle down. The children in the 5+ age group had been in the preschool for a longer time, and the teacher was able to do certain activities with them. They were sitting in their respective places and were listening to the teacher when she was giving instructions while distributing the TLM or while she sang the rhymes and drew different objects on the blackboard for identification. On the other hand, the 4+ age children were subdued, and it seemed as if they were trying to adjust to the new environment. The teacher in this group was also more experienced compared to the teacher for the 4+ age group, which was rather chaotic. The teachers took the children for outdoor play on the street which was used for outdoor activities and morning assembly. The teachers organized games such as 'I sent a letter' and '*aankh micholi*' (blindfolding the child and catching the others) during this time. The children enjoyed the games and loved the fact that the teachers were also a part of the game and were taking turns. The children who were crying earlier stopped crying during these activities and became spectators of the games; some of them even joined the game hesitantly. At the time of outdoor play, they were enjoying each other's company and were playing the game with rules. Both the teachers were affectionate and caring towards the children.

The energy of teachers in Nagtalai seemed to be low, when compared to the Amagarh centre. They spent most of their time trying to organize the children. The way they sang and conducted games was not effective in gaining children's attention. It is possible that they felt exhausted as they tried to engage newcomers. Moreover, these teachers had fewer years of experience and were teaching for only one year.

Generally, teachers and children entered the class together and were occupied in cleaning, managing and arranging seating. When taking attendance, the teacher addressed each child individually and asked about their well-being. The teachers interacted with children in a friendly manner and provided them guidance and helped when needed. During lunch hour, the teachers sang a particular song inserting names of each child. Upon hearing their name, the child got up, fetched the lunch box and returned to the seat.

All the activities planned by the teachers were child centred and age appropriate. In one instance, children were given matchsticks and flexible rubber bands to form shapes. Children had sufficient choices to pick objects of their own interest without interference from the teacher. Children did what they wanted to do, for instance, some girls were making earrings out of the material. The teachers did not discourage children from doing anything which was of interest to them. This went a long way in determining the confidence and comfort of children in the classroom. It was found that once the children had completed a particular activity, they were eager and enthusiastic to assist others, displaying a sense of cooperation and sharing which was truly exceptional.

In Amagarh, the fellow teacher of the 5+ age group and the mother teacher of the 4+ age group conducted some of the activities like rhymes together for all the children. The teachers were observed to assist each other while also guiding the children to perform well. For example, during rhymes session, one teacher and the mother teacher combined both groups of children and sat in a large circle. Then the mother teacher began reciting poems with actions, some with and some without music while the teacher moved among the students to ensure participation and also to assist or comfort the children. In Nagtalai as well, the teachers had a very positive attitude towards each other. They helped each other, and it seemed from their interactions that they were friends. They organized joint classes at the time of outdoor play and after school they worked together on developing the lesson plans for the next day. Also, they interacted comfortably with other teachers including the coordinator.

8.8. Role of Teachers in a Community School

A democratic approach was evident in their strong emphasis on community engagement. The Bodhshalas were envisaged as community schools, a platform for members to engage in the education of the children and community development. From the beginning, it was decided that women's leadership was critical to facilitating change. This was achieved primarily through recruitment and training of mother teachers and fellow teachers. They form a bridge between Bodh and the community since they belong to and understand the community and have a deep sense of commitment to their own people. Mother teachers, as a concept, was introduced to involve and educate the women of the community, as along with educating children it was felt that there was a need to create opportunities for educating older women. According to the joint director,

Zyada se zyada mahilaye agar is position main aa paati hai ki wo preschool ko samajhti hai or us main kaam kar sakti hai to obviously jo poori community ka education status hai us main bohot badalawaa sakti

hai ... or larger ek literacy and dialogue ka process ho jis se hum ek karke identify kar sakey or fir hum un ko train kartey jaye.

(If more and more women are able to join this position, understand the preschool and work in it, then the education status of the entire community can change ... and they participate in a larger process of literacy and dialogue as we engage them in training.)

The willingness and enthusiasm of mid-aged women were the criteria for selecting the mother teachers. They were trained in conducting activities only (games, puppet show, rhymes, songs and storytelling). The words of the joint director are reflected in the fact that most mother teachers were illiterate but eventually learned to read and write.

> We chose mother teachers from the community as they had a better acceptance in the community. They had to teach children by doing activities, so literacy did not matter. Every mother teacher taught and worked efficiently. (Programme coordinator)

Initially, it was decided that each mother teacher would work in rotation for only three months at a time. This rotation concept was employed so that most of the women of the community could have the opportunity to get the benefits of education for further dissemination. However, the project coordinator explained that this system could not be sustained for long.

> Later, we increased this time period for rotation to 1 year. The 'mother group' idea worked well for some time but then the mothers got offers for other jobs like 'crystal shining' and doing sequins work on 'sarees' so they stopped attending mother group.

Involving the women in education was a difficult task. In the beginning, mother teachers met with a lot of opposition from the community members who did not respect. It took them a lot of hard work and persistence to establish themselves in the community as teachers. Today, these women have become a source of inspiration and a role model for others. They are respected and consulted by others in many everyday matters. Their self-esteem has changed as they began to feel that they were doing something meaningful, earning and were supporting their homes, including their children's education. The following excerpt reported in *The Times of India*, Aug, 24, 2008 illustrates the significance of this role:

> Batool, a woman in her late 70s living in Amagarh slum of Jaipur, had thought she had learned whatever there was to know about raising children. That was before she became a 'mother teacher' at the Amagarh Bodhshala (school). 'Here, each day is a revelation of fascinating aspects of child development,' says she.
>
> Mother teacher is one of the celebrated innovations that Bodh Shiksha Samiti, the organization that runs these slum schools, has brought about. A mother teacher is a respected, often elderly, woman of the community who is trained to assist the teacher in the pre-primary classes. The children identify with her and the stories she tells while the school is enriched by a resource person who helps build trust with the community. Often, these mother teachers become an important voice in the community, helping solve problems and spreading awareness about why kids, especially girls, should get an education.[3]

The young and energetic women who were once students at Bodhshalas were viewed as a valuable resource by Bodh and were employed in the role of fellow teachers. This concept has merit for both the organization and the person herself (all the fellow teachers are females). Fellow teachers earned as they taught to support themselves and their higher studies. Simultaneously, they gained teaching experience under the guidance of mother teachers and programme coordinators, while the organization was able to recruit teachers who understood the programme philosophy. In the absence of a mother teacher, the fellow teachers with less teaching experience were assigned to the 4+ age groups, and those with more experience were assigned to the 5+ age group. The capacity of fellow teachers was nurtured through an intense capacity development programme, involving training, mentoring and supervision. They benefited from the focus on 'personal development' in the training sessions. The supervisors in

---

[3] https://timesofindia.indiatimes.com/india/Mother-teachers-pitch-in/articleshow/3397770.cms

Bodh followed up on the academic performances of those enrolled in the bachelor's programme.

Fellow teachers were taught to become independent, learn English, do their own work and document it. They also learned skills such as cycling and computers. During the orientation programme, they were asked to write their goals for the year. We met a fellow teacher who was in her BCom second year and was aspiring to become an accounts teacher. The quote below from some of the fellows illustrate the impact of the programme:

> *Jab se main fellow teacher bani hoon, tab se mujh main zyada confidence aa gaya hai. Main pahley kahin bahar nahi nikalti thi, par ab mujhe bus ke numbers bhi pata hai, or main bus main bhi jaati hoon. Shuru se main Bodh main padhi hoon, tow mujhe Bodh par poora vishwaas hai.*

> (Since I became a fellow teacher, I have greater confidence. Initially, I did not go out, but now I can read the numbers on the bus. I also travel by bus. From the beginning, I have studied in Bodh; I have full confidence in Bodh.)

Often, a healthy relationship developed between the fellow teacher and the mother teachers, as they worked together. The mother teacher taught the 4+ age group, while the fellow teachers taught the 5+ age group and had to teach letters and numbers.

During our second visit, we learned that mother teachers were not employed by Bodh that year for several reasons. First, the funding for the programme had stopped. Second, the initial concept of rotation was not being implemented so they were not able to bring in more women in this position. Finally, Bodh wanted the experienced mother teachers to be absorbed in larger roles of community education, vocational training and administration.

The teachers facilitated school–community meetings once a month to discuss aspects such as children's attendance and performance, school administration and welfare of the community at large. Furthermore, parents and other community members were encouraged to visit the school at any time and observe classes, share their suggestions to maintain transparency and create a participatory model.

8.9. Training Is Crucial

All members in Bodh believed that training and institutional support were the strongest pillars of the organization. A learning community was created by carefully planning ongoing training. They had opportunities to learn new information and discuss challenges through reflective dialogues. They read books such as *Bal Hriday ki Gahraiyan*, *Pehla Adhyapak* and *Totto-Chan* in order to develop an understanding about children. Fellow teachers were asked to read about child development, pedagogy and other areas and present the information. Reflexivity was strongly emphasized during trainings. The teachers were encouraged to examine their behaviour and attitude towards the community, children and parents.

The teachers and other staff received regular training organized by Bodh at their main office and also attended trainings, seminars and workshops organized by other organizations in Jaipur. Additionally, teachers attended a month-long workshop before the start of any new academic session and a one-day workshop at the end of each month. The trainings were mainly focused on teaching–learning processes, teaching methods, lesson plans and understanding children and one's own self. The trainings were conducted in the form of workshops where the teachers got hands-on experience. The teachers also developed TLMs.

> Training of teachers in Bodh is not forced. It is a two-way process between the trainers and students. During the training sessions, the actual classroom issues and concerns are also solved and discussed among all the coordinators, fellow teachers and mother teachers. All staff members of Bodhshalas reported being eager and enthusiastic about these sessions as they provide opportunity for improvement and learning. (Fellow teacher, Amagarh centre)

Simultaneously, there was great emphasis on self-development. They were given opportunities to polish their communication, language, speech, self-defence and other skills. During monthly review meetings, the coordinators asked fellow teachers to evaluate their skills and share their progress. The holistic approach to training is reflected in the content areas listed below:

- Their role in preschool (*preschool main bhoomika*)
- Study in the field of education (*shiksha ke kshetra main addhyan*)
- Study in academics (*academic kshetra main addhyan*)
- Mastering English as a language (*Angrezi ke kshetra main addhyan*)
- Keeping scientific point of views (*vaishvik vigyanik kshetra main addhyan*)
- Keeping track of time (not wasting time; *samay ki barbaadi rokna*)
- Excelling in other abilities (*Annay kshetra main addhyan*)
- Study in health, body and mind (*Svasthya, sharirik evam mansik addhyan*)
- Work at home (*Ghar main kaam*)

The coordinators gave the fellow teachers books and encouraged them to read books on general knowledge, literature and science. They said that this would help the teachers to form a scientific way of thinking. The teachers were also asked to keep reading newspapers, especially to acquire scientific knowledge. The teachers and the coordinator had healthy and open discussions on the issues raised by the fellow teachers.

8.10. Democratic Functioning

As evident from its constitutional provisions, the functioning of Bodh was clearly anchored in democratic principles of equality and mutual respect. Much effort was given by the leaders to create a non-hierarchical culture, where all members were given opportunities to voice their opinions and participate in decision-making. This sensitivity to maintaining equal opportunity is a hallmark of the history and organization of Bodh. We asked the coordinator of Nagtalai what motivated him to stay with the organization for 18 years. He replied that it was the 'freedom' to work.

Yahaan kaam karney ki swatantrata hai, koi kisi ka boss nahi hai, main apni tarah se kaam kar sakta hoon, yehi baat mujhe achhi lagti hai.

(Here we have freedom to work; nobody is boss. I can work in my way and that is what I like the most.)

Teachers and the coordinator at Amagarh said that they remained open to hearing the opinions of the community during their meetings and visits. Small details were looked into to maintain democratic principles during every interaction, between organizers and teachers, teachers and community members, and teachers and children. At the headquarters, meetings were decided as per everyone's convenience. The coordinator of Amagarh said that at times they held the meeting in the late evenings because that was the only time when all community members were free from their daily chores.

8.11. Dynamic Family Leadership

Bodh was initially spearheaded by a single person's commitment to the cause of community development and equal right for all, the director, Mr Yogendra. Usually, such organizations are at risk of becoming weaker due to dependency on a single individual. This was not the case with Bodh. The organization thrived because of its democratic principles and as several members of the family joined the organization in leadership positions. Mr Shasha (Mr Yogendra's son) worked as a consultant for Bodh and mentored various programmes. His daughter-in-law, Ms Divya, was responsible for the documentation of Bodh's work. She was also in charge of the 'sponsorship programme' through which people sponsor the children who cannot pay their own fees. Moreover, some of the senior mother teachers who had retired continued to offer their time to the organization. This was seen as a consequence of Bodh's dedication to democratic principles and strong engagement with the community.

8.12. Research and Documentation

Bodh was a research-based organization; decisions were taken based on evidence on the processes, materials, activities and outcomes at the learning centres. The process of research was built into the pedagogy, and students' performances were monitored regularly to make changes. In addition, they collaborated with outside agencies for evaluation. They had established a strong record for their innovative approach to research-based training and curriculum which was later adopted by other agencies like Nidan.

All the teachers and coordinators eagerly accepted the importance of evaluation and documentation. Impact evaluation was an integral part of the programme. Every teacher maintained a diary in which she entered her daily lesson plans. After the school hours, teachers stayed for an extra hour to plan activities for the next day. During this time, they reviewed the performance of children in different activities and planned the activities for the following day based on this information. At the end of month, the teachers usually gave a simple test to children to evaluate their progress. In the monthly review meetings, all teachers were required to share their evaluations and the progress of the class. Decisions regarding ways to address challenges in the class or issues with individual children meetings were taken during this time.

8.13. Preference for Bodhshala across Generations

There were many schools in Amagarh and Nagtalai community, including government, private, NGOs and Anganwadis. Parents repeatedly said that they favoured the Bodhshala over other schools because they felt that other schools could not match the teaching standards. This trust developed over several years, as many parents were themselves students at these centres. The legacy of a strong relationship can be evidenced from the fact that even the grandmothers and grandfathers also favoured the Bodhshala as a place to study for their grandchildren since they had experienced its benefits with their own children. Parents stated in the interviews and focus group discussions that their children visited the Anganwadi only to receive food. We observed that at lunch time, a number of children left to receive the meal at the Anganwadi. However, they returned to the Bodhshala for learning.

We visited some of the nearby schools to understand their preference. The private school in the area was an untidy place and the classrooms had no ventilation. The ECCE classroom had no electricity and did not have adequate space. The children were sitting on a mat, with a lot of old broken furniture piled in a corner of the room. There were two teachers teaching children with books in their hands. Prayas, a school for children with disabilities, was operated by an NGO, and the environment was much more child-friendly. The walls were decorated with children's work and other posters adding to the aesthetics of the classroom. The children were engaged in various activities in an enthusiastic way, such as singing rhymes. The teachers welcomed us warmly to the centre. However, the feeling that prevailed in the Bodhshala centres was of enthusiasm, happiness and collaboration working in synergy towards a specific goal.

8.14. Concluding Thoughts

Several features work in synergy to make Bodh an exemplary organization in the field of education and community participation. A key feature of this organization was the strong dedication to democratic principles which influenced all aspects of their work. This was especially evident in the value placed on community engagement and the participatory approach to decision-making. They demonstrated that it was essential to develop a developmentally appropriate curriculum, a warm nurturing classroom environment, and ensure ongoing training for teachers to develop a strong ECCE programme. Bodh draws its strength from the community in order to provide for them. The key resources that they hinge this dynamics on are the personnel and their training. The presence of a Bodhshala signifies strong community participation.

Bodh realized that women's engagement was essential for community development; thus, they focused on fostering leadership qualities in women of different ages. The mother teachers and fellow teachers recruited from the community reported going through transformations, as they worked intensively with children and the community. However, the assumption that mother teachers do not need to be literate appeared to be problematic based on the existing literature in the field of early childhood. Finally, the dedication to democratic principles prevented the leadership of the organization from being weakened by egoistic concerns, as consistent efforts were made to engage with multiple stakeholders and engage them in the decision-making process.

CHAPTER 9

Educating Children from Urban Dalit Communities

Suman Sachdeva and Ashutosh Mishra

For me, the soul of my work is the child. I would learn all to give my best to the young child so that she can grow up and find a beautiful future for herself in this world where the best is reserved only for the rich. (Teacher)

Nidan's[1] preschool programme was implemented in six urban slums of Patna, the capital of the state of Bihar. Most of the members belonged to the Dalit community, who had historically experienced extreme social and economic marginalization in the Indian society. The organization served 4,558 households with 21,158 members[2] through its intervention. Caste-wise distribution of the population served revealed that 50 per cent belonged to Scheduled Castes (SCs), 15 per cent to Scheduled Tribes (STs) and 31 per cent to Other Backward Classes (OBCs). Members from these communities were often engaged in rag picking, cleaning work, waste works, sweeping, basket making, etc.

---

[1] https://nidan.in/about-nidan/
[2] Data from Nidan records for the year 2012.

These livelihood options are often considered to be at the lowest rung of the caste hierarchy and are therefore vulnerable to discrimination.

It is necessary to note that the education programme of Nidan was developed following a decade-long engagement with the informal sector workers in urban areas. Intensive mobilization of these communities created awareness about the importance of education and led to a demand for preschool centres for young children in 2006. The American India Foundation (AIF)[3] which was funding Nidan's livelihood programme agreed to extend support to its preschool programme and facilitated its linkages with Bodh Shiksha Samiti[4] (BSS) in Jaipur, for teacher training and technical assistance. Thus, the case study of Nidan provides an excellent example of how best practices can be replicated and contextualized with support from the parent organization. This chapter presents various aspects of Nidan's early childhood education (ECE) programme by focusing on the following topics: background, the socio-geographical context, a day in the life of a child, programme replication and contextualization and community-based programmes.

9.1. Background

Nidan was registered in the year 1996 under the Societies Registration Act, 1860. The organization had FCRA (Foreign Contributions Regulation Act) certification along with Sections 12 A and 80 G recognition under the Income Tax Act. Nidan was intensively working with the people employed in the unorganized sector in the states of Bihar, Rajasthan, Delhi and Jharkhand.

The head of the organization Mr Arbind Singh spent his early years in north-eastern Bihar, a hub of first-generation migrants who travelled to the area in search of work. As a student leader in Delhi, he actively participated in drought relief work and played a key role in setting up a youth-led communal harmony programme in a particularly volatile area in the walled city. After completing postgraduation in

[3] http://aif.org/retrieved
[4] http://bodh.org/

legal studies, he felt an innate urge and responsibility to return to his community in order to devote himself to addressing the oppressive practices he had witnessed while growing up.

Upon returning to Bihar, he discovered a severe lack of social services for the urban poor. Following an anti-encroachment drive targeting poor vendors by the Bihar government, he launched Nidan in 1995. It was established with an explicit mission to 'provide quality preschool education services to children from marginalized communities' (interview with the head).

The initial support to Nidan was provided by development organizations like Adithi for activities such as agriculture and dairy industry, tree plantation, tasar (rough) silk, handicrafts, handlooms and horticulture. Integration of women in all these sectors was encouraged by Self Employed Women's Association (SEWA). They nurtured and provided systemic support through financial resources as well as capacity-building opportunities for the young cadre of the organization.

Nidan began by organizing the informal sector workers, beginning with street vendors in 1995. This group was empowered by establishment of market committees, neighbourhood groups, self-help groups, federations, cooperatives, registered society and trade union, and, when need arose, network and coalitions.

In 1997, Nidan started working with home-based workers. In 1998, it began an education initiative for the children of workers from the informal sector. This programme took Nidan to the slums and gradually issues of slum dwellers; that is, shelter, water, health and sanitation became important parts of their agenda. From 2002, they also began working with waste pickers and extended their work to rural areas to cover jute workers, agriculture workers, landless labourers, artisans, etc. Addressing various vulnerabilities and ensuring social security of informal workers became the core concern and expertise of the organization.

The strategy for preschool education as adopted by Nidan evolved over the years. Initially, the programme started with the aim of providing educational opportunity for children who were not enrolled in the mainstream schools. This initiative was an extended component of the organization's livelihood interventions. The very first batch of teachers received training for both pre-primary and primary education, as classes for both levels were conducted in one centre by the same person. The classes supported out-of-school children through a bridge course, and a school-readiness package was used for children in pre-primary classes. Older children often brought their siblings along with them, as the parents left home early for work. With the enactment of the Right to Education (RTE) Act, 2009, in Bihar, preschool activities were retained in the centre, while the primary special training classes for out-of-school children were shifted to the government primary schools.

The preschool centres of Nidan provided an alternative to the government Anganwadis (preschools under the ICDS programme) which were either not functional or not available in these areas. They offered education activities and health check-ups for the children. Moreover, they received support services for their livelihood and health. The communities appreciated their rapport with the organization and the free preschool education which the children received.

The objectives of the programme focused on creating successful preschool education models for children in the vulnerable communities. Specifically, the objectives were

- To advocate and facilitate enrolment of children of all informal sector workers in slums of Patna in formal schools
- To advocate for retention of all enrolled children of informal sector workers staying in slums of Patna in the formal school setting for at least 10 years;
- To facilitate access of children below age of 6 years to ICDS system in operational areas of NIDAN;
- To establish NIDAN as a resource agency in the field of ECCE.[5]

Nidan decided to provide access to pre-primary schooling through an approach based on creating preschools in clusters around major slums with high concentration of children from socially and economically

[5] http://nidan.in/nidanwp/Documents/Young%20children%20young%20minds.pdf

marginalized populations. The organization allocated one teacher per centre, and a teacher–pupil ratio of 1:30 was maintained. They felt that a teacher–pupil ratio of 1:25 would be best for transacting the curriculum but were not able to maintain this standard due to resource constraint. In 2012, there were 30 centres located in 18 slum communities.

The most important component of preschool intervention is the school readiness for three- to six-year-old children. The programme operated with the belief that a child who attends a preschool is more likely to learn and succeed in school. Investing in young children's well-being and development not only benefited the child but also contributed to a more productive population. When children are admitted directly to the primary school, chances of dropping out are higher. Even when children manage to stay in school, persistent patterns of underachievement are major problems. It is in this context that the early childhood development programme of Nidan focused on an inclusive approach towards education. A core concern of the initiative was to ensure a smooth transition from early childhood development settings to primary education. The organization emphasized on the holistic development of children and on making parents and families realize the importance of ECE in their children's lives. It is important to note that this perspective is very similar to that of BSS.

9.2. Programme Structure

An effective intervention needs to have a sound platform for programme management. Nidan had developed a strong system to institutionalize good practices. The roles and responsibilities of the various people engaged in service delivery were clearly articulated. Considerable effort was given to maintain transparency and build shared understanding about the organizational mandates and strategies through regular communication processes. Most of the staff associated with the programme have been with the organization since the inception of the programme (refer to Figure 9.1).

Area supervisors worked directly with teachers to ensure quality in the implementation of the project. The administrative and programmatic responsibilities were led by the programme manager who was supported by the head of programme quality. The RTE coordinator

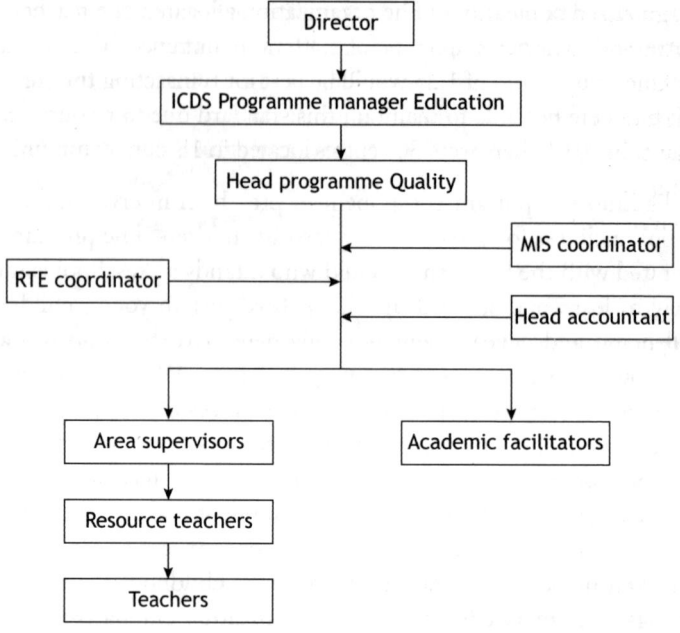

Figure 9.1. *Organizational Structure of Nidan*

facilitated the mainstreaming process by enrolling children from these slums in government schools or under the seats reserved for economically weaker sections in the private schools.

We were able to get a detailed account of the funding sources and the support the organization receives; networking with other agencies was also mapped. Efforts were initiated to change the existing funding structure to mobilize the community and secure funds from them. This additional responsibility was perceived as burdensome by the teachers. The organization had a clear plan for engagement of different personnel and the constitution of the team is reflected in Figure 9.1.

9.3. Socio-geographical Context

There was a dearth of basic health facilities. Small houses with one or two rooms were occupied by large families who lived in cramped conditions. Often, open urinals, defecation, garbage dumps and water logging were observed near the houses. Children and adolescents were found idling or playing outside even during school hours. Girls were observed taking care of their younger siblings and carrying them on their hips. The data from the organization revealed that 11 per cent children had never been enrolled and 7 per cent were irregular. Twenty-two per cent children attended government-run Anganwadi centres, whereas 53 per cent children attended Nidan-operated preschool centres.

Generally, the communities which Nidan worked with were more or less homogenous in terms of socio-economic status and did not report many conflicts. However, subtle power hierarchies were evident as families belonging to higher castes and upper economic strata which did not appreciate preschools being run for the marginalized. They just sent their children to other private schools which ran pre-primary sections. They did resist allocating permanent community spaces or vacant land for the centres, but this too did not come in the way of actually getting the land eventually. As most of the communities belonged to similar castes and were close-knit communities, they seemed to have no issues in sending their children to preschool centres of Nidan. We observed no evidence of exclusion based on caste or gender.

9.4. A Day in the Life of a Child

A young child's day in the slums usually began around 7:00 a.m. in the morning. Many of them went to the preschool centres at around 8:00 a.m. They got ready and had a light breakfast of tea and chapatti before leaving their home. During the initial days the teachers went to each house to bring the children to the centre. However, later children got used to the routine and came to the centre either on their own, with older siblings or were dropped by their parents. After attending the centre they returned home 11 am ate lunch, had bath and then play with neighbourhood children until 4:00 p.m. Their play activities included hide and seek, I spy, running around, playing with clay or sand. Those having television at home preferred to watch cartoons or Hindi films. Some of the children attended coaching centres in the evening. Play resumes for them after coaching classes followed by little study time or television time and most of them were normally in bed by 9:00 p.m.

Girls often helped their mothers in household chores and boys were engaged. Parents were observed shouting or hitting their children sometimes to discipline them.

9.5. Programme Replication and Contextualization

Nidan's programme was nurtured by Bodh, and it is worth noting that the services of both the organizations were anchored in democratic values with a strong emphasis on working closely with the community. The influence of the mentor organization was especially evident in the following principles and practices:

- Importance was given to developing a good rapport with the community and expecting them to engage in the ECE programme.
- Teachers were viewed as key agents of change and were provided necessary academic and administrative supports.
- Teachers were expected to form connections with the community in addition to delivering quality education programme.
- A well-qualified teacher was considered essential to the delivery of a good-quality ECE programme.

9.6. A Community-based Programme

There was considerable importance given to developing a trustworthy relationship with residents in the neighbourhoods. The community was expected to engage and take responsibility for various activities to support the preschools. The community supported the centres by providing land or space to conduct the preschool activities. The community members also dropped in at the centre during working hours, and mothers often got involved in the activities planned for children. Periodic celebrations and meetings were used to strengthen the connections.

However, this approach also posed important dilemmas, as the organization attempted to negotiate the demands of the community and recommendations from the field. Nidan was responsive to requests from the community; for example, children's periodic assessment was introduced as a response to parents' doubts about their children's learning in a 'song and dance'-oriented classroom.

This suggests that parents valued formal learning approaches used in higher classes, and there was a need to explicitly explain pedagogic practices such as play-based learning to parents, especially as such approaches are unique to ECE. In order not to offend the community, Nidan compromised on a critical aspect of its work, that is, holding the community responsible for sending their wards to centres. We found that the teachers spent a considerable amount of time ferrying children from home to school. This practice affected the time available to the teacher for instructional preparation.

9.7. The Role of the Teacher Was Crucial

Like Bodh, Nidan believed that the quality of the programme depended largely on the quality of the teachers. Therefore, recruitment, training and supervision of the teachers were planned with great care. The qualifications of the teachers were given much importance, and only those with at least a graduate degree were hired. This criterion was relaxed in few cases, if there was adequate merit demonstrated by the candidate. Many of the teachers joined the programme due to economic need, but gradually valued the responsibilities and freedom given to them.

> After preliminary screening and shortlisting from the pool of CVs, a candidate is invited to have a face-to-face interaction to gauge their attitudes and knowledge about education and the communities they would require to work with. Having cleared this phase, she is attached to a resource centre and is involved in a week-long rigorous fieldwork. Once this immersion process is completed, the candidate is assessed based on her report and final round of discussions. We want a passionate person to work with the children. We cannot compromise with the quality of the teacher. (Administrator)

An effective supportive supervision system was created to respond to classroom issues. Both supervisors and teachers were encouraged to maintain a daily diary, penning down personal, professional and emotional dilemmas. Diaries were read by the supervisors, and each teacher received individual support on the issues presented. Supervisors provided both mentorship and technical assistance. They helped in making the lesson plans and conducting the classroom activities. Most of the teaching–learning materials used were made by the teachers. Each teacher received ₹500 per month to purchase materials such as posters and charts.

Nidan regularly invested on training and capacity building to maintain high standards in teaching. Teachers found this to be helpful. The academic support to teachers was modelled based on the capacity-building structure developed in Bodh. There was considerable attention given to planning and review meetings. Overall, teachers reported that this was very helpful; however, they occasionally felt that it was also taxing.

9.8. Poor Infrastructure but a Vibrant Learning Environment

We visited three preschool centres and found that all of them had mediocre-to-poor infrastructure. Two centres were close to the main roads, posing a challenge to children's safety. They had temporary structures erected on previously used dumping sites for some centres. Therefore, there was garbage in the vicinity, making the environment dirty and unhygienic. Basic amenities such as dustbins, water purifiers, floor mats, open shelves, trunks and tables were provided in the classrooms. The classrooms were small and sometimes had earthen floors, seepage-ridden walls and broken trunks, although they were clean and hygienic.

> There is need to improve some services at centre. The hand pump besides the school was supposed to serve the children but as of date it is not accessible to them. There is always crowd of community people at hand pump and water logging there. Roof leaking makes the sitting difficult in rainy season. There is always fear of stumbling of smaller kids due to uneven and sloppy flooring. (A mother)

However, one of the centres had better infrastructure. Classes were held in a concrete building, though it did not have proper door and windows. It was an airy, spacious room with large cupboards and trunks to store materials and documents.

Notwithstanding the poor surroundings and infrastructure, it was a completely different experience once we stepped inside the centres. Entering the centres takes you to a different world from what you see outside. There were three teachers surrounded by children belonging to three age groups. They were engaged in various learning tasks using colourful toys, beads and other materials.

Children's work was displayed in various places. Letters, pictures and numbers were painted on the walls, creating a vibrant learning space. The displays on the walls were changed each month. However, some of the displays were not at children's eye level. A lot of teaching–learning material was available and was well organized. Materials such as flash cards, shapes, picture cards, picture charts, number cards, dice and matchsticks were available at the centres. Literacy materials such as worksheets, storybooks, single and double rods for counting, pencils and crayons were used for reading and writing.

9.9. Curriculum

Nidan adapted Bodh's curriculum for ECE, which was based on the National Curriculum Framework. It was designed for children in three age groups: three-, four- and five-year-old children. Activities were planned for 12 months for each age group. The nature of tasks children needed to master moved gradually from simple to complex concepts. Emphasis was given to early literacy and numeracy skills to promote school readiness and prepare children for Grade 1.

The pedagogy used in most classrooms was an amalgamation of free play and guided activities for individuals and small and large groups. These activities provided multiple opportunities for interactions between the child and the teacher and also between children. The seating was arranged keeping in mind the need to have adequate space for children to move around and have opportunity to play with materials. Children's engagement was described by a teacher in the following words:

One day when we walked into a classroom, we found that children were busy doing something in a few corners. They did not even look up. We went close to them and found that they were exploring some blocks, beads and wooden toys kept there. Some were trying to solve puzzles or playing with peg boards. These were colourful and well-equipped learning corners organized where the children involved in activities that they liked.

Teaching was rooted in the child's familiar world, and they were encouraged to explore materials from their surroundings. One teacher used objects from children's environment, including food packets, toothpastes, wrappers, bottle tops and flute, to a conduct language art activities in addition to reading local stories. On another occasion, a teacher provided a variety of materials such as pebbles, beads, twigs, leaves and asked children to classify them into categories. In another class, the children were asked to run and touch a person wearing a particular colour.

Children were often encouraged to draw, paint, speak aloud in the classroom, say rhymes and sing songs. We observed them playing with flash cards, geometrical shapes, beads, puzzles and clay items, which stimulate their cognitive processes. The activities conducted for younger children focused mostly on their perceptions of the world, but with older children these experiences were scaffolded to help them develop concepts.

Children were encouraged to express their creativity when they played with clay and beads or were engaged in drawing and painting. Teachers patiently addressed children's curiosity and attempted to follow their interests.

In addition to literacy, the curriculum also addressed social–emotional issues. In one group, the teacher asked children to draw their own faces to express their feelings such as happy, sad, angry or fearful. She then facilitated a discussion about their drawings without judging their work. In a different group, the teacher asked students to draw significant people in their lives, for example, parents, grandparents and neighbours, and talk about the importance of these relationships.

The programme attempted to create a safe and nurturing environment by developing trustworthy relationships. We observed that teachers responded to children's concerns with empathy. When a child came running to a teacher crying profusely, she immediately left her work, picked up the child, cajoled and asked her what was wrong. When she reported that she was hit by another child, the teacher engaged them in a discussion on how to address conflicts. On another occasion, we were engaged in a conversation when a child came and pulled the teacher's shirt to show her the notebook. She first attended to the child, praised her work, sent her back to her seat and then spoke to us. Punitive or verbal punishment was completely banned in Nidan centres.

The children were encouraged to greet elders and be respectful of them. They were encouraged to be sensitive to the rights and privileges of others. This was done in simple situations when children became stubborn and demanded things which others had or places where others sat and so on. Children were told by the teachers to calmly share their views and not to shout or throw tantrums. The teachers were quite adept at handling large classes where conflicts occurred frequently. It was a treat to watch how they helped children to articulate issues, take perspective and engage them to regulate their feelings.

Some activities were conducted to promote muscular coordination, basic motor skills and good health habits. We observed children actively engaged in games where they were required to walk on a straight line and curved lines, and hop and jump using one or both feet with music. Threading of beads and tying shoelaces were conducted to promote fine motor skills.

To facilitate language development, a teacher conducted a game of asking children to first match sounds and letters and then make sentences with those words. She also showed them a picture and asked them to narrate a story around it

Teachers gave them a variety of opportunities to listen to stories, handle and bond with picture books, learn rhymes, be immersed in a language environment, create, indulge in imaginative play, ask and think out answers, solve simple problems, experiment and generally have a 'feel-good' experience for a positive self-image.

In our observations, we noted a number of activities on school readiness focusing on early literacy and numeracy. The pedagogy emphasized learning by doing and discovery through exploration, and viewed children as capable of constructing knowledge. The role of the teacher was envisaged as a facilitator to create an enabling learning environment and scaffold students' learning.

There was a deliberate attempt to address issues of gender, class and caste through the curriculum. Teachers mostly gave non-stereotypical material to both girls and boys, for example, pictures of girls playing football or going to office, boys engaged in cooking or washing clothes, and fathers playing with their girls. They insisted on making all children sit together irrespective of their backgrounds.

A teacher asked the children to visualize a situation when their friend was caught in a fire. What would they do? Then they were asked to visualize a reversible situation and asked what their friend would or should do. Problems were posed which required children to engage in reverse thinking and ideas of conservation.

In one classroom, there were several puzzles laid out before the children, and they tried to work it out in many ways. Many were not able to do it correctly; however, the teacher encouraged them to persist in the task and not give up saying it was all wrong. Children were given opportunities to try out, manipulate, make mistakes and correct themselves. Sometimes, activities were conducted outside the centre to expose them to real life situations and generalize the concepts they learned.

> Preschool means that there should not be any pressure on child and if 'pre' is removed from 'pressure' word, then it becomes 'sure' that child will be able to adapt to the environment in any preschool. (Supervisor)

Children were allowed to learn at their own pace and provided opportunities for cooperative learning. There was also space for children to revisit the concepts and skills along with new learning so that the learning gets consolidated. Monotony was avoided by not continuing any activity beyond 15–20 minutes.

9.10. Curriculum Planning and Assessment

Planning a daily schedule for children attending the balwadi was seen as an essential exercise with a balance of activities around where the content was presented through a mix of activities for individuals, pairs, groups, in both outdoor and indoor environment. These were planned through a participatory process to ensure flexibility in the activities.

> I do not believe in following the rigid structure of classroom trans-actions. If a child is not learning through the method as planned or used earlier, then the teacher should change her way. Joyful teaching and learning are most important. A child should not be scared or bored and must enjoy freedom of doing what she wishes to explore. Children learn through games and sports. Children get attracted towards colourful objects, toys and eatables, and thus I use these articles to interact with them. (Teacher)

A systematic assessment system was instituted to capture children's performance and make curricular changes to address the needs of individual children. Their engagement and mastery of tasks were recorded daily, monthly and annually. A criterion-based assessment form was used to document what children knew or did not know.

Each day, the last one and half hours of the centre timing were devoted to recording and reflecting on the evidence collected on that day, followed by planning for the next day. Observations on each child's participation in games and other group activities were noted in the daily diary. A monthly assessment of competencies acquired was maintained to track progress but was not disclosed to children. Children's progress was recorded in a narrative form under different developmental domains, including language, numeric skills, communication and child's behaviour. An annual assessment was conducted to map each child's progress. The assessment was done in a group of five children along with their parents.

Table 9.1 presents the parameters used in the Child Monthly Evaluation Book and Teacher Monthly Evaluation Report used to track the progress. Teachers met daily to plan for the following day based on their classroom observations, assessment data and suggested syllabus. A weekly review was conducted by supervisors every Monday to guide curriculum planning and provide mentorship. The diary maintained by the teachers and supervisors was an excellent tool for these discussions. Key issues from these meetings were deliberated at

Table 9.1. Evaluation Parameters

Child Monthly Evaluation Book	Teacher Monthly Evaluation Report

• Month
• Name of teacher
• No. of days centre opened
• Child attendance
• Level
• Behaviour and habits
• Cleanliness
• Participation in assembly
• Physical development
• Educational achievement
   ○ Our world
   ○ Games
   ○ Stories
   ○ Environment
• Other observation/comments
	• Month
	• Name of teacher
	• Name of centre
	• Name of group
	• Level
	• No. of children
	• Regular, irregular and dropouts
	• Reasons of dropout and irregularity
	• Behaviour and habits
	• Cleanliness
	• Participation in assembly
	• Physical development
	• Educational achievement
	   ○ Our world
	   ○ Games
	   ○ Stories
	   ○ Environment
	• Organization of centre
	• Community interaction
	• Suggestions

the centre-level monthly review and planning meetings of supervisors, resource teachers and programme manager.

Monthly review meetings were conducted regularly with supervisors, programme manager, RTE coordinators and programme head to take stock of progress, issues and to plan ahead. An intensive organization-level planning and review was undertaken annually in a 15-day review-cum-capacity-building workshop in June, covering both academic and non-academic aspects.

The intensive process of planning and review sometimes dampened the spirit of innovation. At times teachers hesitated to try new techniques or lessons because they perceived the approval process to be burdensome.

Parents' perspectives were considered in the planning process. For example, after getting complaints from the parents that the children were not learning, the organization instituted monthly meetings and an annual review with parents where children's achievements were presented and assessment data was shared. Because of the poverty faced by the families, children were sometimes involved in rag picking, which interfered with their attendance.

9.11. Capacity Development of Teachers

Like the mentor organization, Nidan firmly believed that the quality of the teachers was critical to maintaining the quality of the ECE programme. BSS was engaged in providing technical support to the organization during the inception phase. Experts came to provide training and onsite support to teachers in Nidan. The impact of the mentor organization was evident in the following quotes:

> We found that the system of education at BSS was quite different from what it was in Bihar. All the 24 teachers who had gone with us had never seen such kind of teaching–learning practice in their life. (Supervisor)

> Before the training at BSS, I did not know how to make lesson plans and was not aware about importance of planning before teaching. I came to know about the importance of different activities for teaching–learning after exposure to BSS classroom. (Teacher)

Formal induction training was provided to teachers, supervisors and programme manager, using external resource persons. Moreover, a pool of master trainers was created to provide regular training to the staff. Training and review meetings were conducted at regular intervals every month. Finally, an annual workshop of 15 days was organized to assess the progress, discuss issues and plan ahead.

Teachers were encouraged to identify their weak areas and address them through peer support and consultations at the resource centre. If problems persisted, supervisors and programme managers stepped in to offer support. Some of the senior teachers were trained to become mentor teachers for new appointees. Exposure visits were conducted for teachers and supervisors to enhance their knowledge. One such visit was undertaken to Kerala to observe best practices in ECE.

Experts in the field of education, especially in ECE, from organizations such as Save the Children, PLAN and Aga Khan Foundation were engaged in bringing fresh perspectives. In addition, experts from District Institute for Education and Training (DIET) and other government agencies also provided technical inputs. AIF worked as a financial and technical partner to provide regular trainings to teachers.

The teachers played an important role in developing community partnerships in addition to their engagement in classroom activities. They arrived at centres an hour before the actual start of teaching activities at 8:00 AM and were present there till 2:00 PM. They had the responsibility of cleaning the centre, making the sitting arrangement, and arranging drinking water before visiting the community to bring children. After the classes were over, they were responsible for dropping children home and preparing the centre and the lessons for the following day. They were required to conduct two home visits each day. During the last one and half hours, they completed the planning and assessment.

9.12. A Community-based Project

Parents were consulted for organization of events such as celebration of Children's Day, Independence and Republic Days, any competition, festival and health camps.

Children from these marginalized communities, especially those of the waste workers, often faced discrimination during admission and participation in classroom activities in the existing government schools. However, parents were eager to educate their children. Nidan responded to this demand by establishing ECE centres in a temporary space and later attempted to secure a permanent land.

However, they did not assume that all parents would be aware of the value of education. Nidan conducted a door-to-door campaign and several community meetings to explain the importance of educating children and sending them to preschools. The employees observed that most parents had a strong desire to educate their children, as they did not want them to pursue their professions. However, their poor economic conditions limited their aspirations, and they were reluctant to send their children to school in anticipation of the expenses to be incurred. Free preschool education was provided based on the principles of equity to enable children to enrol and succeed in school.

Strong community participation reduces the capital costs of a programme. The space for all 18 preschool centres was provided by the community. Some of them donated the land, while others made financial contributions for the infrastructure. Both the centres we visited were initially functioning on the streets, under the terrace of government buildings or at times in a private home. People in Kamla Nagar fought a legal battle with the municipality, who were opposed to giving the land for the preschool, and won the case. Later, this centre became a resource centre. In Bahadurpur centre, a poor member donated a small piece of land for the preschool, while others contributed financially to construct the building. Electricity connection at every centre was extended by neighbouring families free of charge. They also ensured the security of the centre in after hours. In some neighbourhoods, people used the centre as a guest room at night.

Bi-monthly meetings were organized to discuss progress and ensure transparency. In one area, dispute over the donation of land for a centre was resolved by the community through public meetings. Members were engaged in celebration of annual events such as Independence Day, Republic day and Children's Day.

The neighbourhoods where the centres operated were highly polarized on caste lines; a school inspector who belonged to the same marginalized community opposed opening a centre, fearing he would lose his status in the area. The support from the community reduced both recurring and non-recurring costs, which had major implications for the sustainability of Nidan's programme.

According to the teachers, the various supports that they received from the community strengthened their commitment and prevented them from leaving the programme, even though they did not belong to that area. The biggest challenge for the teachers was lack of toilets in all the centres. The neighbours allowed teachers to use the toilets in their homes. One of the teachers who was there from the inception of the programme described the hardships that teachers faced. Initially, she held classes on the street, even during monsoon rains and the severe summer and winters in this region. She felt that she was able to sustain her work due to incredible support from the families in the area. She was never harassed and never felt scared going door to door or working late in the evenings when required. From the various anecdotes related with the teachers, it was evident that community support played a key role in retention of teachers for long.

> Once a child after closing of the centre went towards the main road and met with an accident. We were scared expecting trouble from her family members and community. But no one said anything or held us responsible. (Teacher)

Although parents had limited understanding of current educational practices, they often visited centres and participated in the classroom activities. They wanted a programme with a strong academic focus, which was not consistent with what is considered developmentally appropriate in the field. Due to the visits, they began to recognize the importance of learning through play-based activities in a joyful environment.

Parents were largely satisfied and appreciated what children learned in the preschools. Specifically, they mentioned hygiene practices, dressing up, respecting and communicating with elders. The following quote from a mother illustrates their vision of the partnership:

> Education of a child is not only the responsibility of teachers. Teachers here put a lot of hard work in educating these children. But parents should equally take care with the same zeal. They should visit schools and talk to teachers. I do it regularly; that is why all the teachers even in primary schools where my older child is studying are happy with me.

9.13. Collaborations

The costs of operating the programme were reduced through the partnerships developed by Nidan. It is understood that resources are extremely important to establish and test out models, and in this regard, the suggestions from the donors are respected and welcomed. The primary donor AIF supported Nidan to network with other agencies and take advantage of their expertise. Activities such as capacity building of teachers, syllabus planning and pedagogical decision were conducted with support from other agencies.

An important strategy used by Nidan was to diversify sources of funding. AIF covered major costs such as salaries, administrative costs, travel, training, capacity building and miscellaneous. Telecom companies such as Uninor and Reliance supported the centres through a provision of utilities such as water purification system, garbage box and fans. A few private schools in the area organized health camps for children of the centres and ensured that vaccinations were given at regular intervals.

A comprehensive financial planning was conducted annually and was linked to organizational planning. At the beginning of the year, the entire programme management team, including the programme director, programme manager, supervisors and resource teachers, came together and forecasted the needs and requirements of the following year. Since staff from different levels were involved in this process, not many issues emerged during implementation. According to the programme manager, 'This has been possible due to learning from the six years of continuous planning for same project.'

The process was guided by the organization's vision as well as donor commitment. Suggestions from the donors were considered during the planning process.

Salaries of teachers were directly transferred to their accounts through RTGS system to ensure efficiency and transparency. Procurement of materials and goods in the programme was done through empanelled vendors finalized after due diligence each year. Different staff members, ranging from supervisor to the director, were designated for approvals of purchases of varied amounts. Monitoring of income and expenditure was conducted through the accounting software. Daily expenditure was recorded under the planned head, and a report was generated. A monthly report was sent to the donors, so that the system could flag over expenditures at the earliest.

9.14. Concluding Thoughts

The success of the programme may be attributed to four major factors. First, they were able to identify loopholes in the existing system and identify the target beneficiaries who were not able to access government services. They deliberately avoided duplication of services. Second, community engagement was crucial. When there was a demand from the people, it was easier to work on community ownership. A strategy for community mobilization was put in place right from the inception. Third, rigorous financial and academic planning had been a major thrust. Finally, the quality of education generated further demand for expansion of the programme. According to the programme manager, 'The overall environment is very crucial in ECE centres. Teachers, teaching–learning material and methodology of teaching along with quality assessment and feedback processes have given us a wherewithal to replicate this programme anywhere.'

Nidan was contemplating various ways to sustain the programme; they were aware of the vulnerability related to grant funding. First, they were exploring whether the government could take up the programme, given the demand for it. Second, they were trying to put together a corpus fund in consultation with leaders from the community. Third, they were introducing a participation fee. There was no minimum amount, and parents would voluntarily contribute at their convenience. This was introduced to develop a culture of paying for services which the members accessed. Fourth, teachers were given the responsibility to collect funds from the parents. They were also encouraged to contribute a portion of their salary. Combining various models of fundraising and advocacy with the government, they expected to generate sufficient funds a few years down the line to make the centres sustainable.

> Nidan model is being very cost effective as community owns the centre and programme does not have to pay for space or electricity. We are exploring the ways to raise the fund from community which could be used for paying staff salaries and cost of TLM. (Program manager)

CHAPTER 10

Community-based Programme in Urban Slums

Usha Nayar and Reeta Sonawat

Pratham's strongest point so far is its ability to mobilize people. Our capacity to deliver high-quality educational services is limited by the abilities of the very people who provide energy on a large scale. Five years from now, Pratham[1] should be recognized not only for its ability to mobilize people, but also for its ability to build capacities to deliver a high-quality, education-related services.

—Dr Madhav Chauhan, CEO, Pratham
(Stanford Social Innovation Review, 2011)[2]

Pratham is one of the largest non-governmental organizations in India committed to improving the quality of education for children living in poverty. Their goal is to create innovative, replicable programmes to address existing gaps in the education system for children of various ages. They have not only developed programmes to work directly with children and their families but also entered into partnerships with government systems to improve learning outcomes at scale. Pratham's

[1] https://www.pratham.org/programs/education/early-childhood-education/
[2] https://ssir.org/articles/entry/in-depth_interview_dr._madhav_chavan#

work in early childhood education (ECE) began with the launch of community-based preschool centres in Mumbai but expanded considerably over a period of two decades and provides services through the direct approach, Anganwadi support approach and the government partnership approach.[3] Various institutions such as NYU Stern have studied the organizational model adopted by Pratham in the field of education for the disadvantaged children (NYU Stern School of Business, n.d.). Additionally, the organization has been recipient of various awards, including the 2011 Skoll Award for Social Entrepreneurship.

This case study presents a snapshot of Pratham's Balwadi programme in Mumbai, where the initiative began, and the ways it affected the lives of children and families. It is an example of the direct approach taken by the organization, which provides the opportunities to experiment with new ideas and demonstrate best practices. This programme has been replicated in 10 states of India.

10.1. Background

The initiative was started in 1994 with the visionary leadership of Dr Madhav Chauhan and Ms Farida Lambe, along with the active support of the commissioner of the Municipal Corporation of Greater Mumbai, UNICEF, and several prominent citizens of the country. Pratham, a not-for-profit organization, was established as a public charitable trust. The founders of the organization were committed to devoting their resources for children from the disadvantaged sections of society and to bring about a transformation in the field of education through community involvement, with a special focus on the quality of education. A social justice orientation and human rights framework guided their vision for the programme.

'Pratham was established to address the issue of pre-primary and primary education in India'. The various initiatives of the organization were held together by a common set of objectives:

- To increase enrolment of children in school
- To increase learning in schools and educate communities

[3] Pratham website, February 2021.

- To ensure that the education programme reaches children from communities who are otherwise unable to attend school
- To develop methods/models of education which can be easily replicated and scaled across large groups of children, so as to achieve the maximum impact

Farida Lambe, co-founder of Pratham, stated, 'Trusting people's ability, Pratham started community empowered Balwadis in the slums of Mumbai as the first step of education for every child.' The organization works closely with communities in urban slums and rural and tribal areas with an agenda to support people to develop a nuanced understanding of quality of education and motivate members to become advocates for the children in their communities. They connected with local political leaders to create a supportive agenda for the children.

UNICEF funded Pratham during the first three years, considered to be the foundational period. In 1997, ICICI, a private sector bank in India, assumed the main role of providing support. Since then, the involvement of the corporate sector in India increased significantly. At the time of the study, the Board of Pratham India Education Initiative consisted of eminent leaders from the corporate, academic, research and development sectors. The board was primarily involved in overseeing, supervising and guiding the progress of the Pratham movement across India. The board members, irrespective of the companies, were committed towards providing financial, infrastructural and human resources support to Pratham. The organization operated its programmes through decentralized initiatives in the form of local trusts in the entire country. Pratham's simple yet powerful mission statement 'Every child in school and learning well' attracted volunteers from diverse backgrounds.

Pratham approached ECE from an ecological perspective by launching a variety of programmes which addressed the needs of children and families living in vulnerable communities. Therefore, the Balwadis were embedded in a network of other community programmes which addressed related issues and augmented the services provided. Some of the salient programmes on the ground were read India, English learning programme, computer-aided learning, vocational skills programme and mother literacy programme. They also created opportunities for additional reading by setting up libraries for children. Steps were taken to systematically address issues of women's empowerment among the preschool teachers using tools for community participation.

Alternative pathways were created for children who were unable to attend or cope with the demands of regular schools. They were given the opportunity to join open schools, where education was provided based on their abilities and adapted to their needs. In many ways, Pratham has brought about a silent revolution in education in India at the community grass-roots level. The chapter is organized under the following sections: socio-geographical context, home environment, community-based preschool and emphasis on parent engagement.

10.2. Socio-geographical Context

Balwadis were set up across the entire city of Mumbai for children in the age group of three to six years belonging to families living in poverty. The city was divided into four zones, namely:

Zone 1: Colaba and Mahim
Zone 2: Bandra and Borivali
Zone 3: Mulund and Kurla
Zone 4: Mankhurd and Tilak Nagar

Each zone had a programme leader who was in charge of setting up the programme for that particular zone. This individual was responsible for leading a team consisting of area supervisors, coordinators and teachers to operate the preschool centres.

The Balwadi programme was often conducted in the homes of the preschool teachers. While this disrupted the family routine, from the children's perspective, they were learning in a familiar environment in their neighbourhood. The concept of neighbourhood schools was kept in mind, and each Balwadi provided services only to the children living in the surrounding areas. The site of the centres varied greatly; for example, the classes were conducted in temples, community rooms, under a tree or in the house of the teacher or another community member. Generally, they were close to the children's homes, and as already noted, teachers also belonged to the same community. The Balwadi programme was conceptualized to promote the cognitive, language, social, emotional and motor development of children and prepare them for schooling.

After reviewing the list of Balwadis provided by the administration, we visited some of the centres which had been operating for at least five years, to check regularity, accessibility, attendance of children, and the interest of teachers and community members to participate in the study. Based on these criteria, we identified two Balwadis in Zone 2 (Bandra–Borivali). One Balwadi was located at Gilbert Hill, Papdi Chawl, Andheri (West), while the other at Agripada, near Western Express Highway, Santacruz (East). Both the Balwadis were under the jurisdiction of the same programme head.

These centres were located in the slums of Mumbai, often in narrow lanes. There was a serious space crunch, and there was limited access to basic amenities; for example, water and toilet facilities were scarce. Common toilets were available for use by the children. Typically, a small room was provided by the municipal corporations to conduct various social gatherings. Some NGOs and members from active political parties managed these common spaces which were used for multiple purposes. Pratham leaders had to negotiate with various stakeholders including the caretakers to gain access to the community centres.

At Gilbert Hill, Papdi Chawl, the centre was located in the teacher's home. It was a small rectangular room, and she used the space creatively to set up the preschool. To reach the Balwadi, one had to climb a hill which had a kutcha narrow road. Along the road, there was a huge dumping ground and a sewage drain. There were some goats lying on the road, and it was difficult to walk through the remaining space. After climbing down, there was a lane of houses to the right, where the children lived with their families.

The other Balwadi was situated in Agripada on the east side, a slum close to Santa Cruz Western Express Highway. The centre was operated in a room which belonged to Shiv Sena, a political party. The *shakha* (branch) had a very small ground outside, where the children of the community played. The space at the entrance was used as a library where several daily newspapers were available for reading. The space accommodated 15 persons at a time—some were sitting and others standing at the time of our visit. As we entered, we saw a mixed age group of people—young adults, middle-aged and old men—in the library, some reading newspapers and others waiting for their turn to read a paper of their choice. There were no women in the library. Adjacent to the Balwadi, there was a small snacks shop which had biscuits, ready-to-eat items and stationaries. Just outside the Balwadi, there was an open ground which had a big Peepal (sacred fig) tree. It seemed that the Hindu community had probably celebrated the Teej festival in the monsoon season as there were colourful threads tied around the tree.

During the morning hours, the residents were occupied in daily chores in spite of heavy rains—a typical scene in Mumbai during the monsoons. The roads were busy with men and women travelling to various destinations with their umbrellas. We observed many students wearing raincoats or carrying umbrellas as they walked hurriedly to their schools.

One of the Balwadis was located in a predominantly Muslim community, while the other was located in a primarily Hindu community. The Balwadi in the Muslim area was located in the teacher's home, while the Balwadi in the Hindu community was located in a community centre belonging to Shiv Sena. The same building was also used to operate an Anganwadi programme by the ICDS. The reason for Balwadi and Anganwadi to operate at the same time in the same room was not clear. The space was also used by members of the community for various social and political activities. The education level of the fathers in the Muslim community varied between Grades 4 and 9. Most of them worked as carpenters, helpers and spot boys in the film industry. However, the education level of the mothers was comparatively higher and varied from Grades 4 to 11. In the Hindu community, most families belonged to different parts of Maharashtra, but a few had migrated from the Hindi belt. The fathers in this neighbourhood had completed Grade 10, whereas the mothers' education varied from Grades 4 to 10. The fathers worked as peons, electricians and workers at petrol pumps. Most mothers in the two neighbourhoods were housewives. One of them explained, '*Hum toh ghar sambhalte hai aur bachcho ka dhyaan rakhte hai*' (We look after the house and take care of the children).

10.3. Home Environment

We visited the two neighbourhoods where the centres were located to interact with parents and observed children playing individually and in groups with or without toys. It was rather interesting to observe a child pretending to be a teacher and teaching the concepts she had learned at the Balwadi to her younger siblings at home. During home visits, we noticed that some children answered the door more eagerly and communicated freely, while others were hesitant.

The data suggests that children had a rich social life in their family environment in both the communities. This section presents a glimpse of learning materials, daily routine, nature of interactions and disciplining approaches. Children in both the communities had access to a variety of print materials at home. These included school textbooks, picture books, children's storybooks, alphabet/barakhadi/number books, newspapers calendars, religious texts, novels and magazines. In addition, some homes had art and craft materials, CDs/cassettes and board games or equipment for sports.

The older siblings were responsible for looking after the younger children in the mornings and for waking them up, dressing and feeding them. Mothers were usually busy preparing meals during this time. The older children usually left for school earlier. The mother or the grandmother dropped the child to the Balwadi. When the preschool ended, the children would head home and spend their time playing with their peers in the neighbourhood. From interviews with parents, we learned that children in one of the communities needed help when feeding, dressing and using the toilet but children in the other community did not need this support. Some of these skills such as feeding and use of toilet help children to participate more fully in school settings. The reason for these variations was not very clear, as we did not study the child-rearing practices in these communities.

The mothers taught their children at home, took them to the parks and played with them. They tried to take a balanced approach as they negotiated the parental dilemmas to ensure they were neither too strict nor too lenient. This was most evident in how they disciplined their children, which was a priority for the parents. They followed the traditional practice of disciplining their children by referring to their father or teacher as an important authority figure. Conversations with various families indicated that parents did not indulge in corporal punishment to young children, and there may have been changes in disciplining practices, as illustrated by the following quotes:

> Mother: '*Pyaar se seekhati hun. Maaregi toh bachche nahi seekhenge; aur jyada karenge.*' (I try to teach with love. If I hit them, then they will not learn; instead, the problem will become worse.)

> Mother: '*Anushasan ke liye yehi bolta hu ki ye galathaiye nahi karna. Main maarta nahi hu, sirf daanta hu.*' (To maintain discipline, I ask him not to do wrong things. I only scold him and do not hit him.)

> Mother: '*Main toh cheella deti hu. Main aise dhamki deti hu ki main papa ko phone laga rahi hu fir wo aake peetenge ya teacher ko bolungi, toh wo shaant ho jaate hai.*' (I scold them and threaten them that if they don't listen to me, I will either tell their father who will scold them on his return or that I will complain to their teacher. On hearing that, children calm down.)

> Father: '*Jyada shaitaani karti hai to ek side me baitha deta hu aur bolta huu thek nahi; jyada cheellata nahi. Maarke bhi koi matlab nahi.*' (If she is too naughty, I make her sit on the side and tell her that what she is doing is not right; I don't shout at her too much. And I do not see any point in hitting her.)

Parents expected children to learn good manners and respect their elders.

> *Acha swabhaav, achi tarah se rehna, padhna; unko pata chalna chahiye ki kaisa behave karna chahiye mummy–papa ke saath, bade log ke saath … ye sab seekhana chahiye.*

(The children should learn how to behave properly, treat their own parents and elders with respect. These are essential skills that should be taught.)

All parents were interested in educating their children, but some were more competitive. They encouraged their children to learn more than what the teacher teaches and stay ahead of others:

Main chahti hu jo teacher ne padhaya hai wo usse aage badhe, jo pad-haya hai wo uske mind me ghusa rahe ki main ye padh chuka hu, mujhe aata hai. Jaise aaj teacher ne 2 ki table batai hai, to wo 3 aur 4 ki bhi bataye; sab bachcho se mera bachcha aage rahe. Main bolti bhi hu dono bachcho ko ki school me jo padhate hai, usse jyada seekho.

(I want my child to work harder and learn more than what is being taught at school. I want my child to excel above all the other children. For example, if the teacher has taught him the table of 2, he should also on his own learn the tables of 3 and 4.)

10.4. Community-based Preschool

Pratham's preschool programme was clearly grounded in a community participation model. Members of the local community were involved in making decisions regarding the venue and ongoing management of the centres. They identified local women from the community for the position of teachers. In fact, opening a Balwadi, facilitated by Pratham, in their locality was a matter of pride for the local people. During the time of this study, the organization was gradually transitioning from a service-based model to a resource-based model with the intent to provide technical support to government systems.

Young women from the community were trained to become Balwadi teachers. They occupied a leadership position in the community hierarchy and advised parents who interacted with them on a daily basis. Supervisors were also often recruited from the community when possible, except when special expertise was needed. The organization prioritized capacity building by providing skill-based comprehensive training to individuals who acted as change-makers and were not restricted by the physical structure of a Balwadi.

10.4.1. The Classroom

The Balwadi in the Muslim community was located in the home of the teacher. It was a small rectangular room, and there was no space outside. There was no space available near or around the centre for outdoor activities. There were utensils hanging from the wall, and there was a cupboard in the room. There was only one light and one fan which did not provide proper lighting or adequate ventilation for preschool activities. Both the Balwadis faced space crunch, and teachers were challenged to conduct ECE activities in a developmentally appropriate way.

The Balwadi located in the space belonging to Shiv Sena had comparatively more space, and the children's work was displayed nicely. The lighting and ventilation were good, as there were two fans and three tube lights. Neither of the Balwadis had toilet facilities. Since all the children were from the neighbourhood, they went home or outside for toilet.

Pratham provided teaching aids and materials such as puzzles, sewing toys and stacking blocks, rhyme and storybooks, slate and chalk, and materials for drawing, painting and clay modelling to support learning. Apart from the materials provided, the Balwadi teachers themselves occasionally made teaching aids.

10.4.2. Transacting a Preschool Curriculum in Limited Space

A 'theme-based curriculum' was developed by the ECE experts in the organization and shared with different centres. The learning activities were organized to promote development in specific domains: cognitive, language, physical, social–emotional and creative. A key principle was to provide a sequence of activities which began with simple tasks but increased in complexity. The curriculum addressed all domains of development but emphasized academic writing and communication skills. The trainers worked closely with the teachers to plan the monthly curriculum based on the annual curriculum, following which they prepared the weekly schedule for the centre. Thus, the teachers had the flexibility to plan the weekly timetable and schedule of activities for each day.

Both the Balwadis had a good teacher–child ratio, that is, 1:13. Pratham did not enrol more than 15 children in their Balwadis. The age range of children varied from 2.5 years to 5 years in the first Balwadi and 3 years to 4 years in the other. The teachers said that the 'play-way method' was the best way to teach children; however, they did not give further explanation of this approach. One of them felt that it was necessary to be aware of the children's family background and the children' temperaments. We observed that they practised repetition while teaching the children. One of the teachers explained the rationale, '*Jab dohrate hai toh bachcho ko yaad jaldi reh jata hai*' (if we repeat things, then children remember them more quickly). Teachers developed weekly plans which included many creative activities. For instance, a teacher provided materials for engaging in various activities such as drawing, sewing and clay to teach the concept of colour and number. Another teacher provided laced beads, clay, reading books and painting.

In order to transition smoothly, teachers conducted short activities: '*Haath uppar karo, niche karo, taaren chamkao, taaliyan bajao, khade raho, niche baitho, khudi lagao*' (raise your hands up, put them down, now move them like twinkling stars, clap your hands, sit down and jump up). These exercises helped children to relax visibly and get ready for the next activity. It gave them the opportunity to move around, which was important as adequate space was not available to conduct outdoor activities. Gross motor activities were restricted to exercises conducted while standing up or sitting down. Children were also engaged in rolling mats. It was easier to conduct fine motor activities such as crumpling paper, sewing, lacing beads and shoes. The underlying rationale for selecting activities for each day was not always clear.

One of the teachers kept changing the place and position of the children with each activity so they had the opportunity to move and sit next to new partners. The other teacher encouraged children to change postures alternating between sitting and standing during stories and songs. While the teachers in both the Balwadis seemed to have made innovative use of the limited space available, such cramped space do not seem to be ideal for children's development and learning. The fact that the children had to do vertical exercises is an indicator of their physical discomfort which space constraint put on their bodies.

They were multilingual classrooms; teachers used both Hindi and Marathi with the students to maintain continuity between the languages used at home and at the preschool, which helped to create a vibrant environment where children interacted freely with adults and children. Most children conversed in Hindi and Marathi fluently with the teachers. To facilitate language acquisition, the teachers used simple short sentences and repeated certain words in other languages. They used familiar household materials to encourage children to describe the items along with their thoughts and feelings. We observed children narrating stories and talking about various familiar objects in their environment, including fruits, vegetables, animals, vehicles and abstract concepts such as seasons. Children were given the opportunity to choose the stories that they narrated.

A number of activities were conducted to give children the opportunity to learn classification, differentiation, similarities and establishing a variety of patterns. While some children had difficulty in problem-solving games such as puzzles, others were able to complete it with ease. However, we did not see any examples where the teacher adapted a particular activity based on the age or the ability of a child. They engaged in constructing structures with blocks and lacing. However, we noted that children at either centre did not pose any questions to the teachers or to us. It is possible that the emphasis on conformity, obedience, discipline, being good and politeness in many cultures in India may have discouraged them from posing questions.

We did not find any child with disabilities in either Balwadis. However, we did observe them in other Balwadis of Pratham when we initially visited them to select centres for this study. In general, teacher's training materials also included provisions for children with disabilities. We did not come across any teacher or project personnel, in their teaching learning processes, ever mentioning the subject of disability to sensitize the children.

As the teachers belonged to the same community, children appeared to share a bond with the teachers. In the classrooms, children were generally cheerful and often interacted with their peers. They always waited for their turn to speak or participate in any activities. Some of them were shy, but teachers carefully attended to them and ensured they were included in all the group activities. They often encouraged children to share space, food and toys. It seemed that they valued sharing and cooperation and felt it was important to inculcate these values in the children. These qualities were encouraged even though there was no scarcity of materials in the centre. Teachers encouraged children to wash their hands before and after meals and use a handkerchief to dry their hands. Most children were able to open their tiffin boxes without any assistance. We noted that they ate without spilling much food. At both the Balwadis, families were encouraged to provide nutritious food to children and ensure regular attendance. The children were only allowed to bring homemade foods, such as chapatis and vegetables. They could not bring fast foods such as biscuits, bread and jam for lunch.

Supervisors mentored and monitored the Balwadis. They visited the Balwadis once a month to check the curriculum implementation. When the teachers had difficulty, they visited the centres twice a month to work with the teachers and provide the necessary support. The programme manager evaluated the programme based on the children's response and the impact it made on their lives. Therefore, teachers' observations of children's performance in the classroom and during home visits were considered important. These reports gave them an idea that whether the children benefited or not and whether the curriculum was age-appropriate or not. According to the programme manager, the organization attempted to address deficits by appointing a special committee of experts, who reviewed the problems and recommended changes. The Balwadis were visited by ECE experts from time to time, who provided suggestions for the improvement of the programme.

10.5. Emphasis on Parent Engagement

The activities of Pratham were strongly grounded in the principle of community mobilization. This was evident in the multiple efforts to collaborate with parents. Many parents came to drop the children to school and had regular informal conversations with the teachers. The parents who stayed at home participated in the special programmes and festivities. Moreover, the organization deliberately created several formal mechanisms to facilitate interactions between the parents and teachers. These efforts were greatly appreciated by the parents. First, they organized two parent–teacher meetings each month to discuss the performance of the child, the content covered and their teaching approach. Second, teachers were available every Saturday at a designated time to speak with parents for issues that required immediate attention. Third, there was a parent representative who spoke on behalf of the parents who were reluctant to interact. Fourth, a monthly meeting was organized. The importance of these interactions to the parents is evident from the following quotes:

> *Mahine me 2 baar meeting hoti hai. Usme batate hai ki tumhare bachche kaise hai, padhte hai.*
>
> (There is a meeting with the teachers twice a month, in which they tell us how the children are doing and how they are performing.)

> *Teacher ne Saturday ke din special day rakha hai ki jo bhi parents ko milna hai wo uss din 12 baje aake teacher se milenge.*
>
> (The teacher has kept Saturday as a special day, where, if any parents want to meet they will meet the teacher at 12.)

> *Parents me se ek pratinidhi rakha hai ki agar aapko teacher ke saamne nahi jana hai toh wo jaake baat karenge.*
>
> (The parents have kept a representative, so that if you do not want to go in front of the teacher, then they will go and talk.)

The programme manager mentioned that parent–teacher association meetings were held once a month. Additionally, every centre had a library to enhance the reading skills of children. Moreover, camps were organized in each community from time to time, focusing on various issues such as assessment or admission to schools. Parents were engaged in planning these events. Finally, an annual social gathering was organized every year. In fact, the visits of the supervisors were not only to oversee the Balwadis but also to interact with the community on issues concerning the Balwadi and quality of education for the preschoolers.

While few parents had participated in school activities such as preparing children for dance and dressing them up, others were unable to participate in such events. This suggests that it is necessary to create a flexible model for parent participation to engage parents in ways they feel comfortable. Two different scenarios are presented in the following quote:

> *Jaise garba hai toh bachcho ko kaise ready karna, kapde pehnane, kaise handle karna … teacher bolti hai kya karneka, agar kuch banake leke aana hai toh ye sab bhaag rehta hai humara.*

> (If there is garba, then how to help children get ready, making them wear the dresses, how to handle them … teacher says what to do, if something needs to be made, so we participate in this way.)

Other parents did not have time; hence, they could not participate in school activities:

> *Nahi, main nahi leti. Ichcha toh hai lekin time nahi milta, ghar pe kam bohat rehta hai, badi ladki jaati hei mere liye.*

> (No I don't take. I have the desire, but I don't have the time. There is a lot of work at home. My elder daughter goes instead of me.)

10.5.1. Parents' Perspective on the Preschool

Mothers conversed about various ECE activities, including rhymes, songs, colouring, craft, learning counting, the meaning of rhymes and stories, numbers, days and months, paper crumpling, drawing and colouring, thread printing, learning some English words and basic hygiene, which demonstrate the effects of the interactions between parents and the preschool. They mentioned,

> *Humare khayal se teacher thoda time padhate hai, thoda time khelne ke liye rakhti hai, thoda time ache se baat-cheet karna seekhate hai, yehi seekhati hai.*

> (According to us, the teacher teaches for some time and keeps some time for play. She some time teaches how to engage in discussion; this is what she teaches.)

In addition, the parents expected their children to learn good manners and respect the elders in the community. Moreover, their views on the process of how children learnt was consistent with that of the organization. They were aware of the importance of play and role of mother tongue in education of young children:

> *Khel khel me hi seekhana chahiye bachcho ko; kyuki agar aap daant ke seekhaye toh woh nahi karenge. Agar aap pyaar se seekhaye toh ache se seekhenge.*

(Children should be taught through play. Because if you scold when teaching them, then they won't learn. If you teach them with love, then they will learn.)

> *Sabse pehle use humari matra-bhasha Marathi aana chahiye. Baad me baaki sab.*

(The child should learn their mother tongue Marathi first and then any other language.)

Most parents appreciated the Balwadis because of the nature of activities, quality of the teachers and their ability to engage large number of children. All the parents interviewed for the study were happy with the preschool activities:

> *Iss school me saari khubiyan hai. Bachcho ko time se khelne ke liye dete hai. Kabhi khel khilate hai, kabhi dance seekhate hai. Iss school me har suvidha hai. Abhi teacher jo khubiyaan hai, wo thik hi hai; time padhati hai … itne saare bachcho ko saath me handle karna, sab teachers ki baat nahi hoti; jab teacher achi rehti hai toh sab bachcho ko handle kar leti hai. Agar teacher maarti toh bachche nahi aate unke paas.* (Mother)

(This school has all wonderful qualities. The children get to play on time. Sometimes they play, sometimes they are taught dance. This school has all the facilities. The teacher has some good qualities, which are fine. Not all teachers are able to handle so many children. When the teacher is good, she is able to handle all the children. If the teacher would hit, then the children would not have come to her.)

Parents chose schools for the following reasons: It was close to their home; older sibling studied in the same school; other family members also studied there; or it was a known school. They described the changes they observed in their children:

Badlav toh dekha hai. Jo teacher seekhati hai toh bachche jyada seekhte hai … jaise sube uthke bhagwan ke pair padhna, mata–pita ka padhna; prarthna bolti hai.

(We have seen some change. When teachers teach, children learn more, for example, in the morning, touch the feet of the Gods, touch the feet of parents, she says her prayers.)

In the beginning, they hardly spoke at all, but now they had made friends at school and had started speaking with them.

Children enjoyed attending the Balwadi. They followed the instructions of the teacher and tried to remember to wash their hands and keep their uniform clean. Parents were keen to educate children up to Grade 10; they preferred to send their children to Balwadi for preschool or school readiness, and when the child was ready to go for senior nursery class, they moved the child to an established school up to the age of 5 or 5.5 years. The admission in regular schools was very competitive; therefore, they preferred to admit the child from senior nursery rather than Grade 1. The flexible entrance age allowed a greater number of children from the community to enter into the formal school education system and prevented exclusion of children who did not fit the traditional age group for primary education.

Parents informed us that they preferred to choose the Balwadi of Pratham rather than other Balwadis in the neighbourhood. The mothers wanted their children to gain knowledge, which would be helpful for them in future schooling. Mothers felt that the Balwadis should provide nutritious meals, and children should not have to carry tiffin from home. During the study, Pratham was in the process of designing a programme, named as the parent education programme, for educating parents, which was implemented later. A certification programme was also a goal, which included motivating teachers to complete their education, giving them diploma or certificate course in ECE.

10.6. Balwadi Teachers

The recruitment, training and mentoring of women as teachers or supervisors gave an opportunity to the organization to work on gender issues and promote women's empowerment. One of the teachers was motivated to become a teacher from her childhood: *'Mujhe bachpan se teacher banna tha'* (I wanted to be a teacher since I was a child), while the other was encouraged by her family to join the profession. The interest of teachers to work in this field is evident from the following quotes:

> *Main 10th tak padhi hu. Aur uske baad Balwadi ka course kiya, Montessori course. Wo ek saal ka tha. Fir wo karne ke baad maine 6 saal readymade garments me kam kiya. Fir shaadi hogaya. Uske baad maine yaha join kiya. 22 saal se yahi padha rahi hu. Haa, bohat shauk tha.*

(I have studied till Grade 10. After that, I did a Balwadi course and thereafter a Montessori course, which lasted for a year. After that, I worked in the readymade garment industry for six years and subsequently got married. Now from the last 22 years I have been working as a teacher in a Balwadi. I really wanted to teach.)

> *Maine 12th tak padhai ki hai. Fir Montessori ka course kiya jo 1 saal ka hota hai. Lekin uske exam se pehle hi meri shaadi hogayi toh course complete nahi hua. Uske baad main ghar pe tuitions leti thi; aur drawing, craft jaise classes bhi leti thi. 3–4 saal hue hai bachcho ko padhate hue. Mujhe pehle se hi padhane ka shauk tha.*

(I studied till Grade 12, after which I did a Montessori course for a year. Before I could complete this course, I got married, after which I started taking tuition and arts and crafts classes from my home. It has now been three or four years since I have been teaching children in the Balwadi. I have always been fond of teaching.)

Pratham provided initial training for teachers before they began working in the Balwadis. Every six months, a follow-up session was organized. The content focused on characteristics of preschool children, communication with parents and teaching methods. The organization encouraged and supported teachers who were interested in seeking additional training in ECE. As they scaled up the Balwadi programme, Pratham realized the need for trained teachers. They felt that it was necessary to develop a formal structure for training and later developed a programme in collaboration with IGNOU.

Teachers reported that their status in the community had changed because of their work in the Balwadis. They were treated with greater respect in the community. Moreover, their self-esteem had improved because of taking up the teaching profession. Since the teachers were from the same community as the children, they had a nuanced under-standing of the socio-economic, cultural and emotional challenges faced by the children and the families.

10.7. Changes in ECE

The teachers said that they had noticed many changes in the field of ECE. They discussed changes in Pratham's curriculum, in parents' attitude towards education and generally in the emphasis given to reading and writing in the early years. Few teachers observed changes in teaching strategies. They indicated that previously there was no puppet show or educational trips; only picnics were organized. However, they were now required to take children for visits to the zoo to teach about animals or take them to the market to introduce them to different fruits. Simple cooking activities had also become part of the curriculum. There were changes in sports activities as well. Earlier, children had the opportunity to participate in races which involved running, book balance and lemon–spoon, but later activities such as toy race were added.

Some teachers articulated how parents' perspectives had changed over the years. They placed greater emphasis on ECE and education in English medium as suggested by the quotes presented below:

Pehle ke parents itna interest nahi lete the; bachcho ko school me chodne aate the aur lene aate the, koi baat nahi karte the. Lekin ab parents puchte hai ki mere bachche ne aaj kya kiya, tiffin khaya ki nahi … matlab parents chahte hai unka bachcha sabse aage ho.

(Initially, the parents were not much interested in the progress of their child; they used to just come to drop the child to school and pick them up but never spoke. However, these days, the parents are interested and ask questions like whether the child ate their tiffin/food or not or what the child did throughout the day, meaning parents today want their child to do better than the other children.)

According to few teachers, parents aspired to send their children to English-medium schools:

Abhi English medium ka prabhav jyada hai. Parents ko lagta hai ki bachche English medium me padhenge toh hoshiyaar rahenge.

(Nowadays, English medium is a big influence and is in demand. Parents think that if their children learn in an English-medium environment, they will be smarter.)

Few teachers expressed concern regarding the demands on young children to read and write and pointed out that written work was introduced at earlier ages. One of them said, 'Education has changed. Earlier, in nursery class, there was only oral work; now there is oral and writing together. We have to make the children ready for the next class. There is a lot of burden. Many changes I've seen in these 12 years.'

10.8. Concluding Thoughts

Pratham has focused on developing an early childhood programme which can be scaled up easily in different parts of the country. They have achieved this through collaboration, maintaining transparency and accountability. It is a community-driven programme, which is sustainable and has been scaled up considerably in the past two decades. Moreover, the organization obtains funds from diverse sources, including corporations, UN organizations and government agencies.

The primary strength of this organization was their ability to mobilize the community, sustain parent interactions and engage parents in various activities. The preschools provided a strong platform for Pratham to bring together various members of the community, including parents, grandparents and other members, to bring transformation not just in education but also in other areas related to nutrition and health. ECE was linked to other programmes focusing on parents' education, nutrition and English learning. Together, the nexus of programmes facilitated a process of social change in these communities. Their focus on training and supervision of teachers has led to transformation for some individuals. They reported feeling empowered and that their status in the family and community changed due to their position. In fact, a local political leader mentioned that even though his children were not beneficiaries, he supported the Balwadi, as he understood the importance of education and social change. However, there is scope to examine the early childhood programme more critically, avoid duplication of services and strengthen the curriculum. It was not clear why a Balwadi was housed in the same building as an Anganwadi which is mandated to provide preschool education. More nuanced understanding of children's developmental needs in teachers and differentiated teaching approaches can improve the quality of the classrooms. Moreover, a systematic approach to multilingualism would provide teachers with clear guidelines and promote a more evidence-based approach to learning. While there is much emphasis given on the domains of development, the interactions between domains could be explored further by introducing an activity-based approach. The limited space also affected the ability to conduct certain activities, though teachers attempted to address this issue in many ways.

Reference

NYU Stern School of Business. (n.d.). *Pratham detail.* http://pages.stern.nyu.edu/~sternfin/vacharya/public_html/pratham_detail.pdf

CHAPTER 11

Cooperative Preschools in a Cosmopolitan City

Usha Abrol and Chitkalamba N.

MAYA (Movement for Alternatives and Youth Awareness), a Karnataka-based, non-governmental organization, has worked towards the eradication of child labour since 1989. The community-based centres for education programmes were given a separate entity called Prajayatna[1] in 2008. Therefore, Prajayatna is a programme housed in MAYA and was launched, specifically, to develop community-owned centres (COCs). In the course of their work, the organization found that community ownership was generally lacking in most of the programmes for the poor. The organization also realized that the lack of a forum to articulate problems and hold the state accountable alienated the communities. Their experience indicated that without true community involvement, programmes could not be sustained.

The history of COCs can be traced back to the late 1990s, when MAYA was working with the labourers and their families to eradicate child labour. The organization formed women's groups (mahila sanghas) to discuss various problems faced by them. In the meetings of the sanghas, women labourers often expressed the need for full-time care

[1] http://www.prajayatna.org

for their children. The government ran programmes such as crèches and Anganwadis, which they felt were inadequate to meet the needs of children in these areas (MAYA, 2005a).

While working in Girigowdanadoddi village, in Somanahalli panchayat of Bengaluru, which is an urban district, the MAYA functionaries found that there was an urgent need for full-time childcare for the children from two to six years of age. The area was inhabited by casual migrant labourers where both parents worked for long hours. The nearest Anganwadi was 1.5 km away. Their request for Anganwadis was refused by the government because according to the norms of the project, one Anganwadi could be sanctioned for a population of 1,000 households, but the total population of the village was only 450. In one of the village meetings, the MAYA functionaries suggested that the community could start their own childcare centre, and the NGO would support their efforts. After initial hesitation, the group agreed to follow up on the suggestion. It was discussed with the local gram panchayat (village council) and the School Development and Monitoring Committee (SDMC). A volunteer from the community was selected to conduct a survey of the area. Subsequently, a bigger meeting (Makala Araike Mathu Shikshan Sabha [MAMSS]) of all the stakeholders including parents, teachers and gram panchayat members was held. Some active members persuaded the parents to start their own childcare centre and pay a fee to cover the operational costs. They explained that otherwise the village could not have such a facility for their children. Initially, the parents were reluctant to pay the fees and send food with the children, but during the meeting the entire community came together and offered to support the centre by donating mats, low benches, toys, etc. The government school headmaster allotted a room within the school premises; the first preschool was started.

11.1. Expansion of COCs and Setting Up Prajayatna

Encouraged by the success, similar initiatives were undertaken by MAYA in other areas. Naganayakanahalli, another remote village with a population of 97 households, did not have any facility for young children; the nearest Anganwadi was 2 km away. The parents,

SDMC members and mahila sangha (women's groups) got together to discuss the issue of childcare in a bigger meeting (Makkala Aaraike Mathu Shikshana Sabha). The government school provided a room, and the parents agreed to pay the fees, and in this way the centre was started. Similarly, a centre was started at Avalahalli village, inhabited by some 500 households, where mothers were mostly domestic workers and fathers were casual labourers. To expand this model, MAYA planned community interactions in the other areas primarily inhabited by socio-economically weaker sections, including daily wage earners, migrant labourers, agricultural labourers, etc. Following the success of these initial efforts, other communities were inspired to start their own childcare centres (MAYA, 2005b, pp. 16–18).

The steps involved in setting up the centres were as follows:

1. The field coordinators of MAYA with the help of a local volunteer conducted a survey of the area to identify the gaps in services for young children.
2. The field coordinators discussed the issue with major stakeholders including SDMC members, teachers, Masjid committee members, gram panchayat members and selected parents.
3. A bigger meeting of all the stakeholders (Makkala Aaraike Mathu Shikshana Sabha) was organized to make important decisions related to where to start the centre, amount of fee to be charged, selection of teachers, contributions from the community, etc.

By 2006, some 180 COCs were operational in the urban and rural districts of Bengaluru. These centres were given the name Chukkimane (meaning 'house of stars' in Kannada). In the year 2008, the community-based preschool programme became a separate entity and was given the name Prajayatna.

11.2. Programme Philosophy

The concept of COCs was based on the premise that it is important to create a platform to bring together a group of people who are traditionally divided by religion, language, caste and economic status, so that they can engage in discussions on how to address a common problem and take a collective decision. MAYA's philosophy emerged from their experience of working with the marginalized groups living in poverty. While examining various welfare programmes of the government, they observed that the community ownership was severely lacking in services planned for the poor. Equally conspicuous was the lack of any forum to articulate 'concerns' and hold the state accountable. The organization felt that it was essential to involve the community in all the stages of planning and implementation, therefore, they developed a democratic programme structure to address this lacunae.

The organization felt that it was necessary to develop community structures which could manage and sustain the preschools. In this case, the cooperatives of mahila sanghas became the primary structure to start, manage and sustain community-owned preschool centres. Certain structures such as Makkala Araike Mathu Shikshan Sabha, cluster-level committees and preschool committees were created to involve the community in making decisions on crucial issues such as needs assessment and budget planning. MAYA identified parents as the major stakeholders and created a mechanism to document their expectations from the programme, aspirations for the children and budget planning. It recognized the significance of the early childhood period and developed a holistic package focusing on education, healthcare and nutrition. The organization refers to the COCs as a framework, rather than a model, as it cannot be replicated mechanically. The framework is flexible and can be adapted to the context and the community of the preschool.

11.3. Programme Structure

The Prajayatna organization had developed a sound structure for service delivery and community engagement. Figure 11.1 depicts the structure of the programme.

11.4. Preschool Centres in the Two Communities

At the time of the study in 2012, Prajayatna was running 126 COCs in and around Bengaluru. A purposive sample of two centres was selected, representing two types of community settings. The Gnanjyoti

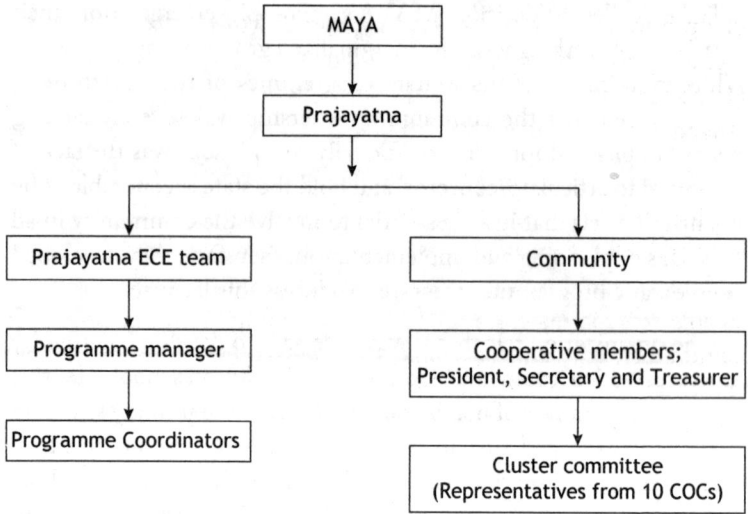

Figure 11.1. *Organizational Structure of Prajayatna*

centre was selected because it represented a community of people from a mixed socio-economic, religious and linguistic background. The children spoke various languages: Kannada, Telugu, Tamil, Urdu and Hindi. The second centre at Madina Cross was located in a homogenous community of Muslim families in Channapatna. The first language of most of the children was either Urdu or Hindi.

The Gnanjyoti centre became operational in 2004. It was located in the suburbs of Bengaluru outskirts, Doddabele Colony, Kengeri. It was located in a residential area, in the house of its teacher in a semi-rural setting. Most people living in the area were daily wage earners, working in garment factories, carpenters, etc. There were two or three small industries and garment factories located in the area in which both men and women worked. Some families kept buffaloes, and their main source of income was selling milk. The total population of the ward was 2,400, constituting 450 households. The population of children between 6 months and 6 years of age was 94 out of them 51 were in the age range of 2–6 years, according to a survey by Prajayatna. There was one government school with a zero grade school (equivalent to pre-school but called zero grade by the Education Department), one private preschool and one Anganwadi. Most children were not attending the Anganwadi due to distance, unsuitable working hours (10 AM to 1 PM), little or no learning activities and the image of the Anganwadi as a feeding centre.

Channapatna, located at about 60 km from Bengaluru, was known for its wooden toy industry. Most of the houses had some cottage industry. All the women were housewives, some worked from home and many were involved in craftwork. This centre provided services to children coming from a Muslim community. It was a close-knit community, where most people knew each other. The teacher and the assistant teacher belonged to the same community. The Madina Cross centre was started in June 2003; it was located in one of the inner lanes (gali) of Channapatna in a rented house. Although it was a congested market area, the lane where the centre was located was free from traffic.

11.5. Preschool Centres

The Gnanjyoti centre was located in the house of the teacher. Preschool classes were held in a room which was about 10 × 15 ft with an attached veranda (courtyard), which was covered. It could accommodate about 30 children but was not big enough to organize activities which required movement. The children sat on a mat on the floor. The room had a lively appearance, as it was well ventilated and a lot of charts were displayed on the walls. The material for teaching and playing was neatly stacked in the cupboards. The courtyard had a small slide and few other outdoor play materials. The covered veranda was used for outdoor play, but only a few children could play at a time. The premise was secured with a fence. Outside the centre, there was a drain which was used by the children as a toilet. Water and soap were available for washing hands. On the whole, the centre was clean and well organized.

The Madina Cross centre, at Channapatna, was located in a rented house. Although the building was dilapidated, it had a big hall for preschool activities. The children could work, play and sleep comfortably. There was no outdoor play area. The centre was lively with charts and paintings done by parents on the wall. The children sat on a mat. There was no proper toilet attached. A drain within the building was used as a toilet for children. Water was stored for washing hands. Both the centres had a lot of indoor play material like plastic toys, blocks and balls. Most of this material was donated by visitors, other agencies or the community. Only the Gnanjyoti centre had few outdoor play equipment.

Printed materials such as the child profile book, the assessment booklet and storybooks were provided by Prajayatna. They also provided some Montessori material. The consumable materials such as paper, colours, pencil, crayons and chalks were purchased after the parents' planning meeting by a committee of mothers, using the money collected from the fee. In addition to a basic learning kit (comprising of materials such as flash cards, picture charts and beads), various teaching aids were developed by teachers during their training. Workshops were held with mothers to develop teaching aids, which further enhanced their participation in the preschool programme.

We visited the centres during the beginning of the academic year, and the admission process was not complete. The Gnanjyoti centre had 23 children and the Madina Cross centre had 19 children according to the attendance registers. The attendance registers of the previous years showed that 39 and 35 children were enrolled, respectively. The centres operated from 9:30 AM to 4:00 PM. Children were allowed to play with the toys as soon as they came, which helped them settle down and learn. The class routine consisted of prayers, songs, storytelling, reading, writing and creative activities. There was a break for lunch where the children ate the food they brought from home, followed by a short nap time. In the afternoon, a hot snack was served to the children. The last activity of the day was craftwork and group games. The centres were well equipped with developmentally appropriate teaching–learning materials.

11.6. A Holistic Programme

The preschool programme of Prajayatna was designed to address the children's need for education, health and nutrition. This holistic approach was developed based on inputs from the parents. The three major components of the programme were as follows:

Preschool education: A thematic curriculum was developed to promote development of motor, cognitive and language domain. The weekly themes and activities were planned in weekly meetings of the teachers. On the days we conducted the observations, the teacher started the day with attendance followed by some simple exercises. The prayers were said in three languages: Hindi, Kannada and English. In Gnanjyoti centre, the weekly theme was water and, therefore, poems, stories, plays and creative activities were organized around this theme. In Madina Cross centre, the theme for the week was domestic animals and, therefore, various activities related to domestic animals such as cats and dogs were conducted.

Nutrition: Parents were primarily responsible for ensuring healthy meals, and children brought their lunch from home. However, supplementary nutrition, in the form of freshly cooked afternoon snacks, was supplied to all the children by the mothers of all the centres. A weekly menu was prepared at the mother's meeting, and they took turns in cooking the afternoon snack. The raw material for the snacks was provided by the organization and sometimes supplemented by the mothers. For instance, sometimes if the quality of rice was not very good, mothers replaced it with good-quality rice. Sometimes they added other nutritive things such as greens and eggs. On the day of observation, children had a snack made of puffed rice at Gnanjyoti and vegetable pulao at the Madina Cross centre. The coordinator reported that information regarding nutritional value of foods, healthy eating habits, etc., was discussed at the parents meetings. The children ate their food sitting in a circle and washed their hands before and after eating. They ate lunch from their respective lunch boxes, and the afternoon snack was distributed by the teachers. They helped the younger children in eating.

Health services: The details of each child's height, weight, nutritional grade and immunization and illness records were maintained at the centres. It was reported by the field coordinators that once in a year, health camps were organized with the help of community groups and the Department of Health and Family Welfare. The COCs supported the programme by bringing children and their families for immunization. Healthcare was considered a responsibility of parents. However, teachers accompanied children and their mothers to events such as immunization or health camps.

11.7. The Curriculum

The emphasis on parent involvement was clearly evident in the way the curriculum goals were decided. In the beginning of each academic year, a meeting was held to document parents' expectations. The coordinators along with the teachers encouraged the parents to voice what they wanted their children to learn in the preschool. Such meetings were primarily attended by the mothers. They identified various goals; for example, the children should learn to speak clearly, be prepared for primary school, and learn alphabets, numbers and concepts such as colour, size and shape. They expected their children to become independent in day-to-day routine activities such as eating on their own, putting on their shoes and taking responsibility for their things such as water bottles and lunch boxes. The parents also wanted their children to develop various social–emotional skills, become disciplined and learn good manners such as wishing visitors and sharing with others. During one of the focus group meetings for the study, parents categorically said that they wanted their children to play and enjoy themselves in the centre. At times, the parents expressed a few specific expectations; for instance, some Urdu-speaking communities wanted their children to learn Kannada and English along with Urdu. These various aspirations were documented and addressed through the curriculum. Prajayatna developed an 'Ability Matrix' each year which provided a broad framework for the curriculum. Some of the criteria from the ability matrix are as follows:

- Ability to perform tasks independently and complete tasks
- Ability to support other children in performing their tasks
- Ability to seek support

- Ability to communicate (develop reading, writing language and numeracy skills; follow instructions; speak and express their individual meaning forms)
- Ability to care for material in their learning environment; share and collaborate with other children

A thematic curriculum was developed in which the activities were planned to foster development in all domains. Themes were decided collectively in a group during the teacher training programmes, with guidance from Prajayatna coordinators and experienced lead teachers. The themes for each week were decided in the beginning of the year; however, the activities and lessons planned were developed during monthly training sessions. These activities included poems, stories, puzzles, games, free talk (conversation using charts) and creative activities such as drawing, painting and collage. For example, in Gnanjyoti centre, the theme was domestic animals and various activities were conducted to develop an understanding of this topic. The teacher told a story about two sheep, recited a poem about cats, showed pictures of common domestic animals and facilitated a conversation. Following this, the children coloured the picture of a dog which was drawn by the teacher. In Madina Cross centre, the theme was festivals and the teacher talked about Eid as most children were Muslim and they were familiar with this festival.

The following principles of pedagogy were shared with all the teachers and reinforced during various trainings and supervisory visits:

- Every child learns differently.
- A non-threatening environment is conducive to learning.
- A stimulating environment supports children's expression.
- Understanding and relating to a child are essential for learning.
- Conversations around experiences, memories, thoughts and ideas of children often allow children to understand a concept.
- Teacher's engagement with the child begins only after the child has had time to adjust to the preschool.

Our interviews with the teachers suggest internalization of these principles. One of the teachers emphasized the need to come down to the level of the child in the following words, '*Unke sath bachcha ban jana chahiye*' (One has to become a child with them). Another teacher said, '*Khel khel mein sikhana chahiye*' (We need to teach through play). These views were echoed by the programme coordinator who emphasized the need to teach according to age and ability and support them to reach the next level in early literacy and numeracy.

The curriculum was culturally responsive and connected to the context of the children. The weekly themes selected were based on the children's experiences in their environment. For example, while talking about the theme 'festival', the teacher referred to Eid, a festival celebrated by the Muslim families in the area. The poems, stories and songs were also selected carefully to reflect the local culture. The medium of instruction was usually the same as the home language. In Gnanjyoti centre, even though children came from a multilingual background, the language did not appear to be an issue. The medium of teaching was in Kannada and most of the children were able to follow it. We observed that the teachers commonly made an effort to use three languages in the class: Kannada, Urdu and Hindi. The prayers, action songs and poems were recited in all three languages. Reading and writing of alphabets and numbers were taught in Kannada as well as English as demanded by parents. In Madina Cross, even though all the children spoke Urdu, the other two languages (English and Kannada) were taught at parents' request.

In both the centres, we observed that children had many opportunities to play and work with other children. Thus, they learned various social emotional skills such as sharing, waiting for their turn and asking questions. The teachers ensured that all the children participated in the activities. In both the centres, most of the activities were organized in groups. Individual activities were minimal at Madina Cross, probably due to large number of children (25 children).

Every day, one hour was devoted to organize the children in three groups based on their ability to do certain tasks. Children moved from one group to the other depending on the activity. The coordinator explained, 'We have a mixed group of children from two to five years of age. Ability grouping helps in organizing age-specific activities for them.' During an activity at Madina Cross centre, children were divided in groups according to their ages for different activities. While one group was engaged in pattern making and peg board, the second group worked on sound discrimination and size, and the third group was involved in basic writing activities. In both the centres, older children were asked to write alphabet (a to z) and numbers (1 to 10). There were several opportunities to engage in early literacy activities. The teacher and the assistant teacher moved from group to group in order to facilitate learning.

The main objective of assessment was to ensure that the parents and teachers were aware of the child's progress and maintain records for school admission. The coordinator explained that the children were assessed twice a year at intervals of six months in the presence of mothers. Only four children were assessed in a day. An assessment booklet was developed by Prajayatna which listed the criteria in each domain of development. The booklet included various items such as identification, matching, naming of objects, identification of objects by sound, counting, and writing the letters in Kannada and English.

11.8. Capacity Building of Teachers

Local women were recruited as teachers and provided training and mentoring for capacity building. Since the teachers were from the same community, it helped them to stay connected with the mothers and fostered a sense of accountability. In Madina Cross, the teacher displayed a strong bond with the mothers and other community members. She said that she took the job because she considered them to be her own people, '*Sab apne hi log hain.*' The background of the teachers facilitated their communication with children and made them comfortable with her. They helped to make the curriculum culturally responsive based on their knowledge of the local community, which was used to identify themes and stories. They were also successful in getting support from the community.

Most of the teachers had completed high school education and were between 25 and 35 years of age. They had lived in the same area for a considerable period of time, and in some places, they operated the preschools in their houses, which could be problematic for several reasons. First, the physical environment of such centres cannot be modified much to provide a rich learning environment. Second, the social boundaries are difficult to negotiate, and it interferes with privacy of the family. Third, there may also be concerns regarding the safety of children. However, such centres were located in the familiar environment of the children, and they probably felt more comfortable. Teachers' salary was decided by the community. The teacher of Gnanjyoti centre stated that she took the job, as her own children had grown up, she had more time and the family did not want her to go out for work. So she started a preschool centre in her own house. The other teacher said that she loved to work with children and also needed to earn.

A decentralized unconventional strategy for training was developed by Prajayatna. After joining, a teacher was given a day's orientation and then placed in a nearby centre for one month. This apprenticeship was considered essential and provided a foundation for the training which followed. The sessions focused on preschool management, health and learning. Training was conducted monthly at the cluster level (1 cluster consisted of 10 centres). Follow-up sessions were conducted weekly at the teacher circle level. The training was individualized based on the level of the teacher and not predetermined based on a specific syllabus. The lead teachers were responsible for assessing the needs and designing the individual training plan for the teacher. Classroom demonstrations were followed by opportunities to conduct the activities. Additional sessions were conducted by external resource persons, and visits to other preschool facilities were used to expose trainees to a range of best practices in the field. A special in-house team of facilitators (lead teachers and coordinators) continuously worked towards improving the skills of teachers.

We observed a circle-level training of 15 teachers. It was facilitated by a supervisor and a lead teacher. The session started at 10:00 AM and ended at 4:00 PM. The trainers used brainstorming, group discussions, planning activities for a week's theme (food) and presentations (mock session) of the planned activities by the trainees in a participatory mode. They were paired up to work on the planning and demonstration sessions. A lot of teaching–learning materials were available to the teachers to conduct activities.

In addition to training, a strong system for mentorship and supervision was developed by the organization. Planning for listing of themes and related subjects was undertaken during monthly meetings of the teachers at the cluster level guided by a lead teacher. Every cluster was supported by a lead teacher who had the experience of organizing preschools within the community and could mentor new teachers. A lead teacher was responsible for the training of teachers from 25–30 preschools. Lesson plans were developed in weekly meetings (in small groups of four–five teachers) based on the theme. This allowed teachers to grasp essential principles of the planning process, which would not be possible if the entire curriculum was constructed in one session. According to the coordinator, 'It is easier for the teachers to learn and implement when they work in groups on theme planning.'

11.9. Collaborative Monitoring

The responsibility for supervision of COCs was shared by the community groups and Prajayatna. The organizational aspects and daily operation of the programme were supervised by the community groups, while the coordinators of Prajayatna were responsible for monitoring academic aspects and capacity building of the teachers. The members of the cooperative monitored the timing of the centres and enforcement of rules. They were also responsible for identifying new COCs and handled issues related to teacher's availability, leave, etc. The parents' committee of each centre looked after day-to-day operation. Each centre had a preschool committee comprising five–seven mothers and the teacher. The members visited the centre twice a week by rotation. They monitored the hygiene, cleanliness, attendance, timings, etc. We noticed that the centres operated in a timely manner. There was transparency in fee and other charges. A committee of two mothers and the teacher purchased the consumable items for the centre. The cluster-level committee regulated the financial matters like utilization of financial resources. The close monitoring and vigil had resulted in a high sense of accountability to the community and fostered regularity in the operation of the centres.

The coordinators of Prajayatna were expected to mentor and train teachers rather than supervise and inspect. The goal was to develop the capacity of teachers so that they were able to run the preschools independently in their community. According to the programme manager, quite a few COCs had become independent and self-sustaining and needed nominal support from Prajayatna. The transformation of these teachers from housewives to independent business women clearly indicated the success of the individualized capacity-building programme.

11.10. Parent Involvement

The parents were identified as the main stakeholders in the programme, and Prajayatna worked closely with them to build capacity and mobilize them to take responsibility for the preschools. Creating opportunities for engagement at various levels helped to develop a sense of ownership and ensure accountability of the programme. Based on our observation of the budget-planning meeting and interactions with parents, we felt that the parents were vocal and aware of the difference between good-quality and poor-quality classroom practices. This was achieved by instituting a number of mechanisms which are as follows:

Parents' expectation meeting: Every year, a parents' expectation meeting was held to map their expectations from preschool and was addressed through curriculum and other services.

Commitment from parents: As soon as a child got admitted in the preschool, the parents made a commitment that they would send the child regularly to the preschool, pay monthly fee, pack nutritious food for the child and attend monthly meetings regularly.

Monthly meetings: Teachers engaged in a dialogue with parents from their centres each month to apprise them of their children's learnings and address problems, for example, late arrival, nonpayment or late payment of fee and need to repair the building.

Preschool committee: Every centre had a preschool committee comprising three–seven mothers and the teacher to look after cleanliness, attendance, etc. It was observed that the preschool centres were regular in opening and closing timings; both teachers and children were punctual. There was transparency in fee and other charges.

Supplementary nutrition cooked by mothers: Mothers took the responsibility of cooking nutritious afternoon snacks for all the children
in a preschool. Each mother took turns in providing snacks.
Parents' workshops: Workshops were organized to engage mothers
in preparing teaching–learning aids and to discuss issues related
to nutrition and healthcare of their children.

The attendance figures indicated the popularity and acceptance of
these centres in the community. The willingness of the parents to
pay the fees and fulfil other requirements like active participation in
planning and management of the centre indicates the acceptance and
appreciation of the programme.

11.11. Role of NGO in Community-owned Preschools

All the COCs were started in response to the demand of the parents
in their areas where there were no childcare facilities. During the
village-level meetings of mahila sanghas, the need for care and education of young children was often discussed. MAYA viewed its role as
a secondary stakeholder, an external agency which needed to create
a platform for community-driven processes and provide technical
assistance for ECCE. Many communities were traditionally divided
by caste, religion gender, etc., which prevented them from coming
together to discuss issues. Based on their experience, Prajayatna felt
that the communities do not usually come forward to discuss issues
and concerns on their own; they have to be brought together on a
common platform and discussions have to be facilitated.

The first step towards developing COCs was organization of a
village-level meeting known as Makkala Araike Mathu Shikshana
Sabha. All the stakeholders including parents, school teachers,
Anganwadi workers, elected members of gram panchayat, village
elders and others irrespective of caste, religion or gender participated
in the meeting. The primary agenda was to build a common vision
for a community-owned preschool. The need for childcare and availability was discussed with the members. Important decisions related

to selection of site, identification of teachers and resources were discussed. In some villages, the school headmaster allocated rooms for starting the centre and, in others, the local groups made a commitment to find a place for the preschool. The two centres studied were started in this manner. The teacher at Gnanjyoti was selected in the gram sabha (MAMSS), and it was decided in the meeting that she would conduct the preschool in her house. At Madina Cross, the gram sabha selected the teacher, and the Masjid committee members, who were present in the sabha, identified a place and offered to pay the rent. The organization believed that to participate in discussions and advocate for the community, it was necessary to create opportunities for capacity building.

While working with the community, Prajayatna recognized the need for strong community institutions and structures to enhance their capacity to manage the preschools. Therefore, several structures were developed to institutionalize services such as the following:

Cooperatives: MAYA worked with mahila sanghas evolved and developed into women's cooperatives with large membership and a legal base. During the years 2001–2003, the number of preschools managed by the cooperative members increased significantly. The MAYA facilitators played a strong role in interacting with parents and convinced them of the need to send their children to preschool, train and orient the teachers to work with children and enable the women's cooperatives to effectively manage the centres.

Cooperatives, thus, became the primary structure of the community preschool model. The organization then took upon themselves the responsibility of training the cooperative members on the basics of child development, managing a preschool facility, planning logistics, etc., and to build their capacity for decision-making and problem-solving. The cooperatives played a significant role in identifying the need for a preschool, finding space, selection of teacher and overall supervision of community-owned preschools. Each cooperative had 15 board members and 3 office-bearers (president, secretary and treasurer) who were responsible for supervising the preschools. Issues such as replacement of poorly performing teachers, finding a substitute teacher, increasing their monthly honorarium and relocation of a centre were decided by the cooperative members along with the parents.

Preschool committees: The second important structure was a preschool committee for each centre, comprising three parents and the teacher. Its main role was to identify and mobilize local resources, in addition to monitoring day-to-day operations. They were involved in purchase of teaching–learning materials.

Cluster-level committee: Every cluster consisted of 10 preschools; 3 parents and the teacher from each of the 10 schools came together to develop plans for their preschools including the budget. Each cluster maintained a bank account. Representatives were elected to be the signatories of that account and monitored the earnings and expenditure.

11.12. Mechanisms for Mobilization of Resources

A study conducted by MAYA revealed that the parents' perception of ownership was based on factors such as paying school fee, providing nutrition, ensuring children's engagement and participation in meetings.

Budget planning meetings were organized by the coordinators at each preschool to discuss the fee structure and operation costs for teaching–learning material, infrastructure development, etc. It was mandatory that one parent from each family attend the meeting. Prior notice was given to the parents informing them of the timings of the meeting. The decisions were recorded and minutes were maintained. We observed such a meeting at Madina Cross which was attended by close to 30 women. The money to be collected as school fee and expenditure were discussed in detail. A small committee of two women and the teacher was constituted to purchase the material. The local councillor (elected representative of the municipal corporation of that area) joined the meeting as a special invitee. The teacher explained the need to repair and paint the building, and he agreed to meet the cost.

The local community also came forward to mobilize resources whenever needed. For example, in Madina Cross, the fee collected from parents was not sufficient to meet the rent of the building. The local Masjid committee agreed to pay the rent of ₹700 per month. The teacher informed that she was anticipating that she may need to shift the centre; however, she was not worried as she was confident that the local people would help her find a new site. However, community participation was stronger at Madina Cross, where the community was a more homogenous group compared to Gnanjyoti, which had migrant population from various areas.

11.13. Role of an NGO as an External Agency

Prajayatna observed that communities usually do not come forward on their own to articulate their concerns and needs in programmatic terms. Therefore, the NGO plays a critical role by creating a platform to initiate dialogue on issues of young children and empowers the community by providing technical assistance by sharing information on available options and resources. The community mobilization processes such as MAMSS, budget planning and involvement of cooperatives were organized by the NGO to mobilize the communities and empower them. They played an important role in convincing parents regarding the need for preschool, trained local women with modest education to become teachers, enabled the women to form cooperatives and assumed the responsibility to manage and supervise the centres.

The entire programme was divided into two circles, and a programme coordinator was allotted for each circle and was responsible for the following:

- Capacity building of teachers and focusing on children's learning and community work
- Organization of three meetings with the parents in each centre, budget planning, health and nutrition and assessment of children
- Two observational visits to every centre in a month
- Conduct four–five monthly meetings with the mothers

However, in practice, they went beyond these stated objectives to become a friend, philosopher and guide to the teachers by spending quality time with them.

11.14. Challenges and Opportunities

A programme like community-owned preschool, though very innovative, faced many challenges. The interviews with the programme manager, coordinators and teachers revealed the following challenges:

1. In a dynamic urban context, the parents' aspirations for their children and expectations from the programme kept changing. They often referred to private schools which had much better resources.
2. Another major challenge was that the parents' expectations were sometimes developmentally inappropriate. The coordinator pointed out, 'The parents were obsessed with formal teaching, especially learning to read and write in English. It is difficult to convince them about the needs and the capacity of the child during this age.' Sometimes, parents sent their 4+ year-old children for private tuition to address this issue. The teacher of Gnanjyoti said,

   > Parents look at these preschools as merely day care centres where children play, eat, sleep and learn and stay away from home for some time, which will help them to adjust in later schooling. They only expect good day care for their children in their absence. By five years of age, most children are withdrawn and sent to private schools where they are enrolled in LKG. After the centre closes at 4 PM, most children go for tuition where they learn formal reading and writing.

   We confirmed this information during interviews with parents.
3. Children as young as two years of age were attending the preschool. The coordinator said, 'There are hardly any children in four–six years of age, requiring us to make our preschool programme more suitable for younger children.'
4. It was difficult to make the programmes self-sustaining. The programme manager mentioned that only a small number of COCs became independent and required no support from Prajayatna. A few centres were converted to Anganwadis, but this did not happen very frequently.

5. Teacher turnover was another major concern of coordinators. Some of them left to join private schools which offered better salaries; a few of them joined the ICDS for job security and better pay.
6. The use of local women who did not have comprehensive training in the area limited the quality of the programme. We observed that teachers were not very confident in concepts related to 'ability grouping', assessment of children and use of Montessori teaching–learning material, which requires a higher level of education and teaching experience.

In spite of the above challenges, the model developed by Prajayatna has some unique strengths, which are as follows:

1. The programme coordinators perceived the teachers' love and affection for children as the major strength of the programme. Equally important were the community bonding and democratic processes like budget planning and, last but not least, teacher's accountability to the community.
2. The strategies for capacity building of the major stakeholder—parents, cooperative members and teachers—facilitated active participation and empowered them to operate the programme. Moreover, some of the teachers were able to join private schools and Anganwadis because of the high quality of training and mentorship they had received.
3. A decentralized concurrent training strategy designed for modestly educated women helped to address quality in the preschools.

11.15. Concluding Thoughts

On the whole, the fact that Prajayatna facilitated the launch and operation of 180 COCs in different districts over a period 5–6 years indicates that the model has potential for scaling up. The framework required a 'bottom-up approach' based on the assumption that each community was different with distinct features of their micro environments. Replication of a community-owned model requires institutionalization of 'community structures' like women's cooperatives for their sustenance. Based on their experience, Prajayatna also worked with

ICDS from 2007 to convert 305 Anganwadis into vibrant community-based preschool centres. However, a major paradigm shift was needed in ICDS to scale up such a programme, as parents and community members usually are not responsible for managing the resources, neither is the Anganwadi worker accountable to the community.

As an external agency, Prajayatna played a critical role in bringing the community together, to initiate discussions, provide technical assistance and plan for sustainability. However, only a few communities operated the community preschools completely independently, which suggests some degree of dependency on the agency on a continued basis.

An individualized capacity-building approach allowed women with moderate level of education to become preschool teachers. However, the fact that parents moved children to private schools as early as four years or enrolled them in tuition classes suggests that they were not fully satisfied with the quality of education. Although Prajayatna tried to introduce some new inputs such as the Montessori Method of teaching and learning in the curriculum and the concept of ability grouping, they were not very successful in centres where the teachers were moderately educated and had less teaching experience. Many of those who could imbibe these concepts moved over to private schools or Anganwadis, where the salaries were better. The model of requiring teachers to operate the preschool centres from their home, due to shortage of space in urban slums, needs to be especially examined as it is difficult to create a developmentally appropriate learning environment in the teachers' homes for a large number of young children. However, the Prajayatna model has shown a clear advantage in creating awareness in the communities for the need to develop caring and developmentally appropriate learning environments from the early age to facilitate the psychosocial and cognitive development and promote school readiness.

References

MAYA. (2005a). *Baseline study of 204 AWCs in Bangalore.*
MAYA. (2005b). *Early childhood care and education.*

CHAPTER 12

Diffusion Model

Scaling Up Quality in Tribal Areas
Venita Kaul and Preeti Mahalwal

12.1. Introduction

In 2010, the Centre for Learning Resources (CLR), a non-governmental institution in Pune, with long years of experience in providing technical support in early childhood education (ECE), was invited by an alliance of five corporate houses known as Bhavishya Alliance to support the ECE component of their development initiative in the Dharni block of Amravati district in the Melghat region of Maharashtra. CLR considered this as an opportunity to demonstrate a coherent model for ECE within the Integrated Child Development Services (ICDS) framework, as it would be in partnership with the directorate of ICDS. As clarified by Dr Zakiya Kurien, a founder director of CLR,

> The way this project was structured was very different. The Commissioner, WCD, earlier stationed in Mumbai is now based in Pune and there is more direct interaction and participation with us; the department sends out circulars, deputes personnel for training, and has brought in AWTCs and MLTCs also in the ambit of the project.

Initially supported by the alliance through ICICI, the project was after a year taken over and voluntarily sustained by the Ratan Tata Trust for a period of 3 years, initially with 70 per cent of the funding for the first year and then with full funding. The project was supported by a grant of ₹10.64 million for a period of three years, that is, from January 2011 till December 2013.

12.2. Socio-geographical Context of Dharni

Dharni block, a part of the Amravati district of the Melghat region of Maharashtra, is largely populated by diverse tribal communities, including Korku, Gond, Gavli, Kewat and Gavlan tribes, each of whom speak their own language or dialect. The region is known for its endemic malnutrition, especially in the tribal communities.

Dharni block shares its border with the state of Madhya Pradesh (MP) on the one side and, on the other, it is a three-hour-long drive away through dense forest area from Amravati. Thus, although a part of Maharashtra state, due to the proximity with MP, the language spoken by the majority in Dharni is Korku or Hindi. Hindi is also the preferred language over Marathi, which is unfamiliar to most families, since the trade and interaction are primarily with MP. This creates a significant challenge for children's education in Dharni, since children come into the formal school system without knowing Marathi, which is the medium of instruction, while the teachers, who are from outside the block, speak Marathi and not Korku. The implications of this challenge are discussed later in this chapter.

12.2.1. Childhood in Dharni

A child's day usually starts early in the morning, as s/he eats a lefto-ver roti/bhakri and then spends time roaming around, following the animals while the mother gets ready to go to the farm or lights the morning *chulah* (stove). There are no toilets in the homes; it is common to see children relieving themselves in the open. In most homes, there is no luxury of water either. Children often accompany their mothers or older girls to fetch the water and/or collect cow dung. Their play consists of some 'pretend play', climbing, running around, playing with sticks and strings, *stapoo*, marbles and so on. We were told that the children go to sleep soon after sunset. Use of physical force for disciplining children is the accepted mode.

12.3. Integrated Child Development Services

We were told that Dharni was one of the first 35 blocks in which the Central government's flagship programme ICDS was implemented in 1975. The scheme through its six services strives:

1. To improve the nutritional and health status of children in the age group 0–6 years
2. To lay the foundation for proper psychological, physical and social development of the child
3. To reduce the incidence of mortality, morbidity, malnutrition and school dropout
4. To enhance the capability of the mother to look after the normal health and nutritional needs of the child through proper nutrition and health education

Given the poor health status of children in this age group, ICDS in practice is heavily tilted towards the health domain. As a result, the ECE component of the scheme has been largely overlooked in many locations, including in Melghat.

12.4. Project Concept and Plan

12.4.1 Objective of the Project

The project aimed to support and facilitate good-quality ECE for local, predominantly tribal population of Dharni block in Amravati district, by demonstrating good practice and strengthening local capacities in the ICDS Anganwadis in that context.

This was envisaged by CLR by:

- Enabling Anganwadi workers (AWWs) to become competent early childhood educators
- Equipping district-level training centres and ICDS supervisors to train and mentor AWWs towards improving their ECE practice
- Organizing parents and communities to own and actively participate in the educational activities of the Anganwadi centres (AWCs)

As Zakiya Kurien explained, 'Our objective was that it should be a project with additional human and financial resources which can enable us to demonstrate a coherent model for ECE at the district level.'

12.4.2. Project Scope and Design: A Diffusion Model

The core strategies adopted by CLR in the project were primarily to (a) develop model centres as training spaces to demonstrate an ECE model on the ground and in action, (b) strengthen capacities of all functionaries in the system through a process of recurrent training and close onsite mentoring and (c) adopt a sustainability plan over the three phases by initially building capacities, then involving and supporting the supervisors in conducting training and mentoring and by the third phase handing over the Anganwadis' training and mentoring entirely to them.

12.4.2.1. Development of Model Centres

CLR's rationale for developing model centres has been that unless we can demonstrate what is meant by developmentally appropriate or play-based ECE on the ground, the training cannot lead to change. CLR had already developed a field laboratory of Anganwadis in Mulshi block near Pune in 2008, which served as a demonstration-cum-training site for CLR as well as a site for developing and testing of mentoring and monitoring tools and for development of audiovisual aids and teaching–learning materials.

12.4.2.2. Project Design

The Dharni block in total had 215 AWCs. The project adopted a 'diffusion model' to promote systemic reform in ECE across the block in three phases over the three years of implementation. The three phases are described below:

Phase I: The initial phase involved creation of 19 model AWCs in the first year of the project through direct and intensive support of the CLR staff with provision of materials, training and onsite coaching. These centres were envisaged to serve as observation Anganwadis (OAs) for the subsequent phases so that other AWWs could observe 'good practice' and learn from them.

Phase II: Seventy-two contiguous Anganwadis (CAs) were identified close to the OAs to demonstrate the 'necessity of dedicated and skilled institutional supervisory support'. This was proposed by:

1. Building the capacity of ICDS supervisors to provide training and ongoing teaching–learning support in the centres, based on learning from the first phase.
2. Intensive and ongoing teaching–learning support to the 91 AWWs by a block-level resource team (BRT). This BRT was proposed to be comprised of five block-level staff from CLR, coaching and working alongside nine supervisors from ICDS.
3. In addition, broad teaching–learning support was to be made available to all AWWs in the block through monthly circle meetings/trainings.

Phase III: The 124 remaining Anganwadis (RAs) along with all CAs and OAs were proposed to be covered to demonstrate the viability of decentralized local-level support by:

1. Intensive and ongoing teaching–learning support.
2. Community facilitation by ICDS supervisors only, with remote and periodic support from CLR.
3. Intensive engagement with the ICDS state- and block-level machinery to educate them and advocate for structural and

procedural changes within ICDS, which are desirable for achieving effective AWCs. This may be considered a 'handing-over' phase or the exit strategy.

The project had a well-laid-out evaluation design, with the expected outcomes and indicators clearly defined as follows:

1. *Children:* Children in OAs would demonstrate 75 per cent and in CAs 50 per cent improvement and some improvement in the RAs in cognitive abilities of classification, seriation, basic concepts, number readiness and language skills, including verbal expression and reading readiness against the baseline.
2. *Anganwadis:* Sixty-five per cent of OAs, 25 per cent of CAs and at least 10 per cent of RAs would demonstrate improved quality of ECE with regard to parameters related to domains of learning space, materials, instructional time, classroom processes and knowledge, skills and attitudes of AWWs as compared to the baseline.
3. *Community:* The community would be aware of the importance of ECE and be supportive of it in at least 50 per cent of the villages with OAs, 25 per cent villages with CAs and 25 per cent in the RAs in terms of awareness and 25 and 10 per cent respectively in terms of involvement.
4. *Functionaries and larger system:* The project would demonstrate a decentralized training model through capacity building of Anganwadi Workers Training Centre (AWTC) trainers, supervisors and block resource development players.

12.5. Organogram

CLR engaged a composite and well-defined team for the Dharni project, with a central team based in Pune at the headquarters for mentoring and supervision and the other, that is, the project team, stationed closer to implementation, that is, in Dharni district itself, to ensure proximity to the field. Figure 12.1 depicts the organogram for the project.

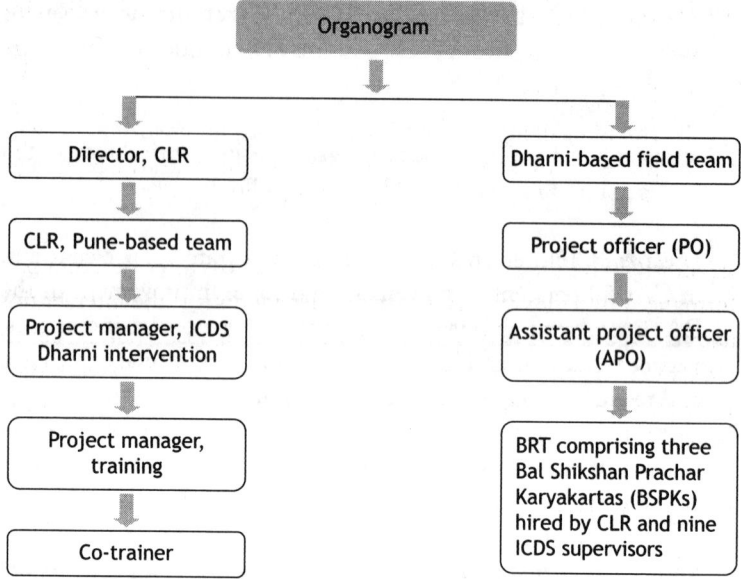

Figure 12.1. *Organogram*

12.6. Methodology for the Case Study

The methodology agreed for all case studies under this qualitative research project was followed.

12.6.1. Sampling Process

12.6.1.1. *Selection of Centres*

The selection of the following two AWCs for the study from among the 215 AWCs in Dharni block was done in consultation with the project team including programme director and programme manager:

- *Dahinda AWC:* Selected as one demonstrating good practice due to the following reasons:

    1. The AWW was rated as a motivated and experienced AWW.
    2. It was an OA.
    3. AWW conducted developmentally appropriate activities.

- *Harda AWC:* Selected as challenging due to the following reasons:
  1. It was a CA.
  2. It had challenge of multilingual classroom environment with presence of Kevati, Korku, Hindi and Marathi languages resulting in home language and AWC language divide.

In addition, five more AWCs were observed across three different performance categories to have a better understanding of the intervention and its impact. The AWTC, Amravati, and mid-level training centre (MLTC), Nagpur, which were involved in Phase I of the intervention were also visited along with their lab centres to assess the extent to which they had adopted the CLR approach.

12.6.1.2. Selection of Children

Six children, three from each centre, were selected for assessment of school readiness and adaptive behaviour. The following points were considered while selecting the children:

- Regular attendance
- Age: five years; if not available, then four–five years
- One better performing child to assess the benchmark
- Gender diversity

In addition to the above, the school-readiness instrument (SRI) was also administered on five more children in lab of AWC in Mulshi and MLTC, Lonar, to get a more varied view of the extent to which the quality reform is impacting children's outcomes.

12.6.1.3. Identification of Interviewee/Key Informants for Interaction

In order to explore the extent of understanding, ownership and impact of the programme by diverse stakeholders, we interacted with parents of the selected children and others, AWWs, paraprofessionals/helpers, supervisors, primary school teachers, CLR programme manager, field officers, programme officers, Bal Shikshan Prachar Karyakartas

(BSPKs), child development project officer, chief executive officer (CEO), and MLTC and AWTC training personnel.

12.6.2. Field Visits for Data Collection

Data collection was carried out over two visits, that is, from 12 to 17 March 2012 and from 5 to 10 August 2012. Both the visits were finalized in consultation with and facilitated by the CLR team. Since neither of us spoke Marathi and Korku (tribal language), we sought their help for interpretation and the assistant project officer (APO) from CLR, who is stationed in Dharni, helped us as interpreter for tool administration. For interviews and focus group discussions (FGDs), the other CLR field team members supported us, as and when required.

The case study exercise was initiated with a visit to the CLR in Pune where we interacted with the project staff and former and current directors of CLR. The interviews focused on understanding the initial conceptualization and vision for the project and how the envisaged processes have been communicated to all levels of management and implementation.

We also visited CLR's field lab and demonstration area in Mulshi on the outskirts of Pune and observed an Anganwadi for the full day to understand the 'CLR model of ECE' and the pedagogical approach. We administered the SRI on three children to assess the school-readiness levels. This was followed by an FGD with AWWs from four lab Anganwadis in Mulshi.

During the second field visit, the ICDS MLTC in Nagpur and the AWTC in Amravati were visited, and job and refresher trainings of supervisors and AWWs observed. We also interviewed the principals and training staff in both institutions and visited their four lab/model AWCs for detailed observation. In addition, we interacted with the CEO of the district panchayat at Amravati.

12.6.2.1. Observation of Centres in Dharni

In the Dharni block, as mentioned above, a total of seven Anganwadis were observed over the course of the two visits. Of these, in two AWCs, Dahinda and Harda AWCs, which were studied in greater detail, participant observations were carried out for the full day on both occasions, using the Early Childhood Education Quality Assessment Scale (ECEQAS) developed by CECED, and the SRI was administered on three children selected on a random basis from each centre, as per the agreed methodology. Video documentation of classroom processes, trainings and FGDs were carried out to capture the richness of data.

Detailed interviews of the AWWs and helpers, the child development project officer and the CLR field staff members based in Dharni were also conducted. In addition, FGDs were conducted with all the supervisors and community members at both sites. A monthly circle-level training conducted by a supervisor and the BSPK was also observed to assess the extent to which the supervisors were enabled to conduct the training. The purpose was also to judge how the programme philosophy and methodology articulated by the CLR leadership and higher-level managers had percolated through the different levels.

12.6.3. Analysis of Data

After data collection, the qualitative as well as quantitative data was organized. The recorded qualitative data was transcribed and coded using etic and emic codes to form categories. Thereafter, codes were grouped together to form themes. Once the themes were identified, 'claims' were developed around them, keeping in mind the guiding questions to describe the cardinal findings of the study. These findings were supported by triangulation of data from multiple sources.

12.6.4. Findings from the Case Study

Overall, we came away from Dharni with a clear understanding that the project had been very well conceptualized by CLR, with a planned approach towards systemic reform in the area of ECE. This was reflected in its comprehensive design, which included, on the one hand, an incremental and phased approach in terms of the 'diffusion model' and development of decentralized capacities and, on the other, a systemic approach in going beyond the field site to include the MLTCs and AWTCs, which prepare the AWWs and supervisors through job and refresher trainings and can be expected to have larger impact on the district as a whole. The fact that these complementary features reflect an effort to address important issues of scalability and sustainability of the project upfront needs to be appreciated.

While the project design was comprehensive and systemic, its strength lay more significantly in its commendable and detailed attention to processes, which in turn provide some very useful learnings for the system. The reflective and responsive attitude of the project management and staff towards project implementation was a commendable feature of this project.

While the project had a clearly spelt out implementation strategy aimed at gradually moving from reform of the 19 OAs to all the 215 Anganwadis in Dharni block, the project's strength also lay in the capacity of the project managers and coordinators to reflect continuously on their predefined strategy vis-à-vis expected process outcomes and their willingness to consider and make mid-course changes, if required, in response to emerging challenges.

The attention to detail comes through clearly in the overall training strategy, which was recurrent and onsite and was planned keeping in mind realistic learning goals for the trainees. Based on the trainees' existing practices, it was designed to handhold them step by step and enable them to move from 'familiar to the unfamiliar', rather than overfeed them with new information. Along with this slow but steady approach, the entire training was demonstration based, in actual model Anganwadi situations, which not only facilitates hands-on experience but also tends to sensitize the workers and others who are being trained through this 'practice-mediated' approach. This is particularly facilitated when the trainees are able to observe the positive response of children to good child-centred teaching–learning situations. CLR has a very-well-designed kit of materials to back up this practice.

The project also demonstrates the critical importance of mentoring, follow-up and maintaining regular communication with the field workers, in addition to recurrent training, a provision completely lacking in the larger regular system. Another commendable feature of the project is its emphasis on learning from demonstrated good practice, the rationale for developing model OAs. While the project provided several positive learnings, there were also some gaps, particularly with regard to ensuring ownership of the approach and the need for community involvement, which indicate the critical importance of these factors in terms of sustainability and scalability of the model.

Each of the above elements lead up to some significant claims, based on evidence from the field, and point to some useful learnings for the system. These are discussed further in detail.

Claim 1: Demonstration of Good ECE Practice through Model AWCs-enabled AWWs and All Levels of Functionaries to Develop a Common Vision of Good-quality ECE Classroom Practice

The CLR 'model of good practice' is of a field-tested, developmentally appropriate ECE curriculum which, as articulated in the project documents, reflects a 'cognitive, ecological and sociocultural perspective taking into account the local context'. In its more visible form, it laid emphasis on a structured two-and-a-half-hour-long preschool education programme, an attractive classroom layout with activity corners and in particular an improvised doll's corner, display of children's work and a CLR kit of play-based learning materials and age-appropriate activities for different aspects of development and school readiness. The day in the OAs began with a half hour of supervised free play in activity corners, which was thoroughly enjoyed by the children. Children were seen running to the Anganwadi in the morning to be in time to make their choice of the activity corner. This was followed by attendance through a beautiful pre-literacy activity in which children 'read'/recognized their name cards through some cues without yet being able to even recognize the alphabet!

The rest of the day saw a balance of developmentally appropriate activities, some individual but mostly group, related to language and cognitive development. After lunch, the four- to six-year-olds were engaged in school-readiness activities through cards and on the blackboard in a play-based mode, while younger children played outdoors or went home.

These activities were considered essentials for all Anganwadis under the project, and the aim was to upgrade each of the 215 Anganwadis to the level of being able to demonstrate all these features.

The model demonstrated by the OAs, as seen in Mulshi as well as in Dharni, was indeed very impressive, especially for a low-cost Anganwadi programme. The activities, processes and interactions among AWWs and the children which were observed were not only very developmentally appropriate but also in some cases very innovative.

The play-way approach in which attendance was taken, the excellent organization of free play activity, innovative conduct of some of the school-readiness activities, as well as the skills and attitude demonstrated by the AWWs and helpers, deserve special mention. These were intensively observed for the duration of an entire day's programme with the help of ECEQAS, and we found that these centres rated significantly higher than scores obtained on this tool from other preschool education programmes in other states.

Moreover, the scores on SRI clearly indicate better school-readiness levels in children from OAs of Dahinda and Mulshi as compared to the other Anganwadis. Interestingly, the children from Dahinda, which is a Korku tribe, scored the best, with their scores better than the Mulshi children, despite the latter being a more peri-urban site and nearer to a metro city like Pune; the latter would have been expected to perform better due to better exposure. The programme content in the Dahinda Anganwadi was observed to be more focused on school-readiness parameters, thus explaining this advantage. In both cases, the children's ages were comparable. While the poorer performance of children in MLTC and AWTC Anganwadis and in Harda could be attributed to these Anganwadis being qualitatively less effective, another factor could be the timing of the assessment, which was in August when children had just come in to the new term, whereas in Mulshi and Dahinda the children were assessed in March, just before they were to go to school. This could be a significant factor influencing the scores as well.

The importance of setting up these model Anganwadis is key to the entire project design. As Dr Zakiya Kurien articulated, 'Unless you can model a programme, how do you encourage a community to send children regularly to ECE?' The programme officer at Dharni was convinced that 'one remembers more of what one sees and not just of what one hears'. He believed that this concrete model also enabled him to make concrete suggestions for the programme to the AWW.

Karyakaram se unko dekhne ko mila hai ...to wo unke dimag me hai.
(Project officer, Dharni)

(They see and they retain.)

One may well say, 'seeing is believing', especially when one sees some good practice in a remote tribal area and that too conducted by an AWW who has studied up to Grade 10 only. Our own perception of the programme was determined not only by the practice demonstrated by the AWW but more by the positive response of the children to the programme, which makes it very convincing. In an overall ICDS scenario where a minimalist programme of a song and a rhyme get accepted as ECE, this balanced, planned and child-centred practice is very commendable.

Offering a model for demonstration is possibly also the most efficient way of diffusing the message and getting other centres to emulate. This was evident from our observations that the different categories of centres visited had adopted the 'model practice' in varying forms. While the OAs were demonstrating it more innovatively, the CAs were doing it in a more structured way and the RAs had got the physical layout to an extent but were still to internalize the processes and activities. What appeared was that they were all on the same track, though at different milestones, within a period of two years. This could be attributed to a considerable extent to the fact that they all had been able to form a common vision.

The MLTC and AWTC visited in Amravati and Nagpur also had a 'mock Anganwadi', which had a similar layout, and the training of supervisors and AWWs was done in these rooms with materials so that the trainees could experience the desired classroom practice themselves. They referred to it as the 'CLR model'.

Claim 2: Recurrent and Onsite training and Follow-up Led to Deeper Levels of Capacity Strengthening of AWWs and Supervisors as Evident in the AWCs

The fact that the project could demonstrate changes in classroom practice within a short period of time, albeit to varying extent, is also attributable to the training approach in the Dharni project. This can be best understood in terms of deconstructing it into some subclaims, which provide useful learning for planning 'training for transformation'.

Subclaim 2.1: Setting Realistic Goals for Training, Keeping in View the Context and Level of the Trainees, Made the Training More Effective

The envisioned reform and the training to bring about that reform are clearly located within the ICDS context and take into account the provisions already under ICDS and work around these. This is very evident in the design of the model centre which prescribes a curriculum for just two hours, as mandated for preschool education in the ICDS; it takes into account the constraints of AWWs who are not very skilled and are also required to undertake many other multisectoral tasks, as also the limitations of space and materials.

Dr Kurien again clarified, 'Knowing the constraints of this worker we have designed … we have set 2 to 2 and a half hours of a preschool programme which is limited … that is the time she has, since she can be doing other things….'

The programme coordinator emphasized the need to set realistic goals or expectations from the training: 'For each BSPK, there are going to be 3 Anganwadis where community participation will be stressed … because all of them have 12 Anganwadis, we cannot start working on all immediately.'

This principle is evident in the overall design of the project where the diffusion is expected in phases, as described above. While the OAs were those with a higher baseline and could be brought to a certain standard within the first phase, the CAs had constraints and needed more time. This was provided for in the project design itself.

Subclaim 2.2: Giving Small and Simpler Dosage Recurrently Rather Than a Lot of Information Together Worked Better

In the FGD with the BSPKs, we were told:

Ek sath bhot sara nahin ... dimag mein rakhne ki ek limit hoti hai.

(We should not give too much in one shot.... There is a limit to what one can retain.)

This incremental approach to training was possible because there was a provision for recurrent training, so that the modules could get distributed and phased out. This incremental approach did show dividends in that across all levels from the programme team in Dharni to the supervisors and AWWs, they all had a common vision and vocabulary at least of the basic features of the model. Their levels of understanding may have been different. However, this claim is also indirectly substantiated by the fact that the MLTC and AWTC lab Anganwadis showed less understanding of the approach, because they had only received an initial training since the CLR team was concentrating on the Dharni block.

Subclaim 2.3: Observation of 'Real-time' Process with Children Sensitized the Trainees Better, Enhanced Their Understanding and Changed Attitudes

The BSPKs' training provides a good demonstration of this principle as their training spanned over four phases. In Phase I, which was for five days at Dharni, they did two days of actual observation of OAs to understand the model to be promoted. Further, they observed some non-project Anganwadis for two days to get a comparative sense of what happens on a more regular basis in the system and then for one day they actually worked in an OA with children. In Phase II, they spent 11 days in Mulshi lab area, where for the first 3 days they were exposed to a situation analysis and an overview of ECE, followed by a 1 full-day observation of Mulshi OAs and for the last 3 days they worked in Mulshi Anganwadis and did activities with children and discussed their experience.

The training concluded with a four-day perspective building and skill development. In Phase III, they worked in the OAs for all the five days. In Phase IV, they had a joint training of five days with the supervisors.

The BSPKs shared with us,

> *Mulshi ki Anganwadis humko batayi gayi.... Observation karne ko bola.... Phir baad mein activities lene laga vaha kendra mein ... bachche kaise hote he ... wo samaj muje aayi ... voh bahut jaruri tha samajne ke liye ... varna agar mujhe theoretical sab bataya jata tha to shayad nahi samaj ata tha muje....*

(We were taken to Mulshi Anganwadis and asked to observe. We learnt what children were like; mere theory would not have given me that understanding.)

The impact of this intensive, hands-on process was very evident in the confidence level demonstrated by the BSPKs in both planning and conducting the monthly meeting of the AWWs and in the mentoring process. It was also reflected in their capacity to analyse their own experience in the project critically, as evident in discussions with them.

Subclaim 2.4: Opportunities for Peer Learning Helped Trainees Learn from Each Other—Again a More Effective scaffolding

The 'demonstration and diffusion model' adopted by CLR itself rests on the principle of peer learning. The intention was to get the contiguous AWWs to learn from OAs and RAs from the contiguous in a relay mode. To some extent, this had now been built into the monthly circle meetings too of the AWWs, so that by rotation one or two AWWs would volunteer to demonstrate some good practice with children and others critique it and learn from it.

> *Training is liye jaruri hai kyun ki, kucch log accha kaam agar kar rahe hai to usko to hum exposure dete hai ki unhone kya kya kiya jiski vajah se baki ki sevika ho unko kucch madad mil sake, vo kucch unse sikh sake.*
> (FGD, BSPKs)

(Training is necessary to give opportunity for the AWWs to learn from those who are doing good work.)

This was also evident in an informal way in RAs which were visited without warning, where some good practice was visible, although the worker had not yet received any training. She confessed that she had learnt it from the neighbouring CA!

Subclaim 2.5: Recurrent Training and Follow-up Helped to Establish a Relationship and Bring in Accountability

The programme officer placed a lot of emphasis on the need for follow-up and constant communication. He reflected on this process in comparison to the more common 'one-shot training' in government programmes.

Jaise pehle training hote the aur Amravati ka training lia 1 din ka ...
wapas aaye fir koi dekhne ko nahin aaya lekin abi to ye shuru ho gya ...
fir 10 din me ek bar to jana to unko laga ye to abi problem ho gya hai....

(Earlier they had training for one day and the trainers never came back to follow up, but that's not so now. Every 10 days there is a follow-up.)

Follow-up visits by the BSPKs and the programme manager gave them a sense of purpose and commitment towards the reform. An AWW said that she felt, 'These people are working so hard, coming to see our work so we should also do our best.' BSPKs also did handholding and confidence building for them as they moved forward with what was to them a different approach to preschool education. It was important for them to know whether they were on track. If challenges were encountered, there was an opportunity to get clarifications or find solutions jointly with the other AWWs, supervisors and BSPKs.

Claim 3: Follow-up Was Found To Be More Effective because It Involved Not Only supervision but Also Close and Effective Mentoring

The key role played in bringing about change by the reflective, recurrent and hands-on design of the training was supplemented by regular mentoring and handholding by the programme team. The programme manager himself mentored the OAs along with the deputy programme manager, while the CAs were jointly mentored by BSPKs and supervisors.

Each of the mentors was expected to spend a full working day in the Anganwadi and support and demonstrate good practice as per the model. The process of mentoring was also reflective of the attention to detail in the programme in making it more effective. Some mentoring principles learned from the observations and discussions are discussed further.

Subclaim 3.1: Mentoring Process Should Not Impose Ideas from Outside, but Build on Existing Resource and Practice

The approach adopted by the mentors was very congenial and collegial and not in the least officious. The principle of moving from familiar to unfamiliar was followed very carefully, as evident from the following quote:

> *Jo unke pas tha wo dena shuru kiya .... gaane khel shuru kiye ... to jaise circle me bithana pehle to wo ... diwar ko chipak ke baithate the, lekin circle me bithana ... bataya.* (Programme officer, Dharni)
>
> (Started with what they were already doing and suggested changes in that; for example, they used to get children to sit along the wall, demonstrated to them how to make them sit in a circle.)

The mentoring process rested on the understanding that appreciation of effort is more important than criticism, and any suggestions need to build on this principle, so as to enable the AWWs who are on a new track of Practise to develop self-confidence and motivation.

Subclaim 3.2: Mentoring Was Effective because It Focused on Demonstration and Not Instruction

The guiding principle for the mentors was that they should not instruct but demonstrate any suggestions that they may have for the AWW—an emphasis on 'do how' and not 'know how'!

As the programme officer expressed this principle, '*Instruction se nahin lekin sath me kaam kar ke...*' (Not through instruction but by working along with them....). This was further endorsed by the ECE coordinator in Mulshi who followed a similar approach there.

In the course of our visit too, we noticed that the BSPK in-charge of the Anganwadis we visited would quietly sit at the back and on one visit during a circle activity sat in the circle with the children and followed the AWW's instruction and participated like the children. There was no attempt to comment or criticize the worker while she was doing the activities—the stance was very much of the proverbial 'fly on the wall'! Even while our team was observing, there was no effort on his part to seek attention and he sat in a very unobtrusive manner. After the children had left, we observed him talking with the AWW and demonstrating an activity. She was also freely sharing her views with him. There was evidently a cordial relationship between them. It is again important to note that the programme team was able to demonstrate mainly because of the intensive 'hands-on training' they had been given which prepared them for the role.

Subclaim 3.3: Regular Mentoring and Communication with the Field Workers and a Non-hierarchical Relationship Was Effective in Helping Build the Mentor–Mentee Relationship

Regular visits and maintenance of other regular modes of communication were observed to be key factors in building this important relationship.

> *Mera to 10 baje se pura Anganwadi shuru hone se Anganwadi ka samay khatam hone tak pura samay wahan rukna tha aur uske baad bhi kuch uski mansik tayari hai to kuch uske sath material development.* (Programme officer, Dharni)

> (I would spend the whole day in the Anganwadi and help also with material development and planning.)

Despite the difficult terrain, regular communication with the AWWs was possible, since they all possessed mobile phones. The BSPKs had all the phone numbers and knew each worker well, including her family problems! This easy access to BSPKs gave the workers confidence and faith in the mentors, and this evidently contributed to the positive and constructive relationship between them.

Claim 4: Mentoring Was Effective because Mentors Were Also Provided Mentoring

The success of the project could be attributed to a significant extent to the different levels of resource support available to the project, right from CLR faculty to programme coordinators in the field to supervisors. While the programme team, that is, the coordinators and BSPKs, were providing mentoring in the field, they also received continuous mentoring and handholding from the CLR team which was visiting initially every month and then every quarter.

The relationship between the CLR team and programme coordinator and BSPKs was observed to be as non-hierarchical as was theirs with the AWWs. It was a very good example of 'walking the talk'. This came through not only in the nature of their interactions but also in the collective analysis and reflection which we observed often happening among them about any issue in the field and how to address it. We observed the BSPKs also giving ideas on how the problem needs to be addressed.

Claim 5: The Recurrent Training and Mentoring Not Only Had a Positive Impact on the Programme and on the Supervisors but Also Led to the AWWs' Self-transformation

The positive, constructive approach with a focus on relationships in the project approach led to a very visible impact on the self-esteem as well as confidence levels of all functionaries, especially the supervisors and the AWWs, who had to ultimately sustain the initiative. Supervisors were enabled to play the role of trainers, rather than only collecting and submitting data and examining records. As the programme officer indicated, this is reflected in their motivation:

> *Supervisors ka motivation usme bhot badha. Supervisors ki position badhi unko lagta ki ye mere position ka kam hai; ki pehle to thik hai data collect karo, compile karo aur office me do uske alawa as a trainer wo khadi ho gayi aur training dena uski tyari karna … wo kam unko acha lgne laga.* (Programme officer)

> (Supervisors' motivation was enhanced as they were given responsibility to train workers which they felt was commensurate with their job level, rather than just collecting and posting data!)

We saw evidence of this self-confidence in the monthly training conducted by the supervisors as well as in the FGD we conducted with them not only in terms of their self-confidence but also in the attitudinal change demonstrated by them towards the preschool education component. They made a strong recommendation that the preschool education component should be made compulsory for Anganwadis, for which we should ask the ICDS directorate to issue an order!

The enhanced confidence level of the AWWs was also very visible. This was more so for the ones who were now being given an opportunity to demonstrate what they could do with children.

> *AWW ko bahot great feel ho gaya hai ki dekho mai kuch alag kar rahi hu na islye log mujhe alag tarike se dekh rahe hai.*(ECE coordinator, Mulshi)

> (AWWs' confidence has gone up as they realize that they are doing something good and people are looking at them differently now!)

They are interested and keen to conduct preschool education now, as an AWW says about this component,

> *Chalta rahega madam ... mera to ye kam hai mein jab tak hu mein ye kam karungi ... bahot sara anubhav mila ... unka margadarshan hona chayiye.* (AWW, Dahinda)

> (I will continue to do this since I have learnt and gained so much experience; we need to continue to get guidance.)

This positive impact is evident not only in their confidence levels to do preschool education, but it also seems to impact their entire personality and make a difference to their emotional status.

The Mulshi AWW and Anganwadi helper shared their own story of having undergone self-transformation. One of them reported,

> I used to be very short-tempered and would fight with everyone ... get regular headaches.... Now after four years of working with children, I find myself more calm and a changed person. (FGD, AWW, Mulshi)

Other AWWs sitting around confirmed that they were witness to this change.

Similar stories were shared by an AWW in Dharni who shared that living alone, her work now with the children had become the focus of her daily life and she was completely dedicated to it. Similarly, another AWW at Harda shared how she also lived alone and how she enjoyed working with children and they had become central to her daily life.

While the project is certainly demonstrating a good practice for ECE, its sustainability and scaling up are significant issues which need to be addressed. Some gaps related to this concern are discussed further.

Claim 6: Timely Emphasis on Involvement of the Families and Community Would Have Led to Greater Probability of the Project's Sustainability

Although mobilizing the community and strengthening community awareness regarding preschool education were parts of the original project design, these aspects were not given due attention, probably due to the incremental approach followed in the project implementation. It was believed that priority should be to first change practice in the centres and use the demonstration of good practice to mobilize and educate the community. However, the interactions and FGDs with the parents and community indicated a lack of awareness of what good ECE is and also of any changes that were visible in the Anganwadis.

A major issue which came up in interactions with the community and in our follow-up with the primary schools was that of the difference between the home and school language. Since Dharni is located in Maharashtra region, the school language is Marathi, while the children we met were either Korku-speaking or Kevati-speaking, but knew Hindi additionally since Dharni shares the boundary with MP and all the trade is with that state in Hindi. Children seemed to have no opportunity to learn Marathi. On the other hand, the AWWs and the teachers in the primary schools were in almost all cases from outside Dharni and were Marathi-speaking, but knew Hindi. They did not speak the children's home language. We were told that they had to be selected from outside the block because there were very few local women who had been educated. However, in our interactions, we did find some daughters-in-law from across the MP border who had studied at least up to Grade 8 if not 10.

Interactions with primary teachers indicated that most children go up to Grades 6 and 7 before they can start understanding Marathi and by then it is too late for them to keep pace with the curriculum. So most of them drop out! The teachers were aware of the challenge but had no solution. When we interacted with the community members, we raised this issue; they seemed to be very accepting of this situation and did not show much concern. We suggested that their fathers may know Marathi and should expose children to this language at the Anganwadi stage.

The mothers seemed to be more aware of the food children were getting rather than the educational content, and there was certain helplessness in terms of their own role. An important factor facilitating sustainability of any such initiative lies in influencing the quality of the demand, rather than merely addressing the supply aspect. Its importance from all angles, ranging from ensuring better child participation to promoting sustainability of the project approach, cannot be overestimated.

Claim 7: The Sustainability and Scaling Up of the Project Will Need Much More Effort towards Creating a Sense of Ownership by the ICDS Department

A significant issue which was observed in the interaction with the CEO, the district panchayat and the block level ICDS functionaries was that while they appreciated the CLR project, there was very little ownership of the work done. The project was referred to as CLR's without seeing their own role or contribution in it. The CEO had very little information on the project, which was to be expected since he had been recently posted in that position. But the officials under him were also not aware of the work in Dharni. The CEO's argument was that with endemic malnutrition in the Melghat region, that becomes a priority and preschool education needs to take a back seat. The CLR material was seen as different from the ICDS materials in the field, including display of two separate time tables, CLR's and ICDS', on the same wall! Charts supplied by the ICDS were not put to use, since the focus was only on CLR material. For any sustained impact, it would therefore be necessary to work on reversing this trend and making the ICDS system own the CLR initiatives as their own.

12.7. In Conclusion

The Dharni case study presents on the whole a very effective combination of (a) a vision for developmentally appropriate preschool education curriculum and (b) a demonstration of the need and importance of paying attention to the detailed processes which go into making of any intervention aimed at quality reform. While undoubtedly the capacities have been created and attitudes changed among the ICDS functionaries at the ground level through this project, given the hierarchical government system, the gains can only be sustained if the concerned departments of ICDS and education make ECE their joint priority. With the new National Policy on Education 2020 in place now, with its emphasis on ECCE as a part of the foundational stage of school education and its underlining of the need for interdepartmental convergence, there is hope that this may happen soon.

CHAPTER 13

Public–Private Partnership for Government Preschools in Rural Areas

Harini Raval

> According to government's guidelines, a supervisor should visit 50 per cent of Anganwadis under him in a month. But here at Bhansali Trust, we have very little work in the office and most of the work is on the field only. The other supportive office work is done by someone else. (CDPO)

The ICDS programme in Sami block of Gujarat was bolstered by three important partnerships, all of which exemplify characteristics which are essential for effective collaboration. One of the key reasons for the success of this two-decade-old partnership was the autonomy provided by the state to the Bhansali Trust, as they recognized the long-term, service-oriented commitment of the organization. This autonomy allowed the trust to create customized solutions for on-the-ground issues, take initiative and remove barriers in service delivery.

In operational terms, the role of the child development pro-ject officer (CDPO) was crucial in building and maintaining the partnership, as she was accountable to both the state government and the trust. The high degree of autonomy granted to the CDPO was unusual but was key to developing a responsive system. She in turn created a respectful environment for other ICDS functionaries and encouraged them to make their own decisions.

This stable long-term partnership created space for the entry of a third partner, the UNICEF state office. UNICEF was able to bring in the technical expertise needed to strengthen the early childhood education (ECE) curriculum. A supportive system was already in place and new feedback mechanism were developed to strengthen the ECE component. This openness and ability to partner and learn from a new player is not seen very often in organizations implementing large-scale interventions.

We visited Vaghapura, a small village 27 km from Sami town, Patan district, Gujarat. The ECE programme was in progress at the village Anganwadi centre (AWC) operating from a two-room structure, as often is the case with AWCs. The bigger room was used to conduct activities and the smaller room served as a kitchen for the Anganwadi helper (AWH). Children had just finished a very active outdoor play with various equipment such as bat and ball, tricycle and a big ball for playing catch and throw. While the Anganwadi worker (AWW) winded up the activity, she guided the children to stand in a queue to wash their hands and feet before the morning meal. Four children were restless waiting for their turn when a child noticed the trail of water coming down the AWC stairs as poured water. He started giggling and put his finger in it to direct the water to the small saplings. The CDPO, had encouraged the AWW to plant a garden. Now each time as water was poured, Sachin and his friends who have joined the play start singing, '*aayoo, aayoo, aayoo … gayoo*' (it's come, it's come, it's come … it's gone). They put their feet across the little stream and watch the water flow down. One of them put his foot in water to stop it from flowing down but it flows over his little foot. He says, –'*ejha dketlu badhu pani piyeche*' (This tree is drinking so much water). Waiting for one's turn is no longer boring.

During our two-day observation in Vaghapura AWC, we observed that children often engaged in such spontaneous play interactions with their peers or with the AWW on many occasions, which provided a glimpse into the learning environment. The preschoolers seemed to enjoy being in AWC and in the company of their friends.

13.1. ECE Programme and Public–Private Partnership

The Bhansali Trust was established in 1969 by a seven-brother family from Palanpur, a town in North Gujarat. The trust was operated by the Bhansali family as a corporate social responsibility (CSR) arm of Bhansali and Co., a multimillion-dollar diamond business established in 1950. The brothers gave credit for their CSR initiatives to their father who believed in sharing whatever little they had even during their lower-middle-class existence. The trust was involved in CSR activities in the areas of health, education, income generation, de-addiction and humanitarian activities including monetary help for the very poor and needy families.

With an agenda to develop public–private partnerships, the Government of Gujarat invited selected NGOs to run the ICDS programme. The Bhansali Trust was invited to implement six projects in Vav, Tharad, Radhanpur, Santalpur, Sami and Haraij, which was soon extended to two tribal projects in Kaprada and Dharampur. In 1991, the operational management of the Anganwadi Workers Training Centre (AWTC) at Radhanpur was also taken up by the trust. The government gave autonomy to the private partner to recruit workers, implement and monitor the programme. In 2012, a total of 1,236 Anganwadis in North Gujarat were operated by the trust.

UNICEF, began supporting the ECE component of the Gujarat ICDS from 2009 to improve quality. This was part of a project supported by the IKEA Foundation in the cotton-growing districts, where children were engaged in labour. The initiative started with developing standards and indicators, preparation of a draft ECE policy for the state and an ECE framework. The aim of the project was to cover six districts where social development indicators were poor. The ECE initiative which began in Kutch and Vadodara was later extended to Patan in 2011. When we visited the two Anganwadis, UNICEF was engaged with ICDS Sami for only six months.

13.2. Socio-demographic Context

This case study was conducted in Patan district in Sami block in the northern district in Gujarat in the year 2012. It is flanked by the Great Rann of Kutch on one side. It was the ancient capital of Gujarat. According to the official government website, the population was approximately 1,181,941.[1] Agriculture and weaving were the primary occupations. Patan's literacy rate was 60 per cent. The official language of the district is Gujarati.

Sami, a rural block in the Patan district, is one of the two blocks which were declared backward based on the human development indicators. At that time, there were 100 villages in the block with the total population of 182,783,[2] predominantly from Other Backward Castes (OBCs). The language spoken was a dialect of Gujarati. The block due to its proximity with the Rann of Kutch faced many challenges, the most debilitating being that of water shortage, resulting in regular droughts. The block scored low on many of the human development indicators such as 47.71[3] per cent female literacy and 49.45 per cent malnutrition. There were limited livelihood earning opportunities, resulting in regular migration of families to greener districts. All these issues had a bearing on the education of children. Additionally, due to the proximity of the village to the desert, the water was very salty.

The Anganwadis studied by us were located in two villages, Vaghapura and Haripura, of the Sami block, one of the eight blocks in Patan. Haripura was going through a drought when we visited it for the study. Most of the villages in the Sami block were declared as 'no water source' villages by the Gujarat government. Even drinking water was not available, leave alone water for irrigation. A long history of water deprivation had weakened these areas economically. Living conditions were very difficult. It being a drought-prone area, vegetables were not easily available. Anaemia and vitamin and iron deficiencies were rampant among the villagers.

[1] patandp.gujarat.gov.in
[2] https://patandp.gujarat.gov.in/gu/taluka/Sami/Taluka-General-Outline
[3] https://patandp.gujarat.gov.in/gu/taluka/Sami/Taluka-General-Outline

13.3. Study of Anganwadis in Two Villages

We followed the research method recommended for all the case studies (refer to Chapter 2). We focused our investigation on three broad aspects: (a) organization and ECE programme, (b) AWC and (c) community. Under the first theme, we explored the programme philosophy and vision, organizational and curricular objectives, organizational structure and programme management processes. For the second theme on the AWC, we focused on the classroom infrastructure and available material, the teaching–learning process and student outcomes, competencies of the functionaries, and their relationship. Finally, the third theme of the community was studied to understand the community support and family involvement in the Anganwadis.

We selected two Anganwadis, one in Vaghapura and the other in Haripura, using the criteria developed for the study, with guidance from the CDPO. The Vaghapura Anganwadi was selected as it was viewed to be effective in circumstances normal to Patan. The Anganwadi in Haripura was chosen as it was viewed to be relatively effective despite concerns related to migration and water shortage. Further, as required by the study, three children between the ages of four and six years from each centre were selected to administer the School-readiness instrument (SRI) and adaptive behaviour scale (ABS). Open-ended interviews were used to explore the first theme along with an expert review of (a) the teaching–learning kit provided by UNICEF and (b) the monitoring checklist and monthly progress report used in the ICDS programme.

Vaghapura was a predominantly upper-caste village inhabited by the Thakur community listed under the OBCs. This village was located about 27 km from the Sami block headquarter and fairly well connected with private and public transport. Agriculture was the main source of livelihood. Tube wells in many of the farms had reduced the intensity of water shortage and dependence on rain. Families migrated for shorter duration, mainly to work in the adjoining greener districts as farm labourers. Most of the homes were pucca, with a veranda in front often used to dry farm produce such as cotton and castor oil seeds or to keep the colourful sankheda[4] crib if there was a baby in the family. The female literacy rate was 47.55[5] per cent and malnutrition in children under five years of age was 51.99 per cent.

Haripura was inhabited by Nirashrit Thakurs, also OBCs, who migrated from Pakistan some generations back. It was one of the interior villages, 42 km from the block headquarter and not very well connected by public and private transport. The biggest challenge that Haripura faced was that of migration; almost 60–65 per cent of the village population was out of the village at the time of our visit. The villagers migrated mainly to the brick kilns for relatively long durations of six–eight months at a stretch. Economic backwardness was accentuated by the prevalence of large families. When families returned to the village, children often lost weight, displayed signs of malnutrition and performed poorly in class. Younger children lost the habit of attending the preschool programme in the Anganwadi. These factors had an important bearing on the health and development of children. The female literacy rate was as low as 9 per cent and malnutrition in children in the age group of birth to 5 years was 68.5 per cent.

We observed that a child's day in the two villages started early when parents left for work in the fields. Breakfast consisted of *rotla* left over from dinner, the night before. Children were seen playing with mud, bricks, cycle tires, etc. Very often these young children accompanied caregivers to the milk collection centre or to the fields where they collected jeera or moth from the fields and exchanged it at the village shop for sweets. During the month of February and March, they went to the fields with older siblings to pluck Pillu, a small red berry-like fruit, children's favourite pass time. Children in Vaghapura regularly went to the village temple for the evening *aarti* (evening prayers) mainly to get *prasad* (food offered to Hindu gods).

---

[4] Sankheda furniture is colourful teak wood furniture of Gujarat, India, treated with lacquer and painted in traditional bright shades of maroon and gold; https://en.wikipedia.org/wiki/Sankheda_furniture

[5] https://www.census2011.co.in/data/village/509012-vaghpura-gujarat.html retrieved on 23.4.2012

Our methods included interviews, semi-structured and structured observation of classroom, student assessment, focus group discussions as well as expert review of documents and artefacts. Open-ended interviews were our chief mode of investigation which we used for exploring almost all the themes.

While exploring various aspects of organization and ECE programme, our first theme, we used open-ended interviews extensively and also conducted an expert review of (a) the teaching–learning kit provided by UNICEF to understand the implicit curricular objectives being promoted under the ECE programme and (b) the monitoring checklist and monthly progress report used in the ICDS programme. We conducted anecdotal observations to understand classroom practices. Moreover, we used the tools recommended for the study to document classroom quality and its effects on children (Chapter 2). Finally, an early childhood expert reviewed the timetable to examine the curriculum. The extent of family involvement and community partnership were mostly understood through focus group discussions.

In order to understand the functioning of the two selected Anganwadis, we interviewed management trustees of the trust—Mr Ashok and Mahesh Bhansali—the CDPO, ACDPO, a supervisor, the Vaghapura AWW and AWH, and the Haripura AWW and AWH, respectively. In addition, we spoke to the education specialist UNICEF, Gujarat, and the UNICEF state consultant. Findings from the study are presented under the three broad themes of:

- The trust and the ECE programme
- AWCs
- Community

13.4. The Trust and the ECE Programme

Our discussions with the trustees—the Bhansali brothers—and CDPO helped to establish that there was a strong value to serve the community across all levels. Both the management trustees were actively engaged with the work of the trust and contributed their share of the family business profits to the trust. The CDPO was highly motivated and had chosen to work with the trust, foregoing the perks and prospect of growth which usually come with government employment. She believed that she could serve more effectively when working with the trust. The quotes below illustrate the dedication at different levels of the programme:

> I had decided that my field of work will be social work. I was a follower of Gandhi ji and read many of his books. In these I came across the idea that not having the responsibility of a family helps better dedicate one's life to social work. I decided at the age of 16 years that I will never marry. (Trustee)

> The reason why I joined this NGO (ICDS programme supported by the Bhansali Trust) is that though the government was offering a similar opportunity, I had very little interest in government files. I had completed my MSW and wanted to work in remote areas. I felt this was a good NGO and work seemed to be good too. It was due to my passion that I joined this NGO. (CDPO)

> I enjoy serving these kids. (AWW)

Both the trustees expressed a commitment to allowing people to make decisions regarding their work. They focused on providing quality training, gave autonomy and created a feedback system to scaffold the growth of the staff. The CDPO shared this belief; she encouraged supervisors to plan based on their priorities within a broad framework. AWWs were similarly encouraged to modify the ECE timetable to accommodate children's needs.

13.5. Change in Organizational Objectives

With engagement of UNICEF and improvement of health in Patan, ECE became a priority. According to the consultant, the priority shifted 'to emphasize on the quality of interaction that should take place in the Anganwadi and the kind of support the child should get (there)'. Programme objectives were defined and enacted by a combination of key players, including trustees, the CDPO and UNICEF. The CDPO explained the dilemmas faced by the project staff and why preschool education was often moved to the back burner in an ICDS programme:

As administrators of ICDS, we find it a little difficult. Education is one aspect out of the six components of ICDS. Naturally, when we focus on one aspect, we cannot concentrate on the other. When the AWW is expected to deliver six services, sometimes she cannot focus on one aspect while she is concentrating on the other. (CDPO)

13.6. Curricular Objectives

UNICEF played a crucial role in developing a curriculum focused on learning concepts through hands-on experiences by engaging in cooperative endeavours with peers, in all the domains of development. A guidebook was developed in Gujarati for the Anganwadi, along with an educational kit. A review by experts indicated that the curriculum for the age group of three–five years was anchored on sound principles of play-based learning and knowledge construction. There was an emphasis on developmentally appropriate practice:

This concept (age-specific activities) was beyond our imagination; but just in a week's time, (the consultant) came to our centre, told us that this can be done and this is how. We could see that within a week's time, the confidence level of our workers had gone up, that yes we can do this. (CDPO)

However, a review of the curriculum indicated that it did not sufficiently address school readiness, emergent literacy, numeracy and cognitive skills, especially for five- to six-year-old children. The UNICEF personnel explained that children above five years of age were not a priority, as they usually attend the primary school. There was a plan to develop a separate curriculum on 'school readiness' for this age group, but this plan did not acknowledge that the foundation for learning must be laid in the earlier years, and it cannot simply be addressed in a year. The shift to ECE was planned in phases. Following are the steps taken in the first phase:

1. All AWWs received a two-day training.
2. UNICEF ECE kit was provided.
3. AWW opened the centre regularly.
4. AWW provided toys and play materials to children every day.

5. Play materials were displayed at a level where children could access.
6. AWW conducted the programme according to the timetable provided by the CDPO.

This led to improvement in attendance and regularity of children. Curricular outcomes for the end of the project were less specific and included achievement of school readiness, more children in school by 2015, more children with higher learning levels, all personnel ready with strong capacities to meet with increased demands of quality education, and trainers with qualities and capabilities to train frontline workers and other personnel in quality ECE. The training of AWWs was planned to address these objectives and focused on the following topics:

1. Importance of early years in the development of child
2. Building rapport with the child to create a stress-free environment
3. What is quality ECE?
4. Demonstration of ECE kit provided by UNICEF
5. Understanding how children learn
6. Enhancing development of children
7. Enhancing physical (motor) development
8. Enhancing cognitive development
9. Enhancing language development
10. Enhancing social and emotional development
11. Use of storybooks to promote language and social–emotional development
12. Enhancing creativity
13. Creating an Anganwadi set-up
14. Developing and following a timetable

13.7. Organizational Structure: Partnership and Autonomy

The organizational structure clearly reflects a strong partnership and autonomy. The ICDS programme was supported by three key partners: ICDS, Bhansali Trust and the UNICEF state office. The partnership was held together in the following ways:

- There was a public–private partnership between the governments and Bhansali Trust; the government contact person was the CDPO.
- UNICEF Gujarat entered into a state-wide partnership with ICDS to improve the quality of ECE.
- Salary of most of the programme staff was paid by the government. However, their services were terminated when the trust stopped the programme.
- Based on requirements on the ground, Bhansali Trust in consultation with the CDPO provided for new roles to be created.

The trust provided additional financial and programme support to strengthen the ICDS programme. The CDPO reported to both the district ICDS and management of the trust. The UNICEF state consultant and the CDPO coordinated the implementation of the partnership on the ground.

The organizational chart in Figure 13.1 presents the structure of this partnership.

A key feature of this partnership was the autonomy granted to the ICDS personnel, especially the CDPO. She was responsible for defining the direction of the programme while addressing the goals of all partners. She invited resource people and as recommended budgetary changes which were usually approved by the trust. She said, 'I knew that for the betterment of the programme, if I put forward a proposal, the NGO (trust) will accept and approve it.'

The ACDPO worked with the supervisors at the block level to address issues related to community involvement and poor performance of AWW and AWH. She also assumed the role of acting CDPO when necessary. The programme team was responsible for achieving the ICDS objectives.

13.8. Effective Programme Management Processes

Programme management processes were examined from two points of view: strategy design and implementation. There was a shift in the management processes over the years, and the trust felt that the

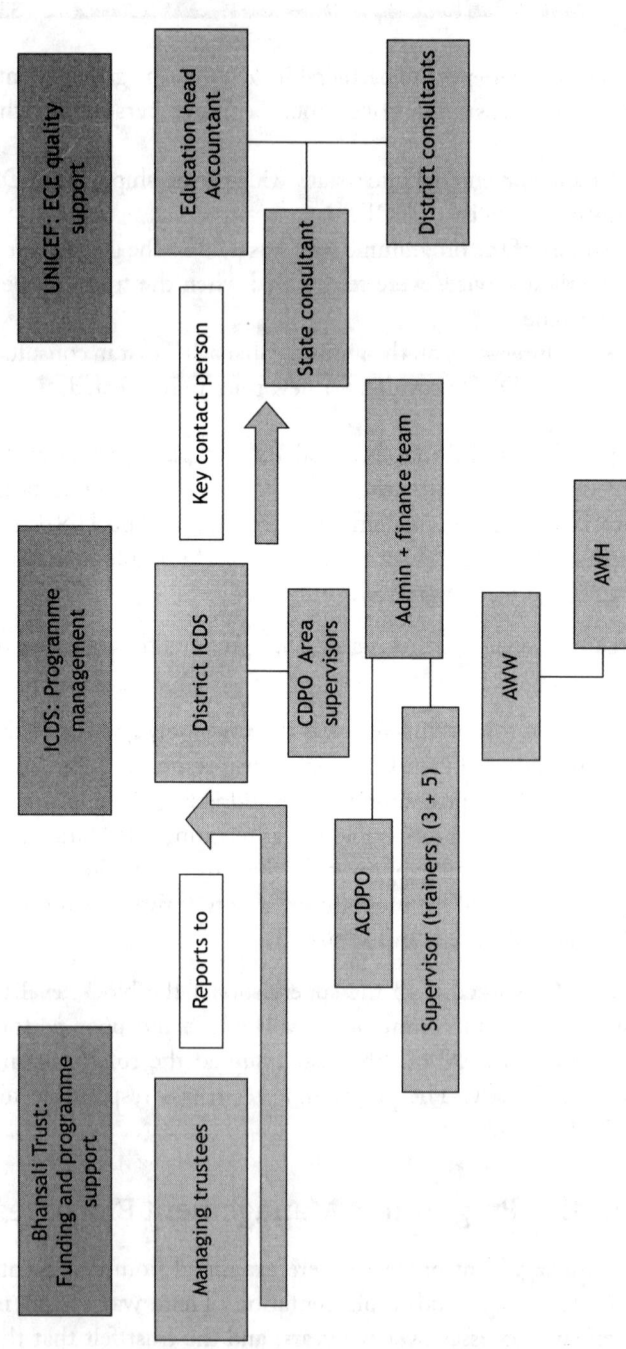

Figure 13.1. Organizational Structure

previous system was more effective. The six key aspects of programme management are discussed further.

1. Recruitment
2. Monitoring and Feedback
3. Capacity Building
4. Staff Motivation and Retention
5. Data Management
6. Budget and Resources

13.8.1. Recruitment

Initially, the programme had a consultative recruitment process undertaken by a committee with representatives from the government and the trust. However, since 2005, the government had taken over the responsibility of recruitment. The management trustees felt that this adversely affected programme quality. They had raised the issue with the government, specifically with the chief minister:

> Having a programme officer in-charge of the programme is okay—it is okay even if the staff is selected by government? Officials are in consultation with us, but they should be considered the trust's employees.[6]

Earlier, recruitment decisions were taken by a committee of five members, of which three were from the trust, which was more effective, as priority was given to local people and those from economically weaker sections. Their performance was observed for a month before a decision was made. The same criteria were applied for recruitment of workers and helpers. The quote below suggests that it was assumed that local women could be trained to conduct the activities.

> At the Vaghapura centre, we initially felt that given her lack of confidence, (the candidate) might be unable to run a centre. We found her kind of weak. But then she did a lot of work.... Then we decided to take her, thinking she could be trained. (Supervisor)

---

[6] Based on the author's discussion with a trustee.

13.8.2. Monitoring and Feedback System

A detailed two-tiered feedback and monitoring mechanism was created. Each supervisor was responsible for 17–18 Anganwadis which they visited every month. Anganwadis were graded in three categories of A, B and C on the observation checklist. The ACDPO played a crucial role in this process:

> I see the checklist (filled by the supervisor) and if there are any mistakes, then we call her (supervisor) and share them with her. Sometimes I cross-check their work. The supervisor does the work but sometimes I follow her and monitor how well she is checking.

In the monitoring tool, UNICEF increased the number of ECE indicators from 4 to 21. The ACDPO, CDPO and supervisors met to debrief regarding the checklist. This was followed by coaching and counselling of workers. The CDPO was involved only when repeated interventions did not lead to improvement in performance. A resource centre was operated by the CDPO and included reading material, activity books, audio tapes and videos in Gujarati.

13.8.3. Capacity Building

The capacity building was conducted through a cascade model with support from UNICEF. The supervisor training was strengthened by making the training interactive, participatory, fun and less material dependent. The CDPO conducted the induction training and focused on developing the capacity of supervisors as master trainers with defined specializations. The quote below indicates the focus of this model:

> Among the supervisors, there are various categories. Some of them need to work on their skills. We sit down and discuss everything in detail with them. Some are very good at reporting, and we need to read only basic details. These are very active; we can identify them during meetings and ongoing training. (CDPO)

The CDPO felt that the trainings led to changes in perspectives of supervisors. They were able to understand the need for:

- Modifying the timetable every two months
- Honouring children's interest and not forcing them to participate in activities
- A helper to support ECE activities even if she is illiterate
- Children's active participation in the process of learning

The CDPO had institutionalized the practice of compulsory coaching by supervisors to demonstrate new ECE activities. They were required to carry out monthly AWW trainings on issues which emerged from the ground. The ACDPO and the supervisor were responsible for the AWW and AWH capacity building. The quote below illustrates the effects of such coaching:

> Even when we went for a visit, she (AWW) would be nervous and she would shiver. We helped her overcome her nervousness; we put all efforts and brought her till here (her Anganwadi now gets an A grade). We met her repeatedly and counselled her. (Supervisor)

13.8.4. Staff Motivation and Retention

A deeply engrained culture of high motivation and commitment was developed over the years and resulted in high retention of staff. This culture was consciously nurtured and promoted by the CDPO. The freedom to make decisions also encouraged them to try new initiatives. Majority of the staff members had worked with the programme for 9–15 years. The CDPO chose to stay with the programme despite multiple opportunities to join the government and had to forego various benefits like promotion in order to continue in a role, which was personally satisfying for her. This culture inspired workers to go the extra mile to solve problems:

The AWW of Vaghapura said, 'I promised the parents that after the Anganwadi hours, I will take their children to my home, where they can play till the parents arrive.'

The AWH of the same centre shared,

> When a child does not come (to the Anganwadi), I go to his house, bathe the child, dress him and bring him here and in the Anganwadi put oil in his hair. If their clothes are not clean, then I sometimes wash their clothes too.

13.8.5. Data Management

Data management and other administrative operations were designed to improve programme operations by reducing paperwork, digitalizing the record keeping and creating a dedicated time slot for the AWW to complete data keeping. The CDPO pointed out that this design enabled the supervisors to increase the number of field visits per month, as illustrated by the quote in the beginning of the chapter. Moreover, she provided insight on the mechanism by which time spent on record keeping was reduced. She explained,

> I personally feel that when you want some work done, then the minimum required record keeping should be in place and should be done on a regular basis. Majority of the time should be spent on the field with the community. So the (reporting) format is computerized and given to her (supervisor) so that she does not have to do too much of writing.[7]

The Bhansali Trust has helped the CDPO in achieving this by providing funds and approving her approach. The trust has clearly communicated that engagement with the community must be given priority, and minor mistakes in record keeping need not adversely affect the work. At the time, the trust was making provisions to computerize the supervisors' reporting system. The necessary infrastructure, training and support staff were already approved by the trust. Additionally, the CDPO had taken a strong stand to prevent duplication of records. She had clearly communicated this policy to the supervisors as well: 'If the same information/record is being asked for more than once or twice, then they should inform me and I will intervene.'

Similarly for the Anganwadi, the time to focus on record keeping was minimized and limited to minimum record keeping, which is done during the Anganwadi hours of 11:00 AM to 2:00 PM. However, it is important to note that there was still considerable paperwork expected from the worker, as indicated in the following quote:

---

[7] Based on interview with CDPO by Harini Raval.

It is true that we have to maintain record, but this can be done after the school hours too. During school hours, I teach the children and take the records such as attendance registers and complete the work at home. After school hours, I go home at 2:00 PM and after lunch I go into the village after 3:30 PM for survey, and I sit in the night and do all the writing work of filling the papers and registers. (AWW)

13.8.6. Budget and Resources

Flexibility was created in the funding system through a unique partnership. While the government was the primary source for funding the programme, the Bhansali Trust and UNICEF state office provided additional resources as needed. Based on the recommendation of the CDPO, new roles were created to increase the efficiency of service delivery, and the salaries for the following additional staff were paid by the trust:

- An ACDPO
- Increase the number of supervisors from three to eight
- Create a dedicated administration and accounts team for the programme

UNICEF provided additional funds for capacity building and provision of training–learning materials to improve the quality of the ICDS programme. Similarly, the trust took care of extra expenses for additional staff, incentives, medical and educational support to staff, interest-free loans for staff, funds for replenishing materials and funding training by external resource persons. The trust released funds based on recommendations from the CDPO. Therefore, a flexible system was created to ensure flow of resources to improve efficiency as needed. The trust made funding decisions based on practical considerations with focus on ensuring delivery of ICDS. For instance, when an AWH was not available, provisions were made for temporary paid help to prepare the supplementary meal. This ensured that the AWW had adequate time for ECE activities, setting up the Anganwadi and looking for an AWH. Mr Mahesh Bhansali said that decisions were taken based on need: 'We have not kept any limit to the amount we will spend. We have not kept any limit in the trust also.'

13.9. The Curriculum

To determine the quality of a learning environment, it is necessary to consider the physical and social environment. The transaction of a curriculum is much influenced by the environment in which learning happens.

13.9.1. Classroom Environment

The scores on ECEQAS indicated that the infrastructure was good for one of the centres but was average for the other. The Haripura centre did not have a toilet, which resulted in lower scores. However, limited outdoor equipment were available, considering the number of children attending the centre.

The quality of the physical environment of the classrooms had improved remarkably due to provision of ECE kit by UNICEF, as children were able to explore a variety of materials. UNICEF provided an ECE kit for the Anganwadis. The kit included materials which addressed developmental domains, were not easily breakable, were safe and could be used in multiple ways. It included activity books for every child. Both centres scored well on items such as learning/play materials, programme schedule and class arrangement. The kit also had supportive documents such as a handout, a parent advocacy booklet and a guidebook for AWWs to support its effective implementation. An expert review of the kit revealed that while the kit was based on sound principles of early learning (play and constructivist approach), there was relatively little emphasis on cognitive development, especially like classification, seriation and one-to-one correspondence. Numeracy skills were primarily taught through activity sheets, and children had limited scope to manipulate objects or picture cards while learning these concepts. The materials displayed on the walls were placed too high and were not at the eye level of the children. This issue was being addressed through training on classroom environment, and the support from UNICEF was crucial to this process.

13.9.2. ECE Activities

The classroom observations and interviews with the functionaries revealed important information on planning of activities, children's engagement and developmental outcomes.

The ECE activities were conducted regularly based on a centrally recommended timetable. A timetable for ECE activities and supplementary nutrition programme was planned by the supervisors based on the contextual realities and was shared with AWWs during the quarterly meetings. The Haripura AWW commented on the importance of the timetable:

It (timetable) is beneficial because all the activities happen every day, and if there is no timetable we would tend to avoid certain activities. Our (CDPO) is very strict about following the timetable. Some do it with fear and some do it for the love of it.

The AWW had the freedom to change the timetable when needed to respond to children's needs and interests. UNICEF brought greater rigour to the process of developing the timetable by providing guidelines for selection of activities.

Classroom observations revealed that there was not much focus on activities for cognitive development, concept formation and emergent literacy and numeracy. The activity books designed for concept formation activities were being used mostly for colouring, and they did not require actual manipulation of objects. The education specialist of UNICEF clarified that age-appropriate teaching of concepts was not envisioned for the pilot phase, but they planned to introduce it in the subsequent phase. For this particular phase, they were satisfied if the children were familiar with the activity books.

13.9.3. Outcomes on Developmental Domains

When we considered the different aspects of development, that is, psychosocial, language and cognitive development, the scores on ABS indicated that the AWWs and parents were able to facilitate psychosocial development. However, the scores on SRI reflected that the support on language and cognitive development was inadequate. During classroom observations, we noticed that no activities were conducted in either Anganwadis for reading, writing and number readiness or for gross motor development. Moreover, in one of the Anganwadi centres, no activities were conducted on developing cognitive skills and concept formation. Less than half the children participated in activities for fine motor skill development, singing and in-action songs, suggesting it may not have appealed to them.

All the six children who were tested on the SRI from the two Anganwadis performed poorly. However, it is interesting to note that while school-readiness scores were very low, the ABS performance was more encouraging. Absolute scores on this scale for children from both the Anganwadis were average. However, both the students from Haripura scored high on the first two parameters of socialization and self-help, and one child from Vaghapura scored average. On the parameter of emotional control, one child from each class had a high score, while all the others had low scores. The children from Vaghapura scored higher on communication, as two children scored average and one child scored high, whereas both the children from Haripura had low scores.

When interpreting the scores, it is necessary to remember that UNICEF was engaged for only six months when data was collected for this study. In revising the curriculum, they had made a conscious decision to begin by focusing on social–emotional well-being and later address issues of school-readiness outcomes. Moreover, none of the children who were tested for SRI had attended the Anganwadi for three full years.

13.10. Roles and Relationships of AWW and AWH

13.10.1. Beliefs, Knowledge and Practices of AWW and AWH

The interviews with the AWWs revealed certain beliefs regarding their roles in the Anganwadis. They felt that it was necessary to emulate the home environment by paying attention to the child, giving time, handholding the child, patiently role modelling good behaviour by encouraging and appreciating the child. In practice, these beliefs were expressed through actions such as ensuring eye contact when conducting the circle time, paying more attention to new students, displaying children's art work and sharing children's performance with parents. The AWW in Vaghapura summed it up beautifully when she said, '(The AWW should be) loving and expressive. The child should feel as if his mother is dealing with her/him.'

Both AWWs also discussed their beliefs about disciplining children. They emphasized the need to promote good behaviour through dialogue with children and parents, and modelling appropriate actions. They were of the opinion that punitive treatment was undesirable, and they advised parents not to resort to such strategies. The Vaghapura AWW felt that it was not useful to be very strict with children. 'Sometimes children are mischievous, I allow them that space—after all they are children—but I keep a check on them.' The AWWs expressed that by encouraging children to participate in caring for the centre, they helped foster an ownership for the Anganwadi and supported children's learning. The workers believed that they could learn from children and encouraged them to share stories and songs that they learned at home. They encouraged children to maintain the cleanliness, decorate the centre and welcome guests. More importantly, AWWs viewed children as active and able participants in the learning process and honoured their perspectives. When asked how she assigns a child to a particular group and activity, the Vaghapura AWW said,

It all depends on what the child likes to do. Sometimes a child changes his group according to the activity going on in the other group. I allow the child to do what he likes.

Moreover, they recognized children's interest in learning and supported them.

Children are also very intelligent. Some of them take chalk from me to write at home. I advise parents to buy a slate and chalk stick for the house, so that the child can write at home as well. It costs a small amount of just five rupees.

The helpers of both the centres felt that they must take full responsibility for children's attendance and development. The helper from Haripura commented, 'In the end, it is my responsibility to take care of these children.' They held themselves accountable for children's attendance and put in much effort to ensure children's arrival to the centre. Both of them visited children's homes in the villages and even bathed and dressed them when required.

13.10.2. Relationship between the AWW and AWH

Interviews revealed a very strong, supportive relationship between AWW and AWH in Haripura and a good, understanding relationship between them in Vaghapura. All four of them believed that a good relationship between the colleagues improves programme delivery.

> (The AWH) does her work well so it gives me a boost to do better. In the morning, (she) comes before I come, and she does all the cleaning and arranging so well, and this inspires me to perform better. (AWW, Haripura)

13.11. Connections with Families and the Community

Interviews with various participants helped us establish that the community and parents accepted and respected the AWW and AWH but had limited engagement with the ECE component.

Most interactions focused on convincing parents to send their children to the Anganwadi regularly. This is especially true for Haripura. Given that it was predominantly a migrant village, the challenges were unique. The AWW usually engaged with the parents to convince them or work out solutions when faced with barriers. However, the socio-economic challenges were formidable as explained by the AWW in Haripura.

> The parents also understand (the importance of Anganwadi) but they are helpless. They generally live on farms of other people (which are far and so parents can't send children to the Anganwadi).

The AWWs succeeded in establishing a relationship with many parents and were able to advise them on appropriate interactions with children. One of the workers described a scenario where a father frequently beat up his son. She engaged in a dialogue and helped the father to take perspective and empathize with his child, and thus motivated him to stop beating. She said,

> Tirath's father used to beat him with a stick. We spoke to his father. We asked him if he remembered how his father used to beat him.

He said, 'Yes, when I was a child I didn't know everything so he hit me, but now I am a grown up.'

With UNICEF's involvement, the ICDS functionaries began to understand the importance of parents' involvement. There were sporadic efforts to engage parents and to keep them informed regarding activities conducted in the Anganwadi.

He (UNICEF representative) said to showcase (Anganwadi activities) in front of the parents and we tried to do that. We cannot say that it was a large-scale effort or that it was done consistently and satisfactorily. We tried to organize programmes where parents also came to see what their children were doing. (CDPO)

The parents and the community contributed more in Vaghapura compared to Haripura. For example, if for some reason, there were no snacks for the children, the community provided food to the centre. Similarly, when there was too much work in the AWC, someone from the village came to help, do the dishes, etc. Occasionally, parents participated in birthday celebrations in both the centres.

13.12. Concluding Thoughts

The rich descriptions of the organizational processes in this case study illustrate four key issues. First, a public–private partnership in the ICDS programme can be especially useful to create a flexible system which is responsive to issues on the ground. ICDS programmes are typically bureaucratic and hierarchical, but a culture of collaboration and autonomy can be fostered through engagement of private partners committed to these values. The programme provided a high degree of autonomy at various levels in the ICDS programme. It is necessary to note that capacity building and monitoring mechanisms required to scaffold such autonomy were also put in place. The data from various functionaries clearly indicate that they appreciate this autonomy, although it demanded greater sense of responsibility.

Programme management processes were flexible and responsive to the ground realities. While provisions for resources were planned ahead by the government, the trust took on the responsibility of providing additional resources as needed to strengthen the programme. Therefore, an adaptive organizational structure evolved organically and was useful in recruiting additional functionaries such as supervisors and creating the new position of ACDPO. The programme ensured the effectiveness of monitoring mechanisms by tying up all monitoring systems to clearly defined follow-up actions. An important loop was developed by linking the monitoring and feedback mechanism to the capacity-building system. The capacity-building interventions such as job coaching, workshops and counselling were informed by the monitoring mechanisms.

Second, the role of the CDPO was crucial in this partnership. The autonomy granted to her to make decisions was essential to develop a responsive system. The CDPO was the nodal person for the government as well as to the Bhansali Trust, and was accountable to both of them. The passion, commitment, sensitivity and leadership skills demonstrated by this particular individual are difficult to find. The changes that the ICDS functionaries experienced as a result of this partnership has been presented in the previous sections.

Third, the engagement of a technical partner like UNICEF was essential to strengthen the component of ECE. During the time of the study, UNICEF had only engaged for a period of six months; therefore, to observe all the effects of this partnership was not fully documented. However, the data from interviews with ICDS functionaries clearly suggests that the introduction of the ECE kit, changes in pedagogy and training were much needed.

Finally, a lot of autonomy was given to the trust and the CDPO. However, changing government rules or approaches can adversely affect the programme functioning. Given Bhansali Trust's position, they were able to raise such issues at the chief minister level and received a positive response. Thus, a proactive strategy for advocacy may be needed to replicate some of these best practices.

About the Editors and Contributors

Editors

Monimalika Day is an Associate Professor at the School of Education Studies in Ambedkar University, Delhi. She specializes in early childhood education (ECE) and has led several research projects at the Centre for Early Childhood Education and Development (CECED). Prior to this, she was an Assistant Professor at George Mason University in the College of Education and Human Development, USA. She has a doctoral degree in Special Education from the University of Maryland at College Park, USA. She has worked at ZERO TO THREE, a national non-profit organization for infants, toddlers and families in the USA. She was the Assistant Director for the Center for Program Excellence, where she provided training and technical assistance to early childhood programmes across the USA. She has a master's degree in Child Development from Jadavpur University. She began her career in Kolkata, where she was the founder and administrator of a drop-in centre for 300 children who lived in the streets. She also taught young children with disabilities at Manovikas Kendra, Kolkata. Her research projects focus on early stimulation, quality of services for young children, inclusion of children with disabilities, teacher education, and collaboration between schools and families. She has authored two books, several chapters and has published in peer-reviewed journals.

Venita Kaul is Professor Emerita, Ambedkar University Delhi. Prior to her retirement in 2016, she was the Founder Director of CECED and Dean of School of Education Studies. Before joining the university, she served as a senior education specialist at the World Bank for 10 years and was a professor and head of Department of Preschool and Elementary Education at National

Council of Educational Research and Training (NCERT) in New Delhi. She has been a member of several advisory committees set up by the Government of India and international agencies, including the National Advisory Committee constituted by the Ministry of Human Resource Development (MHRD) for the implementation of Right to Education (2010), Working Group constituted by the Ministry of Women and Child Development (MWCD) to advise on the development of National Policy on Early Childhood Care and Education (ECCE) (2011–2012) and a member of the committee constituted by MHRD to oversee functioning of the National Council for Teacher Education (NCTE). She was also an expert member on the ICDS Advisory Council and a member of the NCTE Council. At the international level, she has been a member of the Steering Group of Asia Pacific Regional Network for ECD (ARNEC) and an invited member of the Forum for Investing in the Young Child, Washington, DC. She has also been on the boards of a number of well-known NGOs working in the area of education including Pratham, Mobile Crèches and Sesame Street (India). She has led several research projects on the quality of ECE and decentralized planning and convergence of sectoral services for children. She is the author of a seminal book on early childhood programmes which was published by NCERT in 2006 and has several international and national publications to her credit.

Swati Bawa Sawhney is an Assistant Professor (Ad hoc) at Delhi University. Prior to this, she worked as an early childhood consultant at the MWCF under the Strategic Health and Nutrition Partnership programme by the Department for International Development (DFID) to provide support to MWCD, Government of India, through Deloitte-led Technical Support Agency. Prior to working with the MWCD, she was a senior consultant at PricewaterhouseCoopers (PwC) and worked on multiple projects with the Government of India and United Nations. She has also worked at CECED, Ambedkar University, as a research associate.

Her major area of work has been monitoring the status and implementation of National ECCE Policy across states/UTs, guidelines for integrating children with special needs, services for caregivers with children in the age group of 0–3 years on early stimulation and tracking of developmental delay. She also contributed to policy briefs titled 'Unpacking Care: Protecting Early Childhood' and 'Brain Development in Early Years' and research projects 'Preparing Teachers for Early Childhood Care and Education', case study of Uttarakhand Seva Nidhi 'The Balwadi Programme' and 'Link for learning: Action Research in Bihar'.

Contributors

Usha Abrol was formerly the Regional Director of National Institute of Public Cooperation and Child Development (NIPCCD), a lead agency for research and training in child development. She has been a consultant to many international and national organizations and academic institutions in the area of ECCD. She has long experience of designing and conducting international and national training programmes, seminars, conferences, and workshops. She has made valuable contribution in research in ECCD, evaluations of ICDS programme, developmental indicators for children, etc. She has contributed many research reports and papers based on her extensive field experience in ECCD. At present, she is a consultant to many state government departments of child development, serving on advisory bodies of many academic institutes and prominent NGOs, providing inputs in ECCD policy, curriculum development, etc.

Nandita Chaudhary, after a teaching and research career spanning 34 years at the University of Delhi (Lady Irwin College), sought premature retirement to pursue her own academic interests in the year 2017. She now runs a blog and takes on freelance work in publishing, research and lectures in the fields of cultural psychology, child development and family studies in both India and abroad, while continuing to guide doctoral dissertations at the University of Delhi. She has been a Fulbright scholar at Clark University, USA (1993–1994), and a senior fellow of the ICSSR (2012–2014). She is the author of *Listening to Culture* (2004, SAGE), has co-edited five volumes and authored several chapters in books and journals, and serves as associate and guest editor for several leading journals.

Preeti Mahalwal is an educationist with 12 years of experience. She has a master's degree in human development and family studies from Banasthali University (2008). Presently, she is working as a lecturer in Delhi Government School. Prior to this, she was a research associate at CECED, Ambedkar University, Delhi.

At CECED, she was engaged in various qualitative and quantitative research projects. Her research work primarily focused on impact evaluation of ECE programmes, curriculum development and trainings for early years, and case studies of best practice in the area of ECCE.

Ashutosh Mishra is currently working with Kailash Satyarthi Children's Foundation as a Senior Manager, Programmes, and looking after flagship Bal Mitra Gram—The Child Friendly Village and Freedom Fellow programme. He holds a master's degree in social work from Tata Institute of Social Sciences (TISS), Mumbai, and has got over 11 years of professional experience in developmental sector. He worked at policy level in Tribal Department in Gujarat and played a key role in formulation and rolling out of the public–private partnership policy for high-quality Eklavya Model Residential Schools and successfully led the establishment of a series of girls' residential schools' low literacy tribal areas of state. He was part of various strategic forums in CARE India at the time of transition from global to nationalized entity, that is, organization evolution, knowledge management, organization learning, management team, etc. At Bharti Foundation, he led the senior secondary school programme and played a key role in development and roll out of child safety guidelines.

Chitkalamba N. is a postgraduate in life span human development and holds a doctoral degree in the area of moral education and conflict negotiations among adolescents from Bangalore University and is a NCERT doctor fellow. Having begun the career in teaching home science, she moved to the developmental sector, currently working in the area of early childhood development. She is involved in revision of ECE curriculum for Karnataka state. She is also instrumental in designing and implementing large-scale ECE projects across six districts of Northeast Karnataka in collaboration with Hyderabad Karnataka Region Development Board, Government of Karnataka.

Late Usha Nayar received her PhD from the University of Allahabad in clinical developmental psychology. She was the former deputy director and senior professor at TISS, Mumbai, and was holding the Tata Chair position as well as adjunct professor at Adelphi University's Ruth S. Ammon School of Education, New York.

She had published research papers extensively in international and national journals on theoretical, methodological and psychosocial issues related to childhood development and policies in Indian, Asian and international contexts. She was the editor and author of *Child and Adolescent Mental Health* published by SAGE and served on several international journals' editorial boards.

She was working with Hippocampus Norway research project on yoga in schools. It is part of a five countries' study sponsored by the European Union. The participating countries were Belgium, Italy, Spain, Norway and UK.

In addition to the above, she worked with organizations such as UNICEF and World Health Organization, other international agencies, non-profits, academic institutions and national as well as international government agencies on a regular basis. Her association with these institutions in part was because of their unique life-span perspectives to social policy—her specialization. She believed in bringing change by enabling agency in individuals and communities through evidence-based research.

Harini Raval serves as Head of Programmes at the Centre for Learning Resources (CLR), an organization dedicated to leadership capacity building in public education systems and other civil society organizations, providing academic resources for such systems and assisting them in developing programme strategy. CLR's primary operating field is government-run early childhood centres (ICDS Anganwadis) for 3- to 6-year-olds and parenting education and support for 0- to 3-year-olds through government-run home-visit institutions and government-run elementary education schools.

She is deeply interested in capacity-building processes and empowerment strategies for development of various levels of large-scale education system hierarchies. She has also worked extensively with para-educators, developing important insights into effective ways of using this abundant and inexpensive resource. She is deeply committed to finding ways to marry research and ground-level practice in education on an on-going basis and uses the design research approach extensively.

She earned a PhD. for a thesis on professional development of para-teachers from the University of Twente in the Netherlands. Prior to that, she received a master's degree in social work from Nirmala Niketan in Mumbai.

Suman Sachdeva has a Ph.D. in Education and a double Master Degree in Education and Philosophy. Suman is an Education Development Expert, who has more than 25 years of strategic planning and programming experience with UNICEF, International and National NGOs in the areas of elementary and secondary age education, gender and life skills. Currently, she leads the Global Partnership for Education and Quality Education programme in Sierra Leone.

Prior to this, she led the portfolio of quality education, adolescents' empowerment and gender in UNICEF India and served as the Education Lead for the Generation Unlimited partnership/Yuwaah reaching out to the largest adolescent population in the world with many placed in the emergency context.

Earlier, as Director Education, she provided leadership to the education programme of CARE (International NGO) for seven years in India working with the most vulnerable and last mile children, improving opportunities for them through their increased participation in formal and alternative education systems.

Before this, she led the education and an innovative life skills programme, including providing support to the children placed in emergency situations in Afghanistan, Nepal, Srilanka, Bangladesh and India for 7 years, working with Butterlies Programme for street and working children, an Indian NGO.

Shashi Shukla has done master's in Child Development and in education. She taught at Miranda House, University of Delhi for 10 years (2009–2019). She is pursuing her PhD from the Institute of Advanced

Studies in Education, Jamia Millia Islamia, New Delhi. Her research interest is to understand young children in their social context. She has developed module and reading material for diploma in ECCE offered by NIOS along with other publications in child development. She has been actively engaged in several projects with orientation to understand the field of child development. She is a member of Delhi University Women's Association (DUWA) and was co-convener of DUWA's Child Care Centre.

Reeta Sonawat is the Director, Ampersand group, Mumbai. She was the former dean faculty of home science and professor and head of the Department of Human Development, SNDT Women's University, Mumbai. She was selected as a global leader in World Forum on Early Care and Education, Montreal (2005). She is also the Executive Director of Early Childhood Association.

As an international leader in ECCE, she was invited by the US State Department of State Bureau of Educational and Cultural Affair, Washington, DC, in 2009, where she participated in the International Visitor Leadership Program on ECE. For her postdoctoral research, she worked on the project 'Integrated Education in Kindergartens and Primary Schools' in Bremen University, Germany. She underwent training in ECE with reading difficulties at Golda Meir Mount Carmel Institute and Training Center, Haifa, Israel.

She is a recipient of National Award for Teacher Trainer in innovative training for the project 'Improving Classroom Environment towards Quality in Education' and Faculty Research Fellowship by Shastri Indo-Canadian Institute for project titled 'Adolescent of Minority Groups, Sense of Belongingness to Society'. She has published more than 100 research articles in national and international journals. She has authored several books and monographs.

She has given scholarly lectures in University refresher courses, orientation programs, seminars and conferences at national and international level.

Ratnamala Vallury is associated with State Resource Centre, Durgabai Deshmukh Mahila Sabha (DDMS; Andhra Mahila Sabha) as a faculty member and has worked in different positions as ECE specialist under the guidance of Dr K. Lakshmi. She is a postgraduate in English, philosophy and education from Osmania University and has certificates from Indian Montessori Association. By virtue of more than 40 years of experience in the education sector, she has acquired huge experience, especially in ECE. As a part of her association with DDMS (Andhra Mahila Sabha), she participated as a resource person in conducting training programmes for field stakeholders in urban, rural and tribal areas. She conducted onsite training for in-service teachers/student teachers of PG diploma in ECE and BEd students. She participated in research study projects conducted by NIPCCD, NCERT, SCERT and CECED. She participated as research associate in 'Strand B' of the longitudinal study *Indian Early Childhood Education Impact Study* and in 'Strand C' case study of Balwadis of SERP in tribal areas. She participated in developing need-based curriculum for different areas of tribal, rural and urban children. She had been a key resource person for development of activity-based and training material in Telugu language for pre-primary and primary children and teachers.

Index